M000219281

HOW TO

Sell Your Home Fast,
for the Highest Price,
in Any Market

Also by Terry Eilers

How to Buy the Home You Want, for the Best Price, in Any Market

HOW TO

Sell Your Home Fast, for the Highest Price, in Any Market

FROM A REAL ESTATE EXPERT WHO KNOWS ALL THE TRICKS

TERRY EILERS

NEW YORK

All names of companies, products, street addresses, and persons contained herein are part of a completely fictitious scenario and are designed solely for illustrative purposes.

Some of the information contained in this book may be affected by changes in interpretations of the law or deviations in market conditions in specific geographic areas. This book should not be used as a substitute for legal, tax, investment, accounting, or similar professional services. If such services are required, publisher and author recommend that the reader secure the services of a competent professional.

Copyright © 1997, Terry Eilers

All rights reserved. No part of this book may be reproduced in any manner whatsoever without written permission of the Publisher. Printed in the United States of America. For information address: Hyperion, 114 Fifth Avenue, New York, New York 10011.

Library of Congress Cataloging-in-Publication Data

Eilers, Terry (Terry Lynn), 1948–
    How to sell your home fast, for the highest price, in any market : from a real estate expert who knows all the tricks / Terry Eilers—1st ed.
       p.   cm.
    Includes index.
    ISBN: 0-7868-8224-7
    1. House selling. 2. Real estate business I. Title.
  HD1379.E37   1997
  333.33'83—dc20

                         96–34883
                            CIP

Designed by Robert Bull Design

FIRST EDITION

10 9 8 7 6 5 4 3 2

DEDICATION

Many years ago when I began my career in home sales, I faced not only the enormous task of becoming a sales professional but also the incredible challenge of learning the many complexities of the real estate industry. No two days were ever the same, and the questions from buyers, sellers, escrow officers, title people, loan representatives, home inspectors, and other agents were never-ending.

If not for my extremely knowledgeable and patient broker, I am sure I would have become one of the many statistics of attrition in this difficult field. The man's dedication to his family, his clients, his friends, and to each of the many salespeople he has guided to prosperity should be the standard by which greatness is judged.

Thank you, *Bill Elliott,* from all of the thousands of us, including myself, whom you have helped sell our homes, build our careers, and improve our lives.

ACKNOWLEDGMENTS

To Janice Labbé, who is most responsible for this book finally reaching the consumer. Her dedication to quality is immeasurable.

To the many real estate superstar salespeople who have given freely of their ideas to help other agents and home sellers become more successful and sell their homes more effectively.

CONTENTS

CONTENTS

CONTENTS

FIGURES

APPENDIX FIGURES

"Time Is of the Essence"
This phrase is part of every written real estate contract,
and no truer words have ever been spoken when
it comes to selling a home successfully.

PREFACE

For many years I have traveled thousands of miles around the world helping sales professionals improve their knowledge, abilities, and techniques. More important, I have found that the best way to develop expertise in any area is to talk to those individuals who are the peak performers in their particular field.

Let's face it. There are two ways to learn: trial and error, and learning from others' trials and errors. In this book, you have the opportunity to learn from those who have made many mistakes that cost them literally thousands of dollars as well as the people who have become the superstars in real estate sales.

As I have said for years, "There are two actions in life, Performance or Excuses."

Every one of you who chooses to follow the hundreds of suggestions provided in this publication will undoubtedly achieve great success in the sale of your home.

No excuses! If you are going to sell your home, do it right, quickly, and for the highest possible price.

That's performance!

HOW TO

Sell Your Home Fast, for the Highest Price, in Any Market

CHAPTER ONE

So You're Thinking of Selling

WHY ARE YOU THINKING
OF SELLING?

This is the first question you must ask yourself when you begin to think of selling. Break down the question so you really understand the "why." What do you like about your home? What do you dislike? Do you need more room? Less room? Could you make a few changes and be happy with your current home? Is your neighborhood still what you want or need? Are the schools, churches, and amenities what you want? If you remodeled, could you be happier than with a new home? Are you ready to take on the expense of a new home?

WHAT WILL YOU GAIN?

After you have truly spent some time analyzing why you are thinking of selling, you should take some time and consider what you will gain by selling your home. If you will be purchasing a new property, you must decide objectively if the new home and the new payments are worth what you will gain in the new property.

WHAT ABOUT
REMODELING?

If your family is growing or shrinking, you may need to make some kind of a change. In the case of a growing family, remodeling your current home may not be feasible. The layout or building restrictions, not to mention the cost of the remodeling, may prohibit any substantial change in the structure. Most important, the fact that you probably will never recoup all of the cost of the construction when you finally do sell the home could be a deterrent. Figure 1.1 shows the estimated percentage of value that is actually received, compared to the cost of different remodel options.

FIGURE 1.1

THE VALUE VS. THE COST OF REMODELING

Types of Change	% Estimate of Cost Added to Value of Home	$ to Make Change
Bathroom Addition	65	6,900
Bedroom Addition	65	7,400
Swimming Pool	30	26,000
Hot Tub/Jacuzzi	20	5,600
Major 2nd Story Addition	50	35,000
Kitchen Remodel	75	16,000
New Carpet	80	4,200
New Paint	100	950
Professional Improvement		
Exterior Landscaping	30	7,000
Extensive Decking	35	2,500
Garage Addition		
(if no garage exists)	40	6,500

For example, if you installed a pool at a cost of $26,000, you could anticipate recovering only approximately $7,800 when you sold your home.

These figures, obtained from the National Home Builders Association, are based on national averages. The costs may vary in your area. For example, the estimated average cost of a bathroom addition in New York City was $9,700. But in Cheyenne, Wyoming, it was only $3,600.

WHAT WILL YOU NET?

If you have decided that remodeling is not an option, then you also must consider how much money you actually will net when you sell your home.

Many home sellers make the mistake of subtracting their loan balance from what they think their home is worth and base their decision to sell on that figure. Before you make any decision to sell, you must take two very important actions:

1. Obtain, from three reputable real estate professionals, a complete market analysis or estimate of value. As these real estate professionals provide their own estimates of value, do not release their figures to either of the other two agents. However, do advise each of these sales professionals that you are obtaining more than one estimate of value and that you do not want an inflated evaluation. You must make it clear that you are looking for a true estimate of value at which the property will most probably sell in the current market.
2. Prepare a net sheet or estimate of proceeds similar to Figure 1.2, which will give you a good indication as to how much you will actually net.

    Note: Each real estate professional should include a complete net sheet with the market analysis or estimate of value. (See Figure 1.2.)

As you can see by the example in Figure 1.2, although this property sold for $220,000 and the current loan balance was only $110,000, the seller's net proceeds of $92,400 was considerably less than the $110,000 of gross equity. The selling costs equaled approximately 8 percent of the sale price.

WHEN IS THE BEST TIME
TO SELL?

It seems that most sellers believe the only time to sell a home and receive the highest price is during the summer. In some areas, this is true. However, in many locales, homes that are priced properly and

FIGURE 1.2

SELLER'S NET PROCEEDS WORKSHEET

Sale Price $ __220,000__

Closing Costs:

Brokerage Fee	$ __15,400__
Title Insurance	$ __845__
Points (if any)	$ __0__
Escrow/Closing Fee	$ __680__
Document Preparation	$ _____
Fees Paid for Seller	$ _____
Recording	$ __30__
Bonds & Assessments	$ _____
Inspections	$ __150__
Tax Services	$ _____
Repairs	$ __100__
Home Warranty	$ __395__
Attorney Fees	$ _____
Other	$ _____
Total	($ __17,600__)

Liens:

1st Mortgage	$ __110,000__
2nd Mortgage	$ _____
Other	$ _____
Total	($ __127,600__)
Net to Seller	$ __92,400__

well prepared will sell at almost any time during the year. In fact, in many areas such as Arizona, southern Nevada, and Florida, homes actually sell faster in the winter than in the summer. Now, of course, if you live in Alpena, Michigan, and you decide to sell your home during January when there is six or eight feet of snow on the ground, you'll have a better than average chance that it will take a little longer to sell than if you made that decision after spring had sprung.

> **SMART TIP:**
> Homes that are priced right, prepared properly, and marketed correctly will sell any time of the year.

WHERE WILL YOU LIVE AFTER YOU SELL?

Are you going to sell first, then buy or rent? Are you going to sell, then build? Will you buy first, then sell? Will you sell and buy at the same time, closing the transactions simultaneously? In other words, what's the plan?

One major mistake that home buyers make is purchasing a new home with the condition that they will complete the deal only if and when their current home sells.

Under the proper circumstances, having examined all of the options and facts, it is perfectly acceptable to purchase a new home conditioned upon the sale of your current property. However, if you choose to purchase first, then sell, hoping to time your sale and purchase for simultaneous closings, you must become very objective and extremely realistic with regard to price and preparation of your current home. In other words, you must establish a degree of urgency.

Of course, there are many other options you may wish to consider should your current home not sell immediately and you desire to complete the purchase of the new home. Some of these options are covered in Chapters 9 and 11.

> **SMART TIP:**
> Before you ever put your home on the market, make sure you have a structured plan as to how you will make the transition from your old home to your new home.

CAN YOU AFFORD
TO SELL YOUR HOME?

Potential home sellers often fail to recognize all of the costs that may be involved in the sale of their home. Some of the expenses might include: sales fees or commissions (completely negotiable but averaging nationally between 6 and 8 percent of the selling price), repairs, improvements, closing costs you must pay as well as closing costs you may agree to pay, any accrued interest or prepayment penalties on your current loan, moving expenses, costs to purchase your new home, and expenses to make any necessary additions or changes to your new home. New furnishings also may be a major expense, especially if your new home is larger than your current one.

SMART TIP:
Examine closely all of the potential costs that you may incur before you take any step toward actually selling your home.

CHAPTER TWO

A Brief Overview

THE BITS AND PIECES OF SELLING

Here is a short overview of the steps you must take to sell your home quickly and for the highest price. All the following chapters detail every aspect of which you need to be aware if you are to sell your home successfully and achieve the highest financial return.

1. You must *prepare yourself* to sell your home. Realistically and objectively look at the home and be willing to recognize that the general buying public may not view it with the same warm fuzzy feelings and emotions that you feel.

2. The next step to actually getting your house sold is to *prepare the house*. Most sellers do not realize that the average potential home buyer looks at 12 homes before deciding to make an offer. Therefore, sellers must be aware that their home is in competition with at least 11 other homes for every potential buyer.

> **SMART TIP:**
> Learn to ignore your emotional attachments to your house and look at the sale from a business point of view.

   In some cases, the preparation for sale only requires a little polish here and there. However, some sellers may need to make some major improvements before their homes become saleable. The Appendix provides a Home Inspection Form to help you prepare your home to meet the expectations of most potential buyers.

3. Decide if you will attempt to sell the home yourself or if you will hire a real estate professional. Remember, selling may not be as simple as sticking a sign in your front yard and waiting for buyers to begin knocking down your door with offers. *Trying to save a commission may end up costing you a bundle.*

Have you considered the contracts, deposit receipts, addendums, title searches and insurance, points, closing costs, safety and security, loan applications, price and terms negotiations, advertising, calls, showing the property, the many required disclosures, the closing process, the inspectors, the appraisers? WHEW! The list can be overwhelming.

SMART TIP:

As a rule, the average seller is better served, both emotionally and financially, if he or she hires a professional salesperson to handle the sale of his or her home. Statistics show that 90 percent of "For Sale by Owner" homes end up listed with a real estate professional before they are sold. Before you decide to sell your own home, you may want to ask, "Would anyone else have me sell their home?"

4. The next step is deciding at what price you will sell your house. Some sellers believe their home is the nicest home in the neighborhood and that it will sell to the first potential buyer who walks through the front door. Unfortunately, this attitude often creates the misconception that manifests itself in the worst mistake a seller can make: *overpricing property*. Pricing, the most critical action in the sale of your home, must be done objectively and with little emotion or personal feelings. (In Chapter 8 I detail the steps you must take to price your home correctly.)

5. The next step in selling your home is the actual process of advertising and showing. What you should and should not do is detailed in Chapters 11 and 12.

SMART TIP:

It is critical that you price your home no higher than the actual, factually determined market value. Overpricing your home, hoping for an unsophisticated buyer or hoping for that one buyer who can't live without your home, may be the kiss of death with regard to a successful sale.

6. When you have a found a potential buyer, the process of negotiating the sale then takes place. Who will pay for what, what is included, what is not included? All the "what-ifs" must be discussed. You may decide you would be better off having a sales professional handle the sale of your home, which includes the negotiation process. Some states require that a licensed attorney be involved in the

closing process. However, the number of such states is shrinking each year. Unless legally required, the seller and buyer always can decide whether to utilize the services of a lawyer. Chapter 13 will help guide you in the negotiation process.

7. The next step in the sale of your home is the closing process. What do you need as far as paperwork? How do you guarantee clear title? Should you purchase a home warranty package? How will monies be delivered to the closer or escrow holder? How and when will you get your money? If you are purchasing another home, how will you close simultaneously? How will monies be transferred? How will the final walk-through be coordinated? How and when will possession be delivered? Chapter 16 deals with all of the specific steps in the closing process to help to prepare you in advance and to allow you a smooth and effective closing.

> **SMART TIP:**
>
> Should you decide to involve an attorney, make sure he or she is well versed in real estate transactions. Just because an attorney handled your last divorce and did a great job does not necessarily mean that he or she knows real estate law.

8. The last step is, of course, buying your new home. Sellers should do many things far in advance of the actual closing to prepare for the purchase of their new home. A special section of Chapter 14 covers some of the current federal tax laws that affect the sellers and buyers of homes.

CHAPTER THREE

Making the Sales Decisions

BE OBJECTIVE

The following scenario depicts the problem that many sellers face when they decide to sell their home.

Bill and Carol lived in their 30-year-old home for the last 12 years before Bill retired from public service. In a quiet neighborhood of a Southwest city, the couple had greatly improved their property over the years. Some of these improvements included a pool, spa, completely remodeled kitchen, new carpet, new wallpaper throughout, remodeled bathrooms, professionally landscaped front and backyard as well as specialty items too numerous to mention. In other words, Bill and Carol made their home the showplace of the neighborhood. In the three years prior to selling, they had spent nearly $50,000 improving the property. Naturally, they both felt they should recover all of these improvement costs when they sold their home.

After Bill retired, the couple found a locale in another state where they felt they wanted to retire and they immediately purchased a new home, utilizing some of their savings for the down payment. They began moving some of their belongings to the new house, which was approximately a three-hour drive from their first home. During this extended moving process, the couple also called a real estate professional and listed their existing home for sale. Although the sales agent advised the couple that their home should sell for approximately $189,000, Bill insisted that because another home in the same neighborhood, not nearly as nice as their home, had sold for $229,000 within the previous six months, he wanted his home sold for at least that much. The agent showed the sellers figures that indicated that the other home was almost

1,100 square feet larger and had actually sold for $221,000. Regardless of the facts, Bill was insistent that because he had put so much money into his home, he knew *someone out there* would be willing to pay the price he wanted. The agent tried to convince him that most buyers would not care about most of the improvements because they would want to change the home to their own desires. Bill made it clear that his home was different and it would sell at the higher price. If the agent wanted the listing, it would be taken at $229,000. The agent, against his better judgment, took the listing.

During the six-month listing period, the property was advertised, open houses were held, other agents were notified, flyers were distributed ... a complete marketing campaign was utilized, but only two people even looked at the property. At the end of the listing period, the sellers, angry with the lack of results, listed their home for $224,000 with another sales agent. Three months later they received an offer of $189,400 for the property, which they angrily rejected, completing a counteroffer of $220,000. The potential buyers bought another home. After nine months Bill obtained an appraisal from a certified MAI appraiser (American Institute of Appraisers). The value was set at $189,250. *Bill still would not reduce the price.*

To make a long story short, Bill and Carol finally sold their home 16 months after the initial listing for $189,400. They had paid, in the 16-month listing period, over $9,600 in interest on the existing loan, over $3,900 traveling back and forth to their new home, not to mention the wear and tear on their vehicles during the 48 trips they made to their new home. But more than the actual financial loss, Bill and Carol suffered enormous mental strain because they were making their business decisions from an emotional point of view and were not realistic about the facts. Consequently, they paid dearly for their mistakes.

As you begin to prepare yourself for the sale of your home, above all, be realistic and objective. Do not make emotional decisions. Make your decision based on factual information.

ASK FOR OPINIONS

Solicit opinions from the real estate professionals who completed the market analysis or estimates value for you. (This was discussed in Chapter 1.) Ask all these professionals to give you their suggestions as to what they feel you should do to sell your home quickly and for the highest price. And be open-minded. When they give you their suggestions, don't argue or try to explain why you have the bright red velvet wallpaper in the bathroom. Just listen and remember, you have the final decision if you will or will not accept their suggestions. But also remember, most of these professionals are speaking with potential buyers every day and they know how many of these purchasers will respond to different amenities in the home. Make a list of all of the suggestions and begin thinking about which of these ideas you may utilize.

LISTEN TO CRITICISM

Understand, not everyone will speak kindly of your home. *Don't let derogatory remarks affect you.* Sometimes they are right on. Sometimes they are totally off base. Listen to everything, good or bad, and remain objective. *Don't get angry.* You must remember, if everyone had the same tastes, we would all live in the same type of house, decorated exactly the same way, in the same area, with the same ... well, you get the idea.

Now, when someone doesn't like your decorating or the style of your home, he or she probably will tell you. Don't take it personally. It is only that person's opinion, and you should look for the positive that might actually help you sell your home. Who is to say who is right when it comes to the preferences of potential buyers? Maybe your biggest critics will provide the most helpful suggestion when it comes to getting your home sold.

Don't lose sight of the most important fact: You are *not* looking for compliments, you're looking for a buyer.

PEOPLE ARE TRAMPING
THROUGH OUR HOME!

One of the most difficult aspects of selling your home is preparing yourself for the onslaught of sales agents and potential buyers parading through it. Most sellers think that the first person who looks at their beautiful property will buy and that's the end of it. Not so! Remember, as I said earlier, the average buyer looks at 12 homes before deciding to make an offer. Also, many potential buyers will look at the same home two or three or four times before they actually decide to make an offer. So, be prepared. Don't forget, the best thing that can happen is that there is so much interest in walking your property that there is a constant parade of potential buyers through the home.

You need to worry when no one looks at your property.

Certain family members may object to potential buyers touring the home and looking into their most secret and private places. Very simply, have them *get over it!* It is hoped that the invasion of privacy will last only for a short time; until the deal is finalized, you need everyone's patience and cooperation.

CAN YOU MAKE THE REPAIRS YOURSELF?

Some people in this world are blessed with the ability to fix anything and everything. Then there are those people who just think they are one of the blessed fixer-uppers.

For those who are truly excellent handypersons, preparing the home for sale is a breeze. If they can make their list of necessary repairs, put a time schedule together, stick to it, and finish all of the improvements or repairs in a timely and professional fashion, it will save a lot of money, hassles, and headaches while going through the selling process.

However, if potential sellers are among the misinformed, would-be "self-ordained home improvement specialists," look out!

What will probably happen goes something like this: First, these inept handypersons will go out and buy a bunch of tools they think they need but will never use again. Then they will purchase enough paint, wallpaper, baseboards, window caulking, Spackle, wood filler, and cleaning products to prepare the White House for sale. Then they will start 16 projects all at once, so they "don't get bored just doing one job." Several months and several thousand dollars later, when none of the projects is done right, they will realize that they should have just hired someone to do the repair work in the first place.

Don't forget, as I said earlier, the average person looks at 12 homes before making an offer. Your home is competing with at least 11 other homes on the market.

> **SMART TIP:**
> When you start to make repairs on your home, remember, anyone who is interested in your property will not be buying your "Old Home," they will be buying their "New Dream Home" and they will not be interested in shoddy workmanship or an ill-prepared property.

AS A BUYER, HOW DO I SEE THE HOME?

Without a doubt, one of the biggest challenges potential home sellers must face is learning to see their home the way buyers see it.

Sellers have a tendency to look at their home emotionally. They attach their feelings to each and every part of the home. They visualize the window with the Christmas tree glowing, the birthday parties, the spot where Uncle Ralph used to love to sit on the porch in the afternoon sun, the barbecues in the backyard on those great summer weekends, the huge tree in the front yard that used to be just a seedling, the rosebushes they have enjoyed so much, the wonderful neighbors ... all of the individual and collective times of their lives that have made a house their home.

On the other hand, buyers couldn't care less about all those sweet, wonderful times that mean so much to sellers. Potential buyers tour homes scanning each nook and cranny for any spot, blemish, imperfection, and anything else they might be able to use to help with the negotiations.

SMART TIP:

One great technique you can use to help see the home as a buyer does is to create and use a "Buyer's View Box." Simply remove the top of a shoebox and cut a hole about 4 inches wide by 2 inches high in the bottom, center of the box. Using the shoebox as a viewer, start slowly through the house looking at every wall, window, ceiling, crack, and crevice. Record every imperfection you spot. Once you narrow your focus, you will be amazed at how many small and large problem areas you will find that you have lived with for years and never noticed. But believe it or not, buyers will notice every problem area, regardless of how small or inconsequential it may seem to you. Look for everything, from cracked electrical plates, to spots on the carpet, to light bulbs missing over the vanity. When the list is finished (and it may be numerous pages), you'll have a good point from which to start preparing your home for sale.

SHOULD I GET A HOME INSPECTION?

Home inspections are available from local home inspection companies almost everywhere across the United States and Canada. In some cases, particularly with older homes, it may be advisable to consider paying for and obtaining a home inspection before you attempt to sell your home. As a rule, if a home is five years old or newer and is well maintained, obtaining a home inspection may be unnecessary. Be advised, though: Many buyers ask for a complete home inspection as a condition of the purchase of a home.

SMART TIP:

Don't be afraid to negotiate the home inspection fee. You will not be offered a discount if you don't ask for one. Also, if you have listed your home with a real estate professional, have the agent ask the home inspection company for a reduced fee. Remember, the inspection company would like to have more of the agent's future business and may be inclined to reduce a fee slightly at the agent's request .

CHAPTER FOUR

Preparing Your Home for Sale

WHAT AM I LOOKING FOR?

Very simply, you are looking for the three Ds: dirt, damage, and discoloration. Inspecting your home by part of the house rather than by room is easier and more effective. Save the garage and exterior for last. Use the form provided for your inspection. (See Figure A.2 in the appendix.)

According to Bill Bartel of Complete Home Inspections and a Realtor® for over 22 years, the biggest problems a seller can encounter are:

- Badly damaged roofs
- Major plumbing problems
- Extensive problems with the overall electrical systems
- Continual water leakage or drainage into the basement or under the flooring or crawl space of the home
- An inadequate, outdated, or poorly maintained heating or cooling system
- A home that is extensively run down overall.

> **SMART TIP:**
> Remember, you are legally responsible to disclose to potential buyers any problems with the home of which you are aware. If you try to get away with hiding a potential problem area, you may lose a buyer or, worse yet, end up embroiled in a lawsuit!

Floors

Start with floors and baseboards. Using your Buyer's View Box and a notepad, go through each room slowly, noting each spot, tear, loose or broken tile, discoloration, or any imperfection that might catch a potential buyer's eye. Be very critical of tattered carpet and chipped or broken tile. Remember, record everything. Later you can decide which things you will fix.

SMART TIP:

One trick you may use while inspecting your home is to carry small Post-it notes with you. Each time you discover a necessary cleaning task or repair, make a note and post it in the area. Some rooms may end up looking like huge bulletin boards, but you will know exactly what needs to be done without referring back to the inspection form. Also, you may be able to delegate these minor tasks without spending much time orchestrating the process.

Walls and Doors

Next, check the walls and doors. As you did with the floors, go through each room and inspect the walls and doors for cracks, spots, dirt, fingerprints, holes, chipped or peeling paint. If any of the walls have wallpaper, check the seams (top, bottom, sides) carefully.

Make sure all of the doors operate smoothly, the doorknobs turn easily, the hinges are tight and do not squeak, all of the locks (if they are locking doors) work, the paint is not chipped or peeling, and most important, the doors and door frames have no cracks and are very clean (no fingerprints or grease spots).

SMART TIP:

Remove any wild posters, Confederate flags, stuffed animal heads, or animal skins that may be hanging. While you are entitled to decorate your own home as you like, your home will be more salable if it presents neutrally. Why limit the number of buyers who may be interested in your home? Save your personal preference items for your new property.

Windows

First and foremost, are all windows crystal clean? One trick suggested by professional window cleaners is to use window cleaning solution and newspaper to remove the dirt and polish the glass. Newspaper leaves the glass pristine. However, your hands will be black with newsprint ink, so wear gloves or a plastic bag when you complete this task. Are glass panes not cracked and not pitted? Are there cracks in window frames? Do all windows open and close easily? Are all hinges lubricated? Are all latches, handles, and cranks tight, and do they operate smoothly? If windows slide, are the tracks clean and lubricated and do the windows move easily? Most important, do all locks latch easily and lock securely?

Window Coverings

Window coverings are also important. Are all drapes and curtains clean and in good repair? (Even if the window coverings do not stay with the home, they must show well.) Are all louvers, Venetian blinds, or other coverings in good shape, and do they operate properly? Are all pull cords attached properly and operating smoothly? Are all curtain rods clean, straight, strong, and attached to the wall properly? Are there any discolorations or stains on any of the window coverings? (Stains on sheers will really show.)

Ceilings

Next, check the ceilings. Room by room, look for dirt, cobwebs, cracks, chips, or discoloration.

If you have ceilings that are blown acoustic, look for smooth spots where the acoustic has dropped. If there are major holes in the surface covering, you might consider having the ceiling reblown.

> **SMART TIP:**
> If the ceiling or walls have a yellow discoloration, you may have a leak in the roof or exterior walls. You must either repair the leaks or disclose the problem to a potential buyer. Do not just repaint or cover up the discolored area. Doing so could result in problems, or worse yet, a lawsuit, the first time it rains.

Kitchen

The kitchen is your next point of attack. It is critical that you focus on this room and carefully go over each detail.

Clean out the cupboards and drawers and store utensils, pots, pans, and appliances that you may not use on an everyday basis. Make sure doors work smoothly and latch properly. Clean off the countertops so there is a very spacious, open feeling. If the kitchen area is dark, increase the wattage in bulbs and make sure all bulbs are working. If not, replace them. Clean and polish the stove top, sink, faucets, and handles until they gleam. If the handles or faucets are rusted or will not polish well, consider replacing them. Also, if you have a stove top with drip trays, unless these trays are clean and sparkling, replace them. To clean the interior of the oven, use a commercial oven cleaner that removes spots and baked-on food and discoloration. Finally, record any cleaning or polishing that must be done on all of the other appliances, regardless of whether they stay with the home. A filthy toaster, microwave, or refrigerator may turn off a potential buyer. This includes the inside of the refrigerator and microwave. There's no telling what door a nosy potential buyer may open.

Also, if any appliances have a clock, make sure it works and is set at the proper time. Timers on stoves are important to many buyers.

One last item with regard to the kitchen. Make sure the pipes drain well. Many buyers will run the water as well as flip on the garbage disposal. Make sure it works properly. If you have an older home that does not have a garbage disposal, have one put in. This inexpensive improvement will easily pay for itself when buyers start to see your home.

Living and
Family Rooms

Most of the family's time is spent in the living and family rooms. Is there good traffic flow? Is all furniture clean and in good repair? Is there good lighting? Is the fireplace and the area around it clean and in good repair? Do not stack furniture or televisions. Are the drapes and curtains clean and pressed? Are the blinds and other window coverings clean and in good working order? Do not clutter shelves. Make sure that the room is not crowded.

Bathrooms

The bathrooms are extremely important as well. This is another area where you need to be very critical.

Check the faucets. Are there any leaks, and do they clean and shine well? Any cracks in the mirrors, glass doors, sinks, tubs? Do all of the mirrors and glass areas sparkle? Do toilet paper holders roll easily? Are they clean? Are all towel racks, hoods, and drying bars secure, clean and in good shape ... no rust? Are shower curtains clean and spot free? Is there any mold anywhere on the walls, around the tub or sink, or on the ceiling? Are area rugs and tub mats clean and not discolored? Do all cabinet doors work smoothly and latch properly? Is all caulking in good shape, or is it discolored? Do all drains work well and do all toilets flush and refill properly? And last, is the water pressure at an acceptable level?

Bedrooms

On the average, people spend 40 percent of their life in their bedrooms. Make sure that the bedrooms are as appealing as possible. Is there enough room to move around comfortably? If not, move some furniture out. Take out wall hangings or statues that may not appeal to others. Are the dressers clean and neatly arranged? Are the beds made? Are all personal items and valuables stored? Are the windows, windowsills, and window coverings clean and in good repair?

Closets

Closets are another important area. Are they neat and orderly? Do they need to be cleaned out? They will appear larger if they are less full. Also, the floors should be empty. Are the closets well lit? Well painted? Are the shelves in good repair? Do they have an odor of sports equipment, shoes or something old and moldy? Are hanging rods straight and properly connected? Are all hooks secure? Are clothes or whatever hung and stacked neatly? Expect all buyers to look in every closet and cupboard. They are looking for as much space as they can possibly find.

Laundry Areas

Laundry areas can sometimes make or break a sale. An often overlooked area in a home, the laundry area can be very important to a homemaker. Is it clean and lint free? Is it easily accessible, do the doors work right, are the cabinets clean? Is there any floor damage or discoloration from movement of the washer or dryer? If there is a sink in this area, are there any leaks, and are faucets and the sink itself clean and shiny? Any leaks in the hoses or faucets connected to the washer? Are the washer and dryer very clean, inside and out? (Especially if they are staying with the home.) And, most important, is the laundry area well lit?

Staircases

Staircases are often overlooked. Are the handrails secure? (That means *secure*; no movement.) Are all of the stairs tight and free of squeaks or rattles? Are the stairs clean and uncluttered, and, if covered with carpet or tile, is the covering secure? Are there any nails protruding? Are all side slats or vertical rails secure? Are the posts at the top and bottom of the stair handrail tight and immovable? Are all decorative knobs on these posts secure? Is the paint or finish on the staircase in good shape? Are the stairs well lit? If the stairs lead to a basement or to an attic, is there a handrail or something to hold while ascending/descending? Is there plenty of head space at the top or bottom of the stairs? (If not, put up a sign warning WATCH YOUR HEAD! You might be used to the inconvenience and forget to warn a potential buyer.)

Shelves, Bookcases, and Drawers

Next, examine all shelves, bookcases, and drawers. Are they clean, uncluttered, level, and well secured? Are there cobwebs? If there is a covering or finish such as paper or paint on the shelves or in the drawers, is it peeling, cracked, or discolored? Do all of the drawers slide smoothly? Are all handles and knobs tight (especially in the kitchen and bathrooms)? Replacing any worn or loose door or drawer handles is an inexpensive improvement that is well worth the money.

Fireplaces

Fireplaces or woodburning stoves need special attention. At some point you should have the chimney and fireplace cleaned. A good chimney sweep and flue cleaning should be done no less than every two years. If you burn a lot of paper, pitchy wood, or pressed logs, you may need to have this service performed once a year, at least. If the fireplace is not going to be in use while your home is for sale, make sure that it is completely clean. If it does not have glass doors, place a plant or something decorative in the fireplace area to spice up and draw attention to the fireplace.

If the outside or mantel of the fireplace has burn marks or is blackened from smoke, use a commercial cleaner to remove the residue, or repaint if possible.

Electrical System

The basic electrical system should be examined. Do all of the outlets work? (If you are not proficient with wiring or electrical work, do not attempt to make electrical repairs.) Are all wall plates clean and not cracked? Do all switches operate smoothly? If any switches utilize a pull switch, are the pull cords secure and in good shape?

Heating and Cooling Units

Be sure to check the heating and cooling units. Have the filters been replaced recently? Do these units run properly and quietly? Have these units been serviced recently? (If not, have them serviced professionally.) If the home has central heat or air, are all vents in place, clean, and do they open and close easily? If the air conditioners are window units, are they secure in the windows and sealed well? Are all units, vents, and exposed ductwork clean? Do all of the thermostats work properly? Do pilot lights stay lit?

Basements and Attics

Examine basements and attics. Are all areas of the attic and basement clean, uncluttered, and dry? (Do not store all of the clutter that you remove from the rest of the house in these areas!) Do the basement and attic have as spacious and open a feeling as possible? Are there cobwebs? Is there any water standing or leaking into the basement? Are all stairs into and out of these areas in good repair? Do all entry doors work smoothly, especially if they open to the exterior of the house? Are all windows or vents in these areas clean and in good repair?

Note: Make sure there are no little critters running, crawling, or slithering around these areas.

Odors

That's right . . . smell! In interviews with potential buyers, the number-one turn off mentioned more than any other was, for lack of another term, "house-a-tosis," or home odor. Most frequently mentioned smells were animal odors, cigarette smoke, and mold. Nothing will dissuade a buyer faster than walking into a home that smells bad.

Walk outside, take a few deep breaths, then enter your home and shut the door. Walk through the home, room by room, and check for odor. If you can't smell anything, you may just be accustomed to the odor, so get someone other than another family member to do the "smell test" with you.

Once you have identified any ill odors, get rid of the source and air out the house. Do not try to cover up bad odors with strong potpourri or fragrance sprays. Instead, deal with the problem and correct it. Lawsuits have actually resulted from sellers covering up smells that had permeated carpets, flooring, and walls and ultimately resurfaced after the new buyers took possession. Don't get caught in this situation.

Porches, Patios, and Entries

Now check the decks, porches, patios, and entries. Start with the guard- and handrails. Are they tightly secured? Are gates and doors secure, and do they work smoothly? Do all locks and latches work well? If made of wood, is the deck level, and are all of the boards flat and secure? Is the paint or finish on the deck discolored, peeling, or chipping? If a porch is screened, is the screen clean, free of discoloration and fabric tears? Are all built-in barbecues in good working order? Are overhead structures or coverings in good shape? If there is a complete roof, is it free of leaks? Is deck or porch furniture that is built in or stays with the home in good condition? Does the doorbell work?

Garage

The garage is always fun. First, are there any cobwebs up in the beams? Are the walls clean and uncluttered? If the washer and dryer are in this area, are they clean, and is the area around the appliances clean and well lit? Does the overall garage light up well? Are all windows clean? Are the windowsills very clean (especially free of dead bugs and cobwebs)? Are the floors clean and free of grease spots? (Get a commercial cleaner at an auto parts store to clean the spots off the garage floor and driveway.) Are all cabinets and shelves in good order, including handles and doorknobs? If the water heater, water softener, or other appliances are in the garage, are they secured properly, with no leaks? Also, is the area around the water heater clean? Are garden tools and cleaning supplies stored properly? Does the garage door operate properly? Are the springs that lift the door or the garage door opener in good operating order? Are all other doors into the garage working properly, including the locks? If there is an animal door, is it in good shape and does it keep the elements out? If there is a shop or workbench area, is it very clean and uncluttered? Do all electrical outlets and switches work properly? If you use the beam area for storage, make sure it is neat and secure.

Pools, Spas, and Saunas

Pools, spas, and saunas are a special challenge. First, are they clean? *Very* clean? Is the water in pools and spas clear, and does it have the proper chemical balance? Are the pumps, heating units, cleaners, hoses, skimmers, and drains working properly? Are the deck areas clean and free of discoloration? Are the ladders, steps, slides, and diving boards all in good shape? Is all deck furniture neat and well maintained? (Even if it doesn't stay with the home, it must show well.) Is all safety equipment accessible and in good working order? Are all gates, locks, and fences around the pool in good shape? Are all required safety signs visually accessible? Does the lighting work properly in and around the pool, spa, and sauna? Is the interior finish of the sauna in good shape (no splinters, nails, or loose boards)? Are the sauna heating unit, timer, and safety valve all working properly? Does the door of the sauna close and seal tightly? Are all sports equipment, fins, balls, floating toys, and rafts stored or put away? Are all walkways to and from the home neat and well trimmed?

> **SMART TIP:**
> Home warranties are well worth the money, especially if the home has a pool or spa. Make sure the warranty covers these items.

Home Exterior

Now check the home exterior. Check each side of the home completely. Is the stucco, wood, or other exterior finish in good shape? Are there any cracks or holes in the walls? Is there discoloration from water splash, drainage, or sun? Is the paint or finish in good shape? Are the gutters cleaned out, well painted, and secure? Are the eaves peeling, chipping, or moldy? Are the corners of the build-ing chipped? Are all of the window frames caulked well? Are there any cracks in the foundation? If there is a crawl space under the house, is it empty and accessible? (Crawl spaces should not be used as storage.) Are the screens, vents, and crawl space access doors secure and in good shape? Is the area around the house clean and uncluttered? (This also is *not* a place for storage.) If there is a heat-ing or cooling unit situated by the exterior of the home, is the area around the unit clean? Are all exterior doors painted or finished properly (no peeling or chipping)? Are the exterior and the garage doors well finished?

Roof

Inspect the roof. (Climbing up on the roof can be dangerous so you might consider having a professional roof inspection.) Are any tiles or shingles missing or loose? Any leaks that you know of? Are the gutters clean? Is all of the caulking in good shape at the edges of the tile or composition and around any pipes or fireplaces? Are there any trees, bushes, or limbs scraping against the roof?

Yard

The yard may make a big difference to a buyer. Is the grass cut and trimmed neatly? (Make it look like a putting green.) Are all of the bushes and trees trimmed and manicured? Are the bushes trimmed back from the windows to allow light into the home? Are all the leaves picked up? (This may have to be done daily in some areas.) Are all sprinkler systems, including timers, in good working order? Are driveways, walkways, and parking areas clean and free of grease spots? (Use the same cleaner you used on the garage.) Are sidewalks, even if they are supposed to be maintained by the city or county, clean and in good shape? Are all fences, front and rear, in good repair? Is the fence paint or finish chipping, peeling, or dis-colored? Does the front entry and front door area have appeal? Does it invite you into the home? Remove parked cars, snowmo-biles, boats, trailers, and RVs, used or unused, from the driveway or parking areas. Are all animal areas kept clean, especially dog runs? (If an animal has the run of the yard, keep the yard picked up daily. Buyers really love to step in the dog...!) Are all doghouses, children's play houses, swing sets, and tree houses neat and, if they stay with the home, in good working order? Adding a few colorful flowers often can make a house show much better and provide that elusive curb appeal.

WHAT REPAIRS MUST BE MADE?

Now that you have made your inspection, you probably will have to sit down and recover from the shock and depression that has begun to set in. Most homeowners, while living in their home, never realize how necessary cleaning and minor repairs can pile up. When you begin to look at your home as a buyer does, you quickly become aware of the many small problem areas that exist and must be corrected before you put your home on the market. However, don't worry! Many of the things you have discovered recently are simple cleaning tasks. Usually you will be able to make some of the minor repairs yourself, and a maintenance or service person can complete the rest.

As you break down the required cleaning and repairs, room by room, it will quickly become apparent that you face a manageable task. In any case, it is better to discover any existing problems yourself and have them repaired long before a buyer's inspector finds them and blows a deal.

One suggestion: You may want to wait to complete your cleaning until the repairs have been made, especially if they will create a mess while in process.

Now you need to decide what repairs you will make and how you will complete them. This may depend, in part, on how much money you can spend before selling the home. If it is necessary and you can afford to paint, carpet, and have all of the repairs made, your home will show better and probably sell faster. However, if you are limited as to how much you can spend preparing the home, you have several options.

The following list will help you decide what repairs you should make. Please note that ideally you would complete all of the repairs and cleaning; however, some areas are more critical than others.

TABLE 4.1

REPAIRS THAT SHOULD BE MADE

MOST IMPORTANT	IMPORTANT	SOMEWHAT OPTIONAL
• Paint where needed	• Fix discolored flooring	• Fix driveway and side-
• Clean thoroughly	• Repair fencing	walk cracks
• Create curb appeal	• Repair doors	• Refinish wood floors
• Fix leaky roofs	• Repair outbuildings	• Refinish cabinets
• Clean carpet	• Clean ceiling spots	
• Repair tile or flooring	• Repair worn carpet	
• Fix broken windows	and flooring	
• Repair plumbing problems	• Repair sprinkler system	
• Repair electrical problems	problems	
• Fix inoperative appliances		
• Correct heating		
or cooling problems		

Of all these repairs, paint and a thorough cleaning are the two most important. Both will prove to be time and money well spent.

> **SMART TIP:**
> If you paint, use a neutral color, such as off-white. Use proper paint for the proper surface; for example, bathroom and kitchen walls need a different paint from bedroom walls. (Ask at your paint store for guidance.)

WHO SHOULD MAKE THE REPAIRS?

Based on the items in Table 4.1, it will be fairly apparent which repairs you can make yourself and which you will need to hire a professional for. Be objective in your decision about which repairs you will make. If you need to replace a toilet, you may want to hire a plumber or installer. If you start the job and have problems, and then need to hire a professional to clean up your mess, it may end up costing you more than it would have to hire the expert in the beginning.

Also, do not endanger yourself by trying to make repairs that you are not competent to complete. Unless you are well versed in electrical systems, roof repairs, plumbing, and appliance or structural repairs, it is not recommended that you tackle these tasks without professional guidance.

Do whatever cleaning tasks and repairs you are comfortable with by yourself. As I said earlier, start room by room and correct each problem area. Delegate some of these jobs to other family members.

If costly repairs need to be made, such as carpet, tile, or flooring replacement, you may choose to reduce the price of the home by the amount it would take to replace the floor covering. If you choose to do this, make sure you get at least three quotes on the repairs. Have these estimates in writing to submit to buyers, should they ask to see the costs.

> **SMART TIP:**
> One way to save money on needed repairs is to price the home at market value and offer a designated amount of allowance for the repair. As an example, if the carpet is not in great shape but it has two or three years of wear left (no holes or tattered spots and probably would not be tagged by an appraiser for replacement), offer a $1,000 carpet allowance at the close of the transaction. The actual cost of replacing the carpet may be $3,000 or $4,000, but buyers may look very favorably at a seller handing over $1,000 in cash at the closing. Buyers can use the money for whatever they please and the seller saves $2,000 or $3,000!

CHOOSING A PROFESSIONAL

When it comes time to choose someone to make necessary repairs, people always ask whether to use a licensed contractor or hire the local handyperson.

Some considerations should be:

- Is their work guaranteed?
- Do they have sufficient references?
- Do they have insurance if they are hurt on your property?
- Will they help you get permits if they are required?
- Does their work include materials?
- Will they give you an estimate, in writing?

- Can they complete the work within your desired time frame?
- Can they buy necessary material at a discounted price, and will they pass these savings on to you?
- What is your course of action if their work is not acceptable or they do not finish the job?
- Who will actually do the work, the person you hire or some-one he/she hires to subcontract the work?

One very important point to remember is that all repairs are negotiable. Do not be afraid to ask for a lower price if you have reason to believe the estimate may be inflated. However, oftentimes you get what you pay for. If a contractor or repair or service person is honest and reputable, he or she probably will give you a fair estimate and complete the work as promised. Checking a repair person's references can save a seller enormous headaches in the long run. Also, if you use an unlicensed repair person, you may have little recourse if the work is not done properly.

WHAT ABOUT REMODELING?

Some sellers make the mistake of thinking they can remodel their home and make more money when they sell.

In most cases, sellers do not recover all of the money spent when they remodeled. (Chapter 1 covered remodeling and what percentage of the cost a seller can expect to recover.) Two major improvements to a home that almost always pay for themselves are adding a bathroom to a two-, three- or four-bedroom home with only one bath and improvements or upgrades made to the kitchen, as long as you don't get carried away.

SHOULD THE DECOR BE CHANGED?

Some people live in, let's say, very unique surroundings. While this type of decor may be appealing to a few potential buyers, you must remember that you are trying to appeal to the masses. If your home is decorated in a manner that will appeal to only a few select purchasers, change it. You may love the bright gold foil wallpaper with black and silver appointments in the bathroom, but average buyers will go into shock the minute they enter the room.

Don't remodel. Just change what you can comfortably and inexpensively. Try to have your home appeal to as many buyers as possible.

DO YOU NEED TO STORE SOME THINGS?

One of the biggest problems in selling a home is access when showing the property. You may have a lot of beautiful furniture, artwork, and personal items that make your home very comfortable for you. However, a potential buyer may just think it's crowded and too small. You must learn to "undecorate."

An empty or vacant home does not show as well as a home with furniture; however, a crowded home seems small and uncomfortable. Don't forget that it is not acceptable to store half your belongings in your garage or basement. Instead, rent a storage unit for a few dollars a month or store your belongings with a friend or relative and your home will show much better.

Most buyers, unfortunately, are not very creative or imagina-

SMART TIP:
The Two-Suitcase Rule. Hold a large suitcase in each hand and walk slowly through your entire home. Go to each room, around each table and bed, down each hallway, through the kitchen, into the bathrooms, out onto the patio, deck, or porch, down into the basement, up into the attic, and through the garage. This will simulate what it will be like when your home is being shown to two potential buyers. If you can tour your entire home easily, carrying two suitcases, there is probably enough access for buyers to feel comfortable and not crowded. If not, store some furniture or personal items that are not used daily.

SMART TIP:
Tour a few decorated and furnished new model homes and get a feel for the way these properties are shown. They are never crowded and they are usually bright, airy, and comfortable. Take some lessons from the professionals who decorated these homes, but don't get carried away. Builders spend thousands of dollars decorating these houses, and you don't want to get caught in the trap of trying to recover a huge amount of redecorating costs.

tive. The way they see your home is the way they think it is and always will be, so ask for some opinions from real estate professionals who look at your home. Find out what they think you should change, move, redecorate, or replace. Evaluate their suggestions and then decide what items you will change.

(Table 4.2 on page 47 is a list of ways to help sell a home that also may help you.)

CLEANING—THE MOST IMPORTANT REPAIR?

If you can afford to do so, hire a professional cleaning service to go through your house completely. While you may think your home is the cleanest house on the block, you will be amazed at the difference a professional can make. Again, remember that the cost of cleaning your home is negotiable. Don't be afraid to ask for a lower fee, but negotiate this discount up front, before any work is complete. Don't try to renege on monies owed after the fact.

You may want to hire certain professionals for specific tasks. Certainly landscaping, windows, carpet, and drapery cleaning are areas where using a professional should definitely be a consideration.

Whether you decide to hire professionals or tackle the cleaning yourself, pull out your inspection sheet for each room and take each item one by one. If you used the Post-it notes, you already have a pretty good vision of what needs to be done. If other people are doing the cleaning for you, give them free rein. They may see other things that you missed, so make sure they know they are not to be limited to your observations alone.

Rip out any old, peeling shelf paper and scrub out the cabinets, drawers, and shelves. Scrub the walls, sinks, doors, and toilets until they sparkle. Using your inspection form, you should be able to move from room to room quickly and efficiently.

Literally use a white glove or cloth to check every baseboard, cabinet, toilet bowl, windowsill, door frame, dresser, appliance, and anything else that pops into view.

GET RID OF CLUTTER
AND PERSONAL ITEMS

There is a very fine line between sterility and simple neutrality. You do not want your home to seem sterile, but you want it to be very neutral and appeal to a wide range of people. Buyers must be able to "mentally move into your home" when they see it. If they are overwhelmed by your decorating or your massive 16th-century vases and sculptures, they may never be able to picture their furniture or their family in this home.

As mentioned earlier, put away any items that may offend or bother certain buyers. Some of those things may include real stuffed animal heads or fish, outlandish posters, risqué artwork, items that express political or religious statements, or an overabundance of trophies.

> **SMART TIP:**
> Remember, you are not trying to sell your decorating ability or your personal possessions. You are selling your house. Do not distract the buyers from that one important fact: They are in your house to decide if they want to buy it and make it their home. Nothing more.

When it comes to clutter, most people do not see their own. You may need to procure the services of a very forthright friend or your real estate agent to assist you in your task of "uncluttering" your home.

Put away all jewelry, change, brushes, combs, toys, books, glasses, personal items, spray bottles, irons, ironing boards, reports, papers, bills, mail, magazines, match books, workout equipment, and anything else that is lying around not in its proper place.

Desks, kitchen counters, dressers, TVs, bars, basements, attics, and garages are the biggest "clutter catchers." Clean and check them every day while your home is for sale and during the closing process.

> **SMART TIP:**
> Be especially careful to put away jewelry and other valuables. If you do not have a safe, it might be advisable to store these items in a bank safe deposit box until you move to your new home.

Here's an idea: Go through every box, every closet, the basement, the attic, all of your drawers, the kitchen cabinets, and every other place you store your own "personal clutter" and put together a huge garage sale.

Be objective, honest, and relentless! That suit you're hoping will come back into style from the early '60s—out! The snow saucer you haven't used for 15 years—out! The box of baby clothes you are saving in case you have another child . . . and you're now 56—out! The salad chopper you ordered one night a year ago in a fit of insomnia —out! The jeans you're saving for when you are back to the same weight you were in high school— out! Remember, your junk may be another person's treasure.

> **SMART TIP:**
> If you don't want to go to all the effort to have a garage sale (although it may be worth hundreds of dollars for you to do so), donate your clutter to a charity such as Goodwill or the Salvation Army. Not only will this do some good for other people, you also can obtain a receipt for your donation and write it off on your taxes. No more excuses; if you don't use it, wear it, enjoy it, or eat it . . . get rid of it!

WHAT PAPERWORK SHOULD BE ACCESSIBLE?

Buyers may want to see for themselves how much you have paid in property taxes. Even if these taxes are impounded and are paid inclusive with your mortgage payment, you should have available the actual property tax statements.

Buy a small ring binder (2 inches is acceptable) and plastic page protectors. Put all of your paperwork in this binder and have it available for potential buyers. This bit of extra organization will build confidence and help buyers to feel better about your care for the home.

> **SMART TIP:**
> In some states, such as California, property taxes change and are based on the sale price the new buyer pays for the property. In these cases, a current tax statement would not properly reflect the amount the new buyer will pay for the property taxes. However, it is important for you as a seller to be aware of the amount of property tax for which you are responsible, because you may receive part of what you have already paid back, in the form of prorations, at the close of your transaction.

Your agent, should you list the property, will also be most impressed and appreciative.

Maintenance and
Home Improvement Records

Have available all of the records with regard to maintenance service work, warranty work, and improvements that you have made throughout the ownership of the home. Of particular interest will be roof replacement or repair, appliance repair, plumbing service, and electrical work. If you have kept up with the proper service and maintained good records, most buyers will see that as a very strong positive for the house.

Utility Bills

Most potential buyers will want to know the approximate monthly utility bills. If you have all of the bills for gas, electricity, propane, sewage, garbage, and water for the previous year, have them available. If you have not saved your bills, call each utility company and ask for a printout of your bills for the previous 12 months.

Warranties

Have in your binder all warranties still in effect for appliances or other items for the home. This is especially important for roofs, pools, spas, and electrical and major appliances.

LEGALITIES OF
HOME PREPARATION

Defects may not show. As mentioned, some sellers make a severe mistake and try to cover up problems that exist with a home. An example is painting an interior wall to cover up a discolored area caused by a leak in the exterior wall or roof. The seller who thinks a buyer will not take action six months later when it rains and the leak reappears is in for a rude awakening.

Another common mistake sellers make is not advising potential buyers of ongoing plumbing problems with a property. Often these problems are recurring due to tree roots growing into the underground pipes.

Some sellers who have been advised that a heating or cooling unit will need to be replaced in the near future fail to advise buyers of the pending problem and expense.

All of these examples of withholding pertinent information fall under the laws of seller disclosure.

WHAT MUST BE DISCLOSED?

Since the mid-1980s, many states have made it mandatory that sellers disclose, to every potential buyer, any existing problems or defects of which the sellers are aware. As of July 1, 1996, only four states—Alabama, Arizona, Kansas, and Tennessee—do *not* require disclosure. All other states require seller disclosure of any substantial problems or defects that could affect the value of the home. No longer does the Latin phrase *"Caveat Emptor"*—"Buyer Beware" —apply. While sellers can choose to sell a home with many problems and defects or in an "as-is condition," most states require them to disclose every problem area that affects the value of the home.

HOW SHOULD DISCLOSURE BE DONE?

In many states — about 24 as of January 1, 1997 — sellers are required to complete a seller disclosure form. This form covers everything from appliances to roofs, plumbing, flooring, and termites; some even require disclosure with regard to zoning charges or new bonds and assessments that will affect the buyer's valuation of the property. Other areas of disclosure that have become "hot buttons" are environmental hazards such as lead, asbestos, and radon.

Even in states where seller disclosure is voluntary, not required, it is recommended that every seller disclose all problem areas; it is better to lose a buyer than make the sale and end up with years of litigation and expense.

A question that arises periodically is: Are sellers required to disclose strange, bizarre, or possibly offensive occurrences that have been related to or happened in the house? Some examples might be a home where a rape or murder occurred. Someone died in one of the bedrooms from a highly contagious disease. The home is supposed to be haunted. Each state has different rules that will affect your required disclosure. In some states, you are bound by law not to disclose certain occurrences; by doing so you may violate certain civil rights.

To understand disclosure in your area, check with your local real estate professional as to the requirements in your particular state. If the agent cannot provide adequate information, call your state Department of Real Estate and you will be directed to the proper source.

THE SELLER'S DISCLOSURE STATEMENT

The Seller's Disclosure Statement depicted in Figure 4.1 is an example of the form required or used in many states.

When completing the form, be very specific with regard to any problem areas you encounter. As an example, if you indicate on the form that a leak exists in a back bedroom, explain how extensive the leak is, when it leaks, and what damage has been caused.

SMART TIP:

With regard to seller disclosure, you are not warranting anything and you are not agreeing to fix the problem; you are merely disclosing a problem area. Doing so protects you should future problems occur.

REAL ESTATE SELLER DISCLOSURE STATEMENT

Property Address:_____ Inspection Date:_____

The following aspects of the above-referenced property have been personally inspected by the undersigned buyers and their condition noted accordingly on this form.

The disclosure statement concerns the real property situated in the city of _____ , county of _____ , State of California, described as _____ . This statement is a disclosure of the condition of the above described property in compliance with section 1102 of the Civil Code as of _____ , 19_____ . It is not a warranty of any kind by the seller(s) or any agent(s) representing any principal(s) in this transaction, and is not a substitute for any inspections of warranties the principal(s) may wish to obtain.

Coordinate with Other Disclosure Forms: This Real Estate Transfer Statement is made pursuant to Section 1102 of the Civil Code. Other statutes require disclosures, depending upon the details of the particular real estate transaction (for example: special study zone and purchase-money liens on residential property).

Substituted Disclosures: The Seller disclosures have or will be in connection with this real estate transfer, and are intended to satisfy the disclosure obligations on this form, where the subject matter is the same: _____
_____
_____

Seller's Information: The Seller discloses the following information with the knowledge that even though this is not a warranty, prospective Buyers may rely on this information in deciding whether and on what terms to purchase the subject property. Seller hereby authorizes any agent(s) representing any principal(s) in this transaction to provide a copy of this statement to any person or entity in connection with any actual or anticipated sale of the property.

The following are representations made by the Seller(s) and are not the representations of the agent(s), if any. This information is a disclosure and is not intended to be part of any contract between the Buyer and Seller. Seller ❏ is ❏ is not occupying the property.

A. The subject property has the items checked below:

❏ Range	❏ Oven	❏ Microwave	❏ Dishwasher	❏ Trash Compactor
❏ Garbage Disposal	❏ W/D Hookups	❏ Window Screens	❏ Rain Gutters	❏ Burglar Alarm
❏ Smoke Detector(s)	❏ Fire Alarm	❏ TV Antenna	❏ Satellite Dish	❏ Intercom
❏ Central Heating	❏ Central Air Conditioning	❏ Evaporators Cooler(s)	❏ Wall/Wind Air Cond.	❏ Sprinklers
❏ Public Sewer System	❏ Septic Tank	❏ Sump Pump	❏ Water Softener	❏ Patio/Decking
❏ Built-in Barbecue	❏ Gazebo	❏ Sauna	❏ Pool	❏ Spa/Hot Tub
❏ Security Gate(s)	❏ Garage Door Opener(s)	❏ Attached Garage	❏ Not Attached Garage	❏ Carport
❏ Pool/Spa Heater—Gas	❏ Pool/Spa Heater—Solar	❏ Pool/Spa Heater—Electric	❏ Water Heater—Gas	❏ Water Heater—Solar
❏ Water Heater—Electric	❏ Water Supply—City	❏ Roof—Age_____	❏ Fireplace	

B. Are you (SELLER) aware of any significant defects/malfunctions: If yes, list/describe:
_____
_____
_____
_____

C. Are you (SELLER) aware of the following:

1. Substances, materials, or products that may be an environmental hazard such as, but not limited to, asbestos, formaldehyde, radon gas, lead-based paint, fuel or chemical storage tanks, and contaminated soil or water on the subject property. .... ❏ Yes ❏ No
2. Features of the property shared in common with adjoining landowners, such as walls, fences, and driveways, whose use or responsibility for maintenance may have an effect on the subject property................................. ❏ Yes ❏ No
3. Any encroachments, easements, or similar matters that may affect your interest in the subject............................. ❏ Yes ❏ No
4. Room additions, structural modifications, or other alterations or repairs made without necessary permits. .... ❏ Yes ❏ No
5. Room additions, structural modifications, or other alterations or repairs not in compliance with building codes. .... ❏ Yes ❏ No
6. Landfill (compacted or otherwise) on the property or any portion thereof. .... ❏ Yes ❏ No
7. Any settling from any cause, or slippage, sliding, or other spoil problems. .... ❏ Yes ❏ No
8. Flooding, drainage, or grading problems. .... ❏ Yes ❏ No
9. Major damage to the property or any of the structures from fire, earthquake, floods, or landslides......................... ❏ Yes ❏ No
10. Any zoning violations, nonconforming uses, violations of "setback" requirements.. ❏ Yes ❏ No
11. Neighborhood noise problems or other nuisances. .... ❏ Yes ❏ No
12. CC&R's or other deed restrictions or obligations. .... ❏ Yes ❏ No
13. Homeowners' Association that has any authority over the subject property. .... ❏ Yes ❏ No
14. Any "common area" (facilities such as pools, tennis courts, walkways, or other areas co-owned in undivided interest with others).. ❏ Yes ❏ No
15. Any notice of abatement or citations against the property. .... ❏ Yes ❏ No
16. Any lawsuits against the seller threatening to or affecting this real property. .... ❏ Yes ❏ No

Seller certifies that the information herein is true and correct to the best of the Seller's knowledge as of the date signed by the Seller.

Seller:_____ **Date:**_____

50 TIPS TO HELP SELL A HOME

Successful sellers and agents who have sold properties considered "difficult to sell" have provided the following suggestions. While many will seem small and inconsequential, often buyers need just "one more small reason" to decide to make an offer. This list also serves as an excellent recap of the main points you've read so far.

TABLE 4.2
50 TIPS TO HELP SELL A HOME

1. Always look at the home from a buyer's point of view. Be objective and honest with yourself.
2. Stimulate the buyer's imagination by setting scenes: a warm fire, a chair with a quilt, a book on the table.
3. Create a spacious feeling in the home. Leave all interior doors wide open.
4. Post a chart or sheet that identifies and accentuates the positive features of the home. Better yet, use small well-printed signs to accentuate positive features. (Many model homes have these.)
5. Use folded quilts, bright colored pillows, and fresh flowers to draw attention to positive features.
6. Use props such as a bright colored umbrella on a deck to point to backyard positives.
7. Disguise unsightly views, but do not use dark, heavy curtains. Instead, hang light sheers and let the breeze blow in and move them. Never apologize for a poor view!
8. Place 3- or 4-inch glass shelves inside window frames and decorate with small plants or stuffed animals on the shelves but leave lots of light streaming through.
9. Eliminate bad odors. Get rid of the source. Then use Lysol®, potpourri, carpet freshener, deodorized cat litter, and cedar blocks or chips inside closets and drawers.
10. Make sure the front door area is immaculate and not cluttered. Pick up a new door mat. (Avoid cute sayings on the mat.) Make sure brass door knocker is shined. Maybe place some potted flowers by the front entry. Use nice pots and bright-colored flowers.
11. Avoid eccentricities such as beads hanging in doorways, wild posters, black or dark walls, mirrored ceilings, sacred temples, red/gold wallpaper or jars of bugs, spiders, and snakes. Make the home appeal to the masses.
12. Have a garage sale before the home is put on the market.
13. Maintain "comfort" in the home that lies somewhere between clutter and sterility.

50 TIPS TO HELP SELL A HOME *(continued)*

14. Use a "Buyer's View Box." (See Chapter 3, page 22.)

15. Anytime potential buyers may be viewing the home, make the interior visible from the exterior. Clean windows, open drapes, lights on, and soft music playing make a home inviting.

16. If there is space, hang a two-person chair swing on the porch. Maybe paint it a bright color and place bright-colored pillows on the seat.

17. Place photos of the home during different times of the year — Christmas, spring, summer barbecues — throughout the house.

18. Make sure all doors, electric wall plates, and wall corners are clean and free of fingerprints.

19. Clean out closets. Make them feel spacious. Leave room in the entry closet for potential buyers to hang their coats if the weather is cool.

20. Highlight the fireplace or woodburning stove. If the weather is cool, have a fire going when home is shown. If it is too warm for a fire, add color with flowers on the mantel or pillows on the hearth. If the fireplace is not being used, place a large plant or flowers in the burning area.

21. Stand outside the front entry and evaluate the overall "feeling." Is it warm and does it invite you in?

22. Set the dining table. Make it "homey." Use flowers and candles.

23. Create counter space. No dish racks, cleanser, dish soaps or unused appliances.

24. Depersonalize rooms. (An example would be removing a teenager's poster of the latest grunge band from the wall.) Remember, appeal to the masses.

25. Having fresh flowers in the home gives the feeling of life. However, do not let them get stale and create an odor.

26. Increase wattage of light bulbs in dark areas of the home, especially bathrooms, kitchens, closets, and laundry areas.

27. Use color to draw attention to positives. Flowers, pillows, or quilts work well.

28. Make beds appear inviting. Again, pillows and quilts will help.

29. Use bright-colored tablecloths on outside or patio tables.

30. Use track lighting to create moods. It is inexpensive and can work wonders.

31. Use mirrors to make small areas appear larger.

32. Clean off book and wall shelves and make the wall appear spacious.

33. Make sure the garage is spotless and there are no cars inside or on the driveway when the home is shown.

34. Make sure the access through the home is very open and comfortable for at least three people at a time. (See section on "Do You Need to Store Some Things?")

35. Store excessive furniture.

36. Make sure doors open all the way.

50 TIPS TO HELP SELL A HOME *(continued)*

37. Find some way to light or highlight exposed beams.

38. Get rid of video arcades and make sure the television is not the focal point of any room.

39. Make sure any hanging items — plants, pans in the kitchen, soap racks —are very clean and do not have any cobwebs.

40. Make sure all electrical sockets and switches inside and outside operate properly.

41. See that hallways are clear, unobstructed, and well lit. If they are dark, consider some track lighting.

42. Create a "master suite" effect in the master bedroom. Make it look like a bed-and-breakfast bedroom. Magazines are a good source of basic decorating ideas.

43. Make sure staircases are well lit and uncluttered. Also, test that the handrails are secure.

44. Possibly keep underbed storage boxes so the home can be tidied up very quickly if shown on short notice.

45. Be sure that shower curtains and doors are kept clean and unstained. If they are discolored or stained, replace them.

46. Keep porch, deck, and patio furniture clean in case a potential buyer sits down.

47. Clean all grease and oil stains off the driveway, walkways, parking areas, and garage floors.

48. Trim all bushes away from windows for security as well as to allow the light in.

49. Use props to entice the buyer's imagination. Some examples are:

   - Birdhouses in bright colors
   - Swing on the porch
   - Flowers
   - Clean, enticing barbecue
   - Hammocks
   - Dishes of potpourri
   - Glass mirrors or crystal
   - Books on tables
   - Chess or checkers set
   - Set tables or fully stocked bars
   - Potted plants
   - Pillows and quilts
   - Table cloths
   - Umbrellas
   - Logs in fireplace
   - Special soaps and soap dish
   - Large coffee-table books
   - Knitting basket by rocking chair
   - Guitar, piano, music stand and stool
   - Baskets of pinecones, dried flowers, etc.

50. Light one or two candles in the house to create a mood and a nice scent.

Remember: You do not want to create clutter, but you do want to make buyers comfortable—feel at home—and spark their imagination.

CHAPTER FIVE

Should You Sell Your Home Yourself?

THE FOR-SALE-BY-OWNER DILEMMA

Some sellers believe that all there is to selling a home is to throw up a sign, run a few ads, and *whamo,* buyers appear in droves. That is *not* usually the way it happens. In some cases, sellers may be forced to attempt to sell their home themselves, without utilizing the services of a professional real estate salesperson.

This type of situation may occur when sellers have very little equity because they have owned the home for only a short time or because the home has declined in value. In this dilemma sellers may be forced to pay to close the transaction rather than receiving funds from the sale. However, these cases are rare.

For the most part, sellers choose to try to sell their own home to save the commission . . . *no matter what it costs them.*

For many years statistics have shown that the average for-sale-by-owner home sales actually net less than if owners had listed and sold at actual market value utilizing the services of a professional real estate salesperson. Also, remember that over 85 percent of buyers looking for a home go to a real estate agent.

Most buyers who look at properties being sold by owners are doing so because they want a deal. Many of these same buyers are sophisticated enough to know that if sellers sell their property themselves, they will save the commission. These same buyers probably will find out how much comparable homes are selling for in the area and ask owners selling their own homes to reduce their price by 6 or 7 percent to compensate for the lack of commission.

Sellers utilizing the for-sale-by-owner route also lose the advantage of having a third party objectively and nonemotionally negotiate on their behalf. If potential buyers tell you that they have only a slight interest in your property because your color schemes and decorating all stink and it will all need to be redone . . . you might lose a little of your edge when negotiating.

The list of questions that follows may help you decide if you should sell your own home or hire an agent.

Bear in mind that, as in all industries, some licensed real estate agents are not much better prepared to sell your home than you are. However, if you use the criteria shown in Chapter 6 for choosing an agent, you should feel confident that the professional you have chosen will work diligently to get your home sold quickly and for the highest price, ultimately netting you the most money possible.

It is true that approximately one in every six homes that sell is sold without the services of a sales agent. But keep in mind that these statistics include bank sales, attorney transactions, family sales, and direct government sales. In actuality, for normal arm's-length sales, approximately one in 20 actually closes "For-Sale-By-Owner." Over 90 percent of homes originally listed in this way end up listing with sales agents within 90 days.

THE "SHOULD I SELL MY HOME MYSELF" CHECKLIST

Before you make the decision to sell your home yourself, answer all of the following questions truthfully and objectively.

The first 10 questions relate to when you bought your current home.

1. When you bought your home, was it an easy process?
2. Did you easily understand all of the paperwork?
3. How were problems handled and who handled them for you?
4. Who prepared the forms, contracts, and disclosures?
5. How did you decide what to offer for the property? Who gave you the sales data?
6. How did you find your home?
7. Who negotiated the transaction?
8. Who guided you to your loan and assisted with your loan process?
9. Who oversaw the closing process?

10. How did you complete the transaction? (How did you get possession, keys, etc.?)

The following questions relate to your abilities and the actual sale process.

11. Can you advertise your home effectively? Can you write advertising copy?
12. Do you know how to set the price properly?
13. Do you know what repairs should be made and what repairs must be made?
14. Are you willing to spend the money for signs, advertising, and brochures? (This could be hundreds, even thousands of dollars.)
15. Do you know what disclosures must be made?
16. Do you know which inspections are required and which should be done?
17. Can you show your home effectively?
18. Can you screen buyers properly?
19. Do you know what to watch for when rip-off artists or time wasters call you or show up at your door?
20. Can you prepare deposit receipts or purchase contracts that are legally binding?
21. Do you understand good-faith deposits?
22. Do you know under what circumstances those deposits must be returned?
23. Will you be using an attorney to prepare your paperwork or close your transaction? If so, how much are the fees that will be charged?
24. Do you know where to send a buyer for a loan?
25. Can you assist the buyer in loan application preparation?
26. How will the appraisal process be handled?
27. If the appraisal does not come in at or above the sale price, what do you do besides lower your sale price?
28. Do you understand the title process?
29. Do you understand the loan process?
30. Do you understand the closing process?

31. Which types of advertisements attract the most buyers?

32. Which papers, books, or publications are best to advertise your property?

33. What type of brochures are most effective?

34. Where should brochures be placed to attract the most buyers?

35. What color, style, and format of brochure produces the best buyers?

36. What color and size of brochure has the highest readership and the highest response rate?

37. Where can advertising items be sent to produce immediate buyers?

38. How can you negotiate escrow, closing, title, and inspection fees?

39. Do you know how to prepare your home for sale with no help or guidance?

40. If the roof, termite, well, septic, or home inspections turn up with problems, what are your options?

41. How can you get back any overages paid in impounds or special fees?

42. Can you give the closer/escrow officer the proper instructions for closing the transaction?

43. How will you handle the final walk-through process with the buyer?

44. What will you do if the buyer wants to make changes in the terms of the contract before closing?

45. What can you do if the buyer refuses to sign papers or close the transaction?

46. In what cases can you keep a buyer's deposit?

47. What if the buyer has an agent or attorney? Can you negotiate and deal effectively with professionals?

48. Will a sophisticated, professional buyer be able to take advantage of you?

49. Are you flat-out good enough at selling to be able to sell your own home?

50. WOULD SOMEONE ELSE HIRE YOU TO SELL THEIR HOME?

As you can see, the decision to sell your home yourself should not be made without very serious thought.

In the next few chapters I discuss many aspects of the actual marketing, sale, negotiations, and closing process. If you do attempt to sell your home yourself, read all sections completely and make every effort to comprehend all of this information. Also, Chapter 16 covers many of these items in more detail.

If you have decided not to sell your home yourself, the next chapter is unquestionably the most important chapter in this book.

SMART TIP:

If you decide to sell your own home, make sure you have proper sales, marketing, and legal counsel. If you need to sell the home or you are under certain time constraints to get the home sold, set a time limit for your for-sale-by-owner period. And most important, unless you are well versed in real estate and contract law, *never* accept any offer unless it has been reviewed by a professional who understands all of the nuances of real estate law.

Hiring an Agent

WHY DO YOU
NEED AN AGENT?

If you have a good personality, are fairly intelligent, are somewhat versed in sales, have a salable home, are willing to spend the money required to market your home effectively, have total cooperation from your family members, have the time during the day or night to show your home, feel confident writing contracts, have read this book . . . hey, what the heck can an agent do for you?

Understand, this book was written to help you "Sell Your Home Fast" and "For the Highest Possible Price" and to make the selling process easier. That does not mean it was written necessarily to teach you to sell your own home. In the mid 1970s Clint Eastwood movie called *Magnum Force*, Clint, in his inimitable style, drawled, "A man's got to know his limitations." After reading this book, you will know more about selling a home effectively than 90 percent of the people in North America. However, you wouldn't read *Gray's Anatomy* and expect to walk in and perform brain surgery. You might understand the terminology, you may even get a feel for the techniques described, but when it came to do the actual process . . . well, that's a different story. And what if it was your son or daughter or brother or sister on whom you were performing the surgery? Now it becomes even more difficult.

An old adage states, "An attorney who represents himself has a fool for a client." Think about that!

WHAT SHOULD AN AGENT
DO FOR YOU?

As I said before, not every licensed real estate agent is going to do the job he or she should or promised he or she would do for you.

That's why it is critical that you choose an agent who has a proven track record and references to back up any claims made with regard to ability to market your home effectively.

A proficient and professional agent should:

- Give you a complete marketing proposal when you sign the contract. This is prior to actually signing a listing. Later in this chapter I cover what should be included in this proposal.
- Give you references to contact, the more the better.
- Be a full-time professional or have substantial production that qualifies that salesperson as a competent producer.
- Have a complete and competent team of affiliates whom he or she is confident in. (This may include, but not be limited to, assistants, title people, closers, escrow officers, loan people, and office staff.)
- Have contact via referrals, advertising, phone marketing, mail response, and office calls with many potential buyers each day.
- Be proficient in numerous methods or types of transactions and loans.
- Have contact with numerous other agents through computer or listing services such as Multiple Listing Service (MLS).
- Be willing to prepare and utilize brochures, flyers, cards, or other marketing items specifically designed for your property.
- Be willing to keep you informed in writing no less than weekly with regard to the efforts being made to sell your property and what results have occurred.
- Be associated with a national referral service that can refer their buyers to your agent or the agent's company.
- Be able to set your listing apart from the crowd.
- Be able to set your listing price properly with the help of factual data obtained from comparable data services.
- Be willing to provide, in writing, a complete marketing plan designed specifically for your home and be willing to guarantee that plan will be followed unless deviating from it is mutually agreed upon.
- Be willing to guide you on necessary repairs.
- Prequalify any potential buyers before they see your home.

- Help buyers find and obtain any necessary loan money for the purchase of your home.
- Negotiate on your behalf throughout the entire listing, offer, and sale closing process.
- Be present and supervise the closing process as well as handle any problems that might arise after the close.

HOW DO YOU FIND THE RIGHT AGENT?

The easiest way to find the right agent is to look around and ask questions. What agent is selling homes in your area? Not just listing them, *but getting them sold.* Ask your neighbors or your friends who sold their home. How was their experience with that agent? How long did it take to sell the home? Was it a good transaction? Did the agent do what he or she said would be done? Often you will at least find out which agents you do not want to use.

One of the biggest mistakes you may ever make is listing your home with Uncle Morey just to help him "get going" in the business. If you are not in a hurry and you want to be a guinea pig for trial-and-error techniques, list with an inexperienced or inadequately trained agent and hang on for the ride of your life. Either you will feel like the forgotten child or you will swear you've stepped onto a roller coaster, round and round, up and down, no clue what direction you are going and wishing you had never gotten on the ride.

Another place to look for an agent is in your local newspapers, home magazines, or other media advertising.

> **SMART TIP:**
> Do not choose an agent just because you are acquainted with that person through your health club, local restaurant or from your children's school. Check the person out. Does he or she sell homes effectively, and are the clients satisfied customers?

Some agents concentrate on target market areas or groups of people. Some agents concentrate their work primarily in one geographic area. If any of these agents are in your area—they usually refer to themselves as "neighborhood professionals" — you may want to talk with them. But again, do not make a decision or sign a listing agreement until you have reviewed their results, checked their references, and looked carefully at the marketing plan they have for your specific property. Figure 6.1 will assist you in choosing an agent.

FIGURE 6.1

SELLER'S GUIDE TO CHOOSING AN AGENT

Questions to Ask the Agent	What You're Trying to Determine
Do you work full time as a real estate salesperson?	This is critical only if the agent is not a serious professional. A number of agents in the business are what I call "perpetual participants." They are just in the office for something to do and seldom do any business. Some part-time people actually are good producers, so couple this with the questions on production and number of listings and transactions to make a final judgment.
How long have you been a real estate agent?	Again, some people prove themselves quickly. However, you do want someone with some experience. Look at this with the next seven questions for a better overall picture.
What special training have you had?	What sales, listing, contracts, marketing, and other special programs has the agent taken?
Are you a Realtor® or Realtor® associate (a member of National Association of Realtors®)?	The Realtor® designation signifies that the agent is a member in good standing with the National Association of Realtors® and, further, that he or she agrees to abide by the ethics and professional standards established by that organization. Membership in this organization is voluntary. If the agent you are interviewing is not a Realtor® or Realtor® associate, ask why not.
What special designations do you possess (GRI—Graduate Realtors Institute; CRS—Certified Residential Specialist)?	Certain designations indicate that the agent has completed certain training and/or has completed training and a specified number of closed transactions. Both the GRI and CRS are excellent designations.
Has your production gone up or down recently? Why?	Sometimes a very successful agent with a great reputation just stops producing. Maybe it's personal problems, market changes, or just plain burned-out. Whatever the reason, you don't need to be a part of it. You want to see consistent production or, better yet, a continual growth in production.
How many listings have you had in the past six months? How many of these listings sold?	A full-time, good production agent should have a minimum of two to four listings per month. Some agents will have as many as 10 to 12 per month. How many have sold will de-

QUESTIONS TO ASK THE AGENT	WHAT YOU'RE TRYING TO DETERMINE
	pend somewhat on the market situation. However, at least a third to half of the listings taken should be sold or pending sales.
Of the listings that didn't sell, what would you say is the dominant reason?	The most common answer will be "They were overpriced." If that is the answer, ask why the agent took the overpriced listings. Most probably it was to pacify the client, in hopes that he or she would accept a lesser offer if one was written.
How many total transactions have you closed in the past six months?	A full-time, successful agent should close two to 10 transactions a month, depending on the specific market area and the price range of the homes sold. A very successful agent in Beverly Hills may average only one transaction a month and have $15 million in total closed transactions, whereas another agent in Las Vegas may close 50 transactions and only have $6 million in closed sales. Again, how does this agent's production compare to other agents in the area?
Do you have a full-time team of affiliates with whom you work consistently who will see that no details are missed?	Who will the agent recommend for title, escrow or closing, loans for the buyer, and so on? Are these people with whom the agent has worked consistently and feels comfortable? Why are they the best?
How many potential buyers would you guess you personally talk to each week?	Five, 10, 20—more is better.
How many potential buyers would you guess your entire office has contact with each week?	Fifty, 100, 200—more is better.
Do you understand specialized contracts such as seller carry-back, wrap-arounds or cosigner's transactions?	You may never see one of these offers, but if you do you want your agent to be competent to guide you.
Do you belong to Multiple Listing Services?	Absolutely critical! Unless there is no MLS available in your area, walk away from any agent who does not belong. This is where most buyers are found.
In what ways will you encourage other salespeople to push my property?	Pitching at multiple meetings, office meetings and caravans, open houses, special brochures, phone calls to other agents ... in other words, what's the plan, Jack?
Will you make a specialized brochure and/or other marketing material specifically for my home?	In some areas this is critical. In other areas it isn't so important. However, insist on one for your property.
If the answer to the last question was yes, how and to whom will these items be distributed?	One should go to every agent in the area, all of the potential buyers with whom this and other agents are working with, specific buying areas for this price of home (such as condos, apartments, non–owner-occupied homes in the area), bulletin boards in area offices, all relocation directors for any major companies moving into the area, even possibly to hotels where people being relocated tend to stay. Also, a

FIGURE 6.1

SELLER'S GUIDE TO CHOOSING AN AGENT (continued)

QUESTIONS TO ASK THE AGENT	WHAT YOU'RE TRYING TO DETERMINE
	box reading "Brochure—Take One" should be provided somewhere by or on the for-sale sign so potential buyers driving by can pick up a copy. These are only a few suggestions.
How many of these marketing items will be distributed each week?	Answer depends mostly on the area. If you are in Ft. Lauderdale, it may be 2,000 a week. However, if you are in Marysville, California, it might only be 200 a week. Saturation is the key.
Where else will you advertise my home? How often?	Newspapers, home magazines, billboards, computer networks. (See "Performance Campaign" in Chapter 11 for paper exposure techniques.)
How will you set my listing apart from the hundreds of others on the market?	Specialized marketing program designed especially for your property.
What other ways will you expose my property to potential buyers?	Record everything each agent tells you for comparison with other agents you will interview.
In your estimation, what is my property worth?	Don't flinch—just write it down.
What listing price do you recommend?	If it is higher than the last answer, ask why. Remember, overpricing is not a good technique.
How did you arrive at that price?	Comparable market analysis: Is it done using only the local neighborhood? All comparables that an appraiser would use should be utilized.
Can you assist in my relocation plans (if applicable)?	If you are leaving the area, this is very important. It is also a consideration if you are buying another home . Ask specifically if the referral contact the agent recommends is someone whom he or she has worked with in the past, or is it just a name out of a referral book? You want an agent just as competent at the other end of your move.
Do you have suggestions as to how I might save money on sales commissions, title fees, closing costs, repair costs, inspection fees, and moving costs?	Pay close attention! If the agents don't have any suggestions, you will have some for them. Remember, Chapter 15 deals with ways to save money.
Will you give me a written plan of action that spells out exactly what we agree you will do to sell my home? Will you guarantee, in writing, to follow that plan?	If agents hedge about giving you a written plan of action, can them. You want a guarantee they will do what they say they will.
May I have a list of your references, listings you have now, and past clients? May I contact a couple of these people if I choose to?	If they won't give you references, again, get rid of them. If they are new and don't have real estate references but you still want to consider them for the job, ask for personal references.

QUESTIONS TO ASK THE AGENT	WHAT YOU'RE TRYING TO DETERMINE
What is your commission?	Six or seven percent is normal. Don't respond to this. You'll come back to this later.
Why do you feel you and your company would be the best to handle the sale of my property?	Just get a feel for their ability to sell themselves and their company. Remember, no matter what they are selling, they must sell themselves first.

THE DECISION

After you have evaluated each agent, then you must make your choice. Look at the facts, trust your intuition, and go with the agent for whom you have the best overall feeling. Keep in mind that the person you choose is essentially going to be your business partner for at least a few weeks because he or she will get paid only when you get paid.

CHAPTER SEVEN

Listing the Property

WHAT THE AGENT EXPECTS FROM YOU

Before the actual listing appointment you should:

- Have prepared your home for sale as discussed in Chapter 4.
- Have put your paperwork binder together as discussed in Chapter 4.
- Have available all necessary information regarding current loans, liens, and other pertinent information that might affect the sale of the home.
- Be mentally prepared and ready to look objectively at the facts the agent will provide with regard to price and sale information.
- Prepare a fact and information sheet for the agent pointing out all amenities you see as the most important features of the property.

WHAT YOU SHOULD EXPECT
FROM THE AGENT

At the listing appointment the agent should have:

- Information about the entire housing market including but not limited to:
  How many homes have sold in the area.
  The prices at which these properties sold.
- An analysis of the entire local market. (In other words, is the local market hot, cold, a buyer's market, a seller's market, etc.?)
- Any suggestions for improvements that he or she thinks you should make to help sell your home.
- A complete marketing action plan. (Exactly, step by step what he or she will do to sell your home.) You will have some sug-

gestions with regard to this when you have read the section entitled "The Complete Action Marketing Plan" on page 75.

- A complete analysis comparing your home to the other homes that have sold. The comparison should include the number of stories; bedrooms; bathrooms; square footage; special bonus or family rooms; basements; attics; special storage areas; amenities such as fireplaces, pools, spas, oversize garages; list price; time on market before sale; date of sale, and, if possible, how the home sold: Federal Housing Aministration (FHA), Veteran's Administration (VA), conventional, seller financing.

The agent also should recommend what price it would be appropriate to list your home at and should have prepared a Seller's Net Proceeds Worksheet. (See Figure 7.1.)

Some agents might give you a range of prices that may include information with regard to how the home sells. As an example, if the home sold VA or FHA, you might be asked to pay discount points for the buyer to obtain this government loan. (Discount points are fees charged by the lender to offset the lesser amount of interest the buyer will pay on certain loans. Each discount point is 1 percent of the loan amount.)

An agent might advise you that a buyer purchasing with an FHA or VA loan that has discount points of 2 may offer $177,000 for the property. However, a buyer using a conventional loan (where no points were charged to the seller) may offer $174,000, knowing that the seller will save on closing costs by accepting the conventional offer at a lesser price. The discount points charged to the seller in that scenario would amount to $3,440. The seller's net is improved by $440 by accepting the lower sales price and the conventional offer.

Remember, the Seller's Net Proceeds Worksheet is an estimate. It is not a guarantee from the agent as to how much you actually will receive at closing. Rather, it is an estimate that should come close to your approximate net proceeds, assuming no additional, unforeseen costs such as termite damage, roof repair, or additional undisclosed loans.

FIGURE 7.1

SELLER'S NET PROCEEDS WORKSHEET

Sale Price $ _____

CLOSING COSTS:

Brokerage Fee	$ _____	
Title Insurance	$ _____	
Points (if any)	$ _____	
Escrow/Closing Fee	$ _____	
Document Preparation	$ _____	
Fees Paid for Seller	$ _____	
Recording	$ _____	
Bonds & Assessments	$ _____	
Inspections	$ _____	
Tax Services	$ _____	
Repairs	$ _____	
Home Warranty	$ _____	
Attorney Fees	$ _____	
Other	$ _____	
	Total	($ _____)

LIENS:

1st Mortgage	$ _____	
2nd Mortgage	$ _____	
Other	$ _____	
	Total	($ _____)
	Net to Seller	$ _____

FIGURE 7.2
MARKETING PLAN
Schedule of Events

Prepared for _____

By _____

For Property Location at _____

ACTION ITEMS	SCHEDULED	COMPLETED
1. Prepare your home for the marketing process		
• Present marketing plan	_____	
• Review marketing plan schedule of events	_____	_____
• Provide competitive market analysis	_____	_____
• Estimate your net sale proceeds	_____	_____
• Review market conditions and customs	_____	_____
• Discuss financing terms and alternatives	_____	_____
• Review disclosure regulations as required	_____	_____
• Provide you with a Seller Service Survey Card	_____	_____
2. Review professional techniques that can help your property sell faster.	_____	_____
3. Install company yard sign (as agreed upon).	_____	_____
4. Submit property to the local Multiple Listing Service (as available and agreed upon).	_____	_____
5. Arrange for a preview of your property by other real estate professionals.	_____	_____
6. Distribute property description letters or brochures (as agreed upon).	_____	_____
7. Keep you informed as agreed upon.	_____	_____
_____	_____	_____
_____	_____	_____
_____	_____	_____
_____	_____	_____
_____	_____	_____
_____	_____	_____

BEFORE SIGNING THE LISTING: THE MARKETING PLAN

It is very important for you and the agent to agree on what you will expect from him or her.

Most important, you should agree on the marketing plan the agent will follow to get your home sold.

Figure 7.2 is an example of a successful performance campaign that has resulted in the sale of thousands of homes throughout the United States and Canada. Each agent will have his or her own ideas and actual plan, but as the seller, you should not be afraid to make suggestions, and the agent should be willing to listen if the suggestions have merit.

SMART TIP:

Remember, this is just an example of a marketing plan. Do not try to stuff your plan down the throat of an agent who really knows what he or she is doing in your area. If the agent has had good success, trust him or her. However, it doesn't hurt to make suggestions if it appears that you are not getting results.

SIGNING THE LISTING: TYPES OF LISTING CONTRACTS

Once you and the agent have agreed to all of the details, it is time to prepare and sign the actual agreement. Since there are several types of listing contracts, it is important that you understand the pros and cons of each, for both you and the agent.

Exclusive Right to Sell

This is the most common type of listing used by most real estate sales people, and it is the most binding with regard to the agent receiving a commission. No matter who buys the home, even if it is your mother, the agent will still get the commission. Also, all other agents or companies who might sell the property would sell through your agent or broker. (See Figure A.3 in the appendix for a sample of an Exclusive Right to Sell Form.)

SMART TIP:

You can add an addendum to the Exclusive Right to Sell at the time of the listing to exclude a person or persons from this exclusive contract. In other words, at the time of listing you advise the agent that your brother, John Jones, may buy the home from you and, if he does, without the help of an agent, you will not be required to pay a commission to the agent. *Remember, you can add names only at the time of listing. You can't add any names later on.*

Exclusive Agency

This type of listing allows sellers to sell their own home and not pay a commission. As an example, if as just stated, you sell your home to a family member, friend, or anyone else who has not had any contact with the agent, you are not required to pay a commission. However, the agent or broker that you hire has the exclusive agency on the property and any other real estate company or agent who writes an offer on the property would make that offer through your exclusive agent, just as with the Exclusive Right to Sell.

Open Listing

Essentially, you agree to pay a commission to any agent who brings a buyer and handles the transaction. Oftentimes, on commercial properties or open land, you will see two or three different real estate signs on the property. These probably are cases of open listings. The sellers have given all of the agents permission to advertise and sell the property with no exclusivity.

SMART TIP:

If you are trying to sell your home For Sale by Owner, include in your advertising a statement that offers brokers the opportunity to sell the home at a specified commission. This, in essence, makes the property an open listing. Figure 7.4 is an example of a For-Sale-By-Owner ad.

FIGURE 7.3

TYPES OF LISTINGS COMPARISON

EXCLUSIVE RIGHT TO SELL	EXCLUSIVE AGENCY	OPEN LISTING
Pros	**Pros**	**Pros**
Agent: Most exclusive and secure for the agent; therefore, the agent is the most motivated to work on your listing. *Seller:* You will have a stronger commitment from agent.	*Agent:* Agent will get paid if he or any other broker brings a buyer. *Seller:* You can sell your property yourself and not pay a commission.	*Agent:* If the market is good, gives agents another property to show and sell. Agent does not have to spend money on advertising, etc. *Seller:* You can offer the property to multiple agents with no exclusivity. You can sell your home yourself and pay no commission. Broker must be the direct procuring agent to receive a commission.
Cons	**Cons**	**Cons**
Agent: None *Seller:* Must pay a commission, regardless of how a buyer is procured, even if seller finds the buyer.	*Agent:* Not as exclusive as Exclusive Right to Sell and may be less motivating. *Seller:* Agent may not work as hard or spend as much money on your listing.	*Agent:* Few agents will work on this type of listing because there is no exclusivity and little security. With most open listings, sellers are not committed to selling their property. *Seller:* Essentially you are a For Sale by Owner without much more than hope. And hope is a goal without a plan. Most agents will not feel confident showing your property; therefore, they may put it last on the list to show and sell.

FIGURE 7.4

BROKERS WELCOME: BY-OWNER ADVERTISEMENT

NEW ON THE MARKET
For Sale by Owner
Elegant, all cedar, 5-bedroom, 4-bath secluded home surrounded by 60 pine-covered acres, a private trout stream and breathtaking views. Only 10 minutes from town, schools, and shopping. $795,000. Shown by appointment. 000-0000, ask for Dale.
Brokers welcome at 3%.

As mentioned earlier, there are pros and cons both for the agent and seller to each type of listing contract. Figure 7.3 on page 77 will help you understand these deviations.

Most Multiple Listing Services (MLS) will allow Exclusive Right To Sell and Exclusive Agency listings only.

When you do list your home, I recommend that you sign an Exclusive Right to Sell for these reasons:

1. Your agent will make the highest and best effort to sell your home because there is security in his or her efforts.
2. Other agents from the MLS will see you are a committed seller.
3. Your agent will be more apt to spend money advertising your property and pushing every possible buyer through the home.
4. There will be more trust and less opportunity for questionable actions on the part of both agent and seller.

SMART TIP:
When you sign the Exclusive Right t Sell, I do recommend that you include provision requiring the agent to follov the actions or performance campaig you have agreed upon to market and se the home. If the agent does not perforr as he or she has agreed, you can hav your listing back.

WHAT YOU SHOULD WATCH FOR IN THE LISTING CONTRACT

Most agents use preprinted listing contracts that have spaces to fill in any negotiable items such as special clauses, stipulations, and names and addresses.

Some items that you need to pay close attention to are explained in the following pages.

Commission Rate

The most common rates are 6 to 7 percent of the sales price; however, this is totally negotiable. Read Chapter 13 on negotiating techniques, before you agree to the commission rate. Understand, the higher the commission, the higher the agent's motivation to show and sell your property. Do not quibble too much if you are happy with the agent and his or her plan of action, but don't be afraid to ask for a lower commission, as explained in Chapter 9. Most agents will jump at your offer when they understand what you are willing to do to help sell your home.

Term of the Contract

Most listing agreements are written for a term somewhere between 90 and 180 days. Do not sign a listing with an automatic continuation clause or an automatic extension. You want to be able to evaluate the progress if the home has not sold during the initial listing period. It may be in your best interest to relist the property with your original agent. However, you will make that decision just prior to the original listing expiration.

Also, in some areas, especially where homes are priced in the upper range ($500,000 or more), many agents will request a longer initial listing period, up to as much as a year. You will be able to see if this is reasonable if you look closely at the "Days on the Market" section of the "Comparable Sale Report," which the agent should have provided for you. If the homes appear to be selling in 60 to 120 days, there would be no reason for the longer listing period. However, if the "Days on the Market" appear to be in the range of 120 to 240, then it would be perfectly reasonable for the agent to ask for an extended initial listing period.

Agent Protection After the Listing Period

Associated with, but an altogether different issue, is how long after the initial listing period is the agent protected for and how long will he or she still earn a commission on a buyer procured during the term of the listing. In other words, suppose your agent has shown your property to a prospective buyer and the buyer has hesitated in making an offer; then, after the initial listing period has expired, the buyer comes back to you, the seller, or to the agent to purchase the property. What period of time is the agent protected and for how long would the seller be subject to the provisions of the original listing contract with regard to paying commission?

Again, this is an area of negotiation. Normally, the term of after-contract protection is somewhere between 30 and 60 days.

Special Extension Periods

On occasion, an agent may ask you to extend the listing period through the projected sale and closing process. This is actually after the agent has procured a buyer and you are waiting to close the transaction. This is another protection device for the agent; should the initial purchase contract not go through, he or she may have found several other people who are interested in purchasing your property and possibly have made "backup" offers.

If the agent has an extended listing period, he or she could prepare a new contract and restart the closing process with the new or backup buyer. Because you extended the listing period, you still would be bound by the listing agreement even after the first transaction did not close. In most cases, this should be acceptable to you, the seller.

Listing Price

All of the terms of the listing contract are based on the listing price, as indicated in the listing contract. If an offer is received for a lesser amount, all bets are off. You can renegotiate any part of the contract including, but not limited to, the repairs you agreed to make, what personal property stays with the home, even commission ... anything that was predicated on the sale price of the property being the same as the listing price.

Unfortunately, many sellers assume that if a lesser offer is presented and they accept it, all of the other terms of the listing contract are still in effect, which is not the case. The purchase agreement or deposit receipt presented by the buyer or the buyer's agent will include all of the terms and conditions on which that contract is based. The terms of the purchase contract may be totally different from the terms specified by the seller in the listing contract.

Unless an agent procures a buyer strictly in compliance with the terms of the listing agreement, the seller shall not be bound to accept the buyer's offer and pay that agent's commission.

However, in most cases, sellers do accept lesser-priced offers and abide by most of the terms of the initial listing agreement, including the commission percentage originally agreed to by the seller and the agent.

Financing Terms Agreed to by Seller

You may agree to carry-back the deed of trust or mortgage. All terms acceptable to you, the seller, with regard to this type of financing should be stated in the listing agreement, including loan amount, terms of repayment, and interest rate.

The best way to state an offer for this type of financing in a listing agreement is: "Seller may consider owner financing, not to exceed $10,000, with interest of no less than 10%, payments and term negotiable."

Condition of Property at Sale

The listing agreement should indicate all repairs you intend to make, and any financial allowances that may be offered to the buyer for repairs or improvements. In other words, in exactly what condition the seller is going to deliver the home to the buyer at the close of a transaction should be specified.

Personal Property

Another area of consideration is that of any personal property or attachments that will transfer with the home to the buyer. Some examples might be appliances—washer, dryer, refrigerator—chandeliers, window coverings, or area rugs.

For the most part, these personal property items will not affect the sales price or appraisal of the home. However, in some cases, these personal property items can amount to a substantial value. As an example, a home on the water at Lake Tahoe might include dock rights and a boat. In that case, there would be substantial value to the personal property that is being transferred, and these might become negotiated items if a lesser offer was received or the buyer had no interest in the personal property.

If the personal property is a boat, car, or other item that would require registration, it should be indicated in the listing agreement whether the seller is willing to pay the registration or transfer fees or whether the buyer will be responsible for these costs.

Chapter 8 discusses a special sales method that includes the technique of giving away "FREE" personal items or services to assist in the sale of a property that has proven to be difficult to sell.

If you intend to remove items that appear to be attached to the property, this should also be stated in the listing agreement so buyers will not be surprised when they take possession. Examples might be prize rosebushes that will be removed from the ground; a dog run that is attached to a cement base; children's play equipment, tree or play houses; or workbenches in a shop or garage.

If an item is attached to the property, most buyers will assume it stays with the property. Specify in the listing contract if that is not the case.

Special Permissions

This area of the listing contract is important because it details the "Special Permissions" you will give to your listing agent and to other agents who may show the property. An example might be giving your permission to the agent to place a lock box with a key inside, on your property, thereby providing better and easier access. In most areas it is normal procedure to place lock boxes on the listed properties.

Other permissions might include placing a sign in the yard, holding open houses, and entering the premises when the seller is not present. Although most of these permissions will seem obvious necessities, some sellers become irate when they find that the listing agent has placed a signpost in their beautiful manicured yard, which required a post hole 8 inches x 8 inches x 3 feet deep.

No surprises! That is the rule for a good agent/seller relationship. Cover all of the special permissions in the listing contract.

Special Cautions

Another area that should be addressed in the listing agreement is special cautions. If, for example, a seller has prize Dobermans in a dog run in the backyard and these animals are never to be disturbed, put it in the listing agreement. If a caution is so critical that a financial loss could occur, put it in the listing agreement. Just verbally telling the agent "Be careful of the dogs" may not be adequate warning for your agent or other agents who show the property, but if those warnings are a part of the contract, the agents will definitely take heed.

Also, include any of these cautions in the form used to submit the property to the local Multiple Listing Service (MLS).

EXIT AGREEMENT
(GETTING OUT OF THE LISTING)

As discussed previously, when you sign an Exclusive Right to Sell or an Exclusive Agency listing agreement, you should include a stipulation that specifically states that this Exclusive Right to Sell is based on the performance of the agent as agreed upon in the marketing plan or performance campaign. A good, ethical agent will be more than willing to specify the action plan in writing and be willing to agree to follow that marketing blueprint. As part of the listing agreement, it should be stated that if that performance campaign is not followed, this will be justification for you to ask for the listing to be terminated and that the agent will comply with that request.

If you feel that an agent has not performed as agreed in the original performance campaign, you as the seller should take these steps:

1. Identify exactly what actions or inactions on the part of the agent you feel are not satisfactory. If it is just that the agent has not yet produced a buyer, but has followed through completely

with the marketing plan, you should recognize that the problem may be market condition, price, or other circumstances totally out of the agent's control.

2. If it does appear that the agent has not followed through with marketing plan (has not advertised the property as agreed, has not held open houses, has not kept seller informed as agreed, etc.), then it is a different story.

3. Give the agent at least one opportunity to explain or correct the problem areas that you have identified. Be specific. Explain what you want to occur and within what time frame.

If the agent makes the changes that you have requested, within the time frame you have specified, then you are back on track. If, however, you still do not see the action that you were promised previously, it may be time to ask the agent to cancel or terminate the listing. Remember, as I said earlier, there are only two actions in life—"Performance or excuses!" and at this point you may hear a lot of excuses. Be firm and remind the agent that you had an agreement based on performance. That performance has not occurred; therefore, the listing agreement is to be terminated as agreed.

If the agent refuses to release the listing, first call the agent's managing broker. You can get his or her name by simply calling the agent's office or the local Board of Realtors® and asking for the name of the broker of record.

If the broker refuses to terminate the listing or will not return your calls, contact the local Board of Realtors®, the local Better Business Bureau, or the state Department of Real Estate, usually located at your state or province capital.

If you must, become a total pain in the neck to everyone associated with this agent until you get action.

See Figure 7.5 for a copy of an Easy Exit Listing Agreement. Figure A.1 in the Appendix presents a Performance Campaign. If your listing agent does not have similar forms, ask that these be included with your listing agreement. *Do not be afraid to ask for performance in writing.*

The rest of the listing agreement will be self-explanatory, or the agent will be able to answer any questions you may have.

If you are uncomfortable with a clause or portion of the listing contract, tell the agent you would feel more secure having some counsel review the agreement before you sign.

One word of warning: If you seek counsel, make sure you talk to someone who knows the subject about which you are asking. Everyone has an opinion or a theory about how things should be done. Don't make changes just for the sheer sake of making changes or requests. However, don't fall for the old line, "This is the way it's always done." *Find out* if this is the way it's always done.

FIGURE 7.5

EASY EXIT LISTING AGREEMENT

100% GUARANTEED

Most home sellers' worst fear when signing a listing agreement is not being able to rescind the listing agreement for lack of performance by the agent.

You can now rest easy with my listing agreement because it is 100% GUARANTEED. If, for any reason, you are unhappy with my service or performance, you can cancel your listing.

NO problems. NO hassles. ANYTIME.

I am so confident in my marketing campaign, past performance, and professional standards that I am willing not only to GUARANTEE my performance, but to put it in writing.

The truth of the matter is, if I couldn't produce the results, I wouldn't be making the promise. Find out why the highest level of professionalism and service produce the quickest results.

_____   _____
Name   Date

FIGURE 7.6:

SELLERS' ACTION PLAN

on next pages

SELLERS' ACTION PLAN

1. We agree to maintain the property clean, in good condition and ready to show at short notice throughout the listing and sale process. We further understand this "ready-to-show" condition must be maintained even after an offer has been accepted to allow the potential buyers as well as any backup offer buyers the opportunity to see the home.

2. The seller will make every effort to see that the home is easily accessible, including a lockbox and keys provided for the listing agent.

3. The seller will see that all pets are either removed from the premises or caged properly during any potential showing periods. This could include the entire listing period if animals stay in the home during the day when the seller is not present.

4. The seller will work with all cooperating agents who may show the home and will provide for the listing agent all business cards left by these cooperating agents. (Agents should leave a card in the home at every showing to alert the seller and listing agent that the property was shown.)

5. The seller agrees that if the property has sold after the first 60 days of the listing period, seller and agent shall meet to discuss any areas of concern of either party, including but not limited to price, terms, and condition of the property.

6. The seller agrees to help market the property by maintaining a supply of fact sheets or brochures and distributing these sales items to friends, family members, or at any other opportunity that may arise in the normal course of the seller's daily activity. The seller immediately will provide the listing agent with the names of any persons who show an interest in the property.

7. The seller agrees to notify the listing agent if any of the sales or marketing items are damaged or depleted (signs, brochures, etc.).

8. The seller shall expect contact with the agent on a weekly basis. However, the seller shall not deem it necessary to have any excessive contact with the agent unless problems arise or there is a specific reason for the contact.

9. The seller will notify the listing agent immediately if another agent should try to solicit the listing.

10. The seller will provide for the listing agent all real estate solicitation materials that are mailed or delivered to the seller's property.

11. The seller agrees to contact the listing agent before obtaining information on or viewing other properties that the seller may be interested in buying.

12. The seller agrees to notify the listing agent should something occur that may change the seller's motivation, one way or the other, to sell the property (job transfer fell or came through, death in the family, pending bankruptcy, etc.).

13. The seller agrees to notify the agent of any personal circumstances that may change the status of the listed property (lawsuits, separation or divorce, bankruptcy liens or judgments, refinancing or additional financing using the listed property as collateral, change of owners of record, quitclaim deeds or other transfers of title, or substantial change of occupants or tenants).

14. The seller will notify the listing agent immediately if the seller becomes aware of any code violation, zoning changes, or problems or permit requirements that may affect the listed property.

15. The seller agrees to maintain and have available, on request, loan information, utility bills, warranties and service records that might be of interest to agents or buyers. (This may be in the form of an information binder.)

16. The seller agrees not to attempt to negotiate with any potential buyers or other agents unless requested to do so by the listing agent.

17. The seller agrees not to talk to buyers unless agents are present.

18. The seller agrees to return phone calls from the listing agent immediately.

19. The seller agrees to maintain the listed property in essentially the same condition as when the property was listed. The seller shall notify the agent if the furnishings are going to be removed, and the seller will not remove any property deemed as part of the real property. (Examples of real property are built-in cabinets, doors, in-ground sprinkler system, built-in security system, etc.)

20. The seller agrees to notify the listing agent immediately of any significant changes in the property, such as remodeling, new roof, garage torn down, etc.

21. The seller agrees to vacate the property as often as possible when property is being shown.

22. The seller agrees to notify the listing agent if the seller is going to be out of town for more than 24 hours. The seller further agrees to provide the agent with his or her itinerary, including phone numbers, where the seller can be reached during this period. (If an offer is received, time is of the essence. The offer may expire in a matter of hours.)

23. The seller agrees to maintain contact in some way—via voice mail, answering machine, etc.—so that the agent may leave messages for the seller and these messages can be received no less than once per day.

24. The seller agrees to be the agent's silent partner and provide the agent with complete cooperation in all aspects of selling the listed property.

Seller_____ Date_____

Seller_____ Date_____

HOW YOU WILL HELP THE AGENT

Sellers must realize when they list their property with an agent that they must become working partners with that agent. Use a Sellers' Action Plan from Figure 7.6 when you negotiate the commission as indicated in Chapter 13.

This form will surprise most agents; not many sellers make such commitments to listing agreements. As discussed in Chapter 13, many agents will see the true financial value in your commitment and may be willing to reward you for your efforts.

WHAT IF YOU CHANGE YOUR MIND?

Once you have signed a listing agreement and put your home on the market, you can't just arbitrarily decide you've changed your mind and take your home off the selling block.

Most agents will be understanding if unforeseen circumstances arise that change your motivation, such as your job transfer didn't come through, a death in the family, or even that you have just realized you can't afford to buy a new home and make the move. If, on the other hand, you just decide you're too emotionally attached to your neighbors and you change your mind, the agent may not be quite so understanding.

Remember, that agent, from day 1 of the listing, has spent a considerable amount of time and money predicated on the assumption that he or she will recover those expenditures when the property sells.

If the agent were to bring a buyer, ready, willing, and able to purchase your property in conjunction with the terms of the listing agreement, the agent has legally earned the commission and could sue you for the fee. If, under those circumstances, you refuse to sell, you may open yourself up to this and other litigation.

> **SMART TIP:**
> Work with the agent and be honest. If circumstances change and you decide not to sell your property, talk to the agent and see what you can work out.

CHAPTER EIGHT

Pricing the Home

THE MOST IMPORTANT DECISION

Without a doubt, of all of the mistakes a seller can make, mispricing the home either too high or too low is the most harmful and costly.

If you price the home too low, the home will sell, and probably sell quickly, but you will lose money that is rightfully yours.

If you price the property too high, it will not sell. The home will continue to cost you money in the form of interest, repairs, and upkeep. More important, you may experience severe mental and emotional stress that can be much more costly in the long run.

Even if a home should sell at an inflated price, above the market value, the bank or loan appraiser will probably come in with an appraisal that is less than the sale price. At that point, very few buyers ever consider paying more than the appraised value for a home.

Further, a bank, savings and loan, or mortgage company will never base a loan amount on any figure higher than appraised or market value. Therefore, a transaction that is originally structured and based on a sale amount higher than market value most likely will never close.

> **SMART TIP:**
> A property priced correctly, prepared properly, and marketed appropriately will sell in any market, good or bad. Sellers who refuse to price their properties correctly are wasting not only their time but the time and money of any agent who might have potential buyers for the property.

COMMON MISTAKES IN PRICING

The following are the most common mistakes made by sellers and agents with regard to pricing properties.

PRICING CONSIDERABLY
ABOVE MARKET VALUE

Pricing considerably above market value is a mistake made by misinformed sellers and agents for a number of reasons. The most common reason is that sellers, when they first think about selling, sit down and calculate the exact amount they must or would like to receive from the sale of their home. The net figure becomes their one and only concern, and they become blinded to the facts. They add this predetermined necessary net to the sales costs and their current loan balance and the resulting figure becomes their "gotta get price!" It is amazing how many sellers totally ignore the market value facts and say, "We have to get a certain figure or we won't sell!"

The market value or sales price of a property can never be established from the figure sellers feel they must receive as net profit. The home is worth what it is worth, and no matter how much you "gotta get," it will never be worth any more.

Unfortunately, in many cases, when the agent comes to take the listing, the seller gives the agent no choice. The seller says, "We gotta get $270,000 or we won't sell" and the agent says, "Well, okay, we'll give it a try!" This is a fateful mistake on the part of both parties, especially if the highest comparable sale in the area is no higher than $235,000.

Agents worth their salt will simply say "No, I won't take an overpriced listing. Call me when you become more realistic."

However, as I said, some agents will take a listing at any price, hoping and praying with all their might that a buyer from another planet, completely unaware of market values, will pop out of the blue and pay cash for the overpriced property.

Or . . . that the seller will become realistic should some poor soul write an offer at market value.

Neither of these scenarios is very likely.

Another common reason that sellers decide to price their property considerably above market value is that they believe they have "the nicest home in the neighborhood," with the nicest carpet and nicest kitchen, and their home is more wonderful than any other home within 50 miles. And, with all of these upgrades and improvements, surely the home is worth at least $20,000 or $25,000 more than any other comparable sale.

These sellers are not only factually unrealistic, they have an even greater problem: They are emotionally attached to the property.

As illustrated in the story about Bill and Carol in Chapter 3, the cost of improvements made to a property probably will never be completely recovered and most buyers will not see the improvements in the same manner as the seller. Buyers will see the home the way they want to see it, with their own decorating ideas, which may be totally different from those of the seller.

Another common scenario is that a seller just takes the attitude "I want to start high and I can come down if you bring me an offer. I can always come down on the price but I can't go up." This type of thinking will create nothing more than a problem listing.

Most buyers, when they are looking for a home, fix their sights on homes within a certain price range. As an example, if a buyer has been prequalified for a loan of $150,000 and he or she has $30,000 to put down, most buyers will look at homes in the $180,000 to $195,000 price range.

> **SMART TIP:**
> Sellers must realize that with comparable-size homes, the nicest home in the neighborhood will become a victim of regression. The value will be pulled down by the lower-value homes. The least-valuable home will become a product of progression; its value will be pushed up to the higher value homes.

If a seller has a home with a true market value of approximately $185,000 but chooses to price the home at $210,000 in hopes of finding a buyer who will pay top dollar for the property, that seller has probably priced him- or herself out of the market for most buyers who would be looking at comparable properties.

Also, buyers who are looking at the $210,000 range will quickly rule out that seller's property because they can buy so much more elsewhere for the same price.

Underpricing the Home

A home is usually underpriced for one of two reasons:

1. The seller knows that the home needs a lot of work and he or she does not wish to or cannot afford to prepare the home properly for sale. Consequently, this seller will offer the home for sale at considerably less than market value.
2. The seller is ill-educated or uninformed with regard to home sales in an area and simply misprices the home. Also, the seller may have owned the home for a long time and may not be aware of the appreciation that has occurred over the years of ownership.

Lack of market awareness can be overcome by studying the local market, the economy, and all of the comparable sales that relate to a seller's particular property.

With regard to the first type of seller, a good cleaning and a coat of paint often can do wonders for the appearance and value of a home. Because most buyers look at many homes before they make an offer, the home that is not prepared properly for sale or is dirty or ill kept will have very little chance of competing with properties that are in good shape.

Sellers who choose to sell their home in disrepair must realize that the decrease in value will not be a minor figure. Most homes that sell in an "as-is" condition do so at 10 to 15 percent below market value. Using an example of a home with a true market value of approximately $200,000, the reduction in value could be as much as $25,000 or $30,000.

Many real estate investors make their living buying homes in need of cosmetic repairs (cleaning, paint, yard care, etc.). These investors make only the necessary repairs to bring the home up to near market value. Then they sell the home quickly, earning anywhere from $5,000 to $20,000 on each transaction.

A home that is in need of some repair but is in crystal clean condition will probably sell somewhere close to or just below market value, with some allowance for the work that needs to be done.

On the other hand, a home that is filthy and in disrepair will not have a chance of competing with the other homes on the market.

WHY MUST YOU PRICE PROPERLY?

There are four reasons you must price your home correctly from Day 1 of your listing.

Time

Chances are that your home ultimately will sell at its fair market value. Pricing it properly at the outset simply increases the likelihood of a timely sale with less inconvenience and greater monetary return.

Competition

Buyers educate themselves by viewing many properties, and they will always look at a range of homes priced competitively. They know, or learn very quickly, what is a fair price. If your home is not competitive in value with those they have seen in the same price range, it simply will not sell.

Reputation

Overpricing causes most homes to remain on the market too long. Buyers and agents become aware of the long exposure period and often are hesitant to make an offer because they fear something is wrong with the property. Clean, well-prepared homes that are on the market for a long time historically sell for less than their fair market value.

Inconvenience

If overpricing keeps your home from selling promptly, you may end up owning two homes, the one you are trying to sell and the new home you have already purchased. This can prove to be costly, worrisome, and very inconvenient.

Figure 8.1 shows statistically the typical activity that is generated on a property during a standard listing period. As you can see, most of the activity is generated during the first five weeks of the listing period.

Statistics have shown that agent and buyer interest grows as soon as a home is placed on the market, peaking somewhere

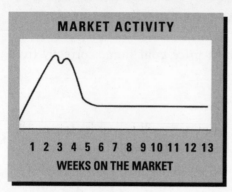

MARKET ACTIVITY

1 2 3 4 5 6 7 8 9 10 11 12 13
WEEKS ON THE MARKET

FIGURE 8.1
MARKET ACTIVITY CHART

around the third or fourth week. Pricing a home properly and then creating immediate urgency in the minds of agents and buyers is critical.

UNDERSTANDING AND USING COMPARABLE SALES DATA

Although professional appraisers consider many factors when they are establishing value of a home, the most important component is comparable sales. If there are numerous comparable sales—or "comps," as professionals call them— pin-pointing a specific home's value will be an easy process.

SMART TIP:
The best pricing analogy for a seller to understand is simply this: If you own stock and it is trading at $72 per share, but you decide you want to sell your stock at $90 a share, who will buy it?

The answer is *NO ONE!* And that is exactly the way sellers must look at pricing their home. If they try to sell their home worth $185,000 for $210,000, *no one will buy it.* Worse yet, no one will even be interested enough to look at it.

The three most critical elements with regard to finding acceptable comps are area or location, comparable amenities in the homes, and size of the home.

Now, just as an appraiser uses comparable sales to establish the value of a home, real estate professionals and informed sellers will use exactly the same data to establish market value and the list price of a potential sale property. Most of the comparable sales data will be readily available to real estate professionals through their Multiple Listing Service. In most cases, this information is maintained current, within at least 30-day periods; in some areas it is updated daily.

Once you understand how to read and utilize comparable sales data, consistently determining proper valuation of properties is a fairly simple process. You are simply comparing "like properties" with "like properties" or homes with somewhat the same amenities in somewhat the same areas.

In a very busy or "hot" market, it is easy to find many "like properties" that have sold. However, difficulty occurs when the market is slower or you have a property that is unique and like properties that have sold in the past six months can't be found.

Most agents believe that the only properties that can be used as comparable sales to establish market value must be strictly within the same area as the seller's home. This, of course, would be ideal if every property placed on the market had three or four perfect comps to use for the valuation process. However, this is not always the case; many agents do not realize that an appraiser, making a valuation on the same property, may go outside of that particular neighborhood and find another "similar" neighborhood. By "similar" I mean homes built at almost the same time as the subject property and with about the same amenities and sale prices as the subject property: equivalent homes with equivalent sale prices.

> **SMART TIP:**
> Remember, you are using properties that have sold *and closed* for comps. Often potential sellers make the mistake of using listing prices to establish the value of their home. Listed properties should *never* be used as comps for valuation of a home because sellers can list their property at any price, as much above market value as they may choose.

For this reason, it is imperative for sellers and agents to look at the total sales market of the entire area, not just the neighborhood prices. This is especially important when comparable sales are not readily available in the neighborhood surrounding the subject property.

The Comparative Market Analysis (CMA) in Figure 8.2 shows the sales data used to determine the market value on the home shown and listed.

As you can see, once you learn to read and understand the comparable sales data, it is simple to determine the current market value of specific properties.

Sellers who, after reviewing comparable sales data, insist that their home is worth more than the comparable sales are simply

FIGURE 8.2

COMPARATIVE MARKET ANALYSIS

COMPARATIVE MARKET ANALYSIS

Date: _1/3/96_   Competitive Market Value: $ _206,000_
For: _John and Mary Doe_   Probable Sale Price: $ _205,000 – 207,000_
Address: _1217 Carbone Way_   Seller's Acknowledgment: _Ed James_
Prepared By: _Bill Smith_

Note: List prices and sale prices add - 000 to each price shown.
        SQ. FT. is price per sqaure foot. This figure is rounded to the nearest dollar.

ADDRESS/ FEATURES	BED RMS	BATH	SQ.FT.	AGE	FAM. RM	DIN. RM	FIRE-PLACE	POOL	GAR.	LIST PR.	SALE PR.	SQ.FT	DAYS MKT.	TERMS	DATE SOLD	REMARKS
SUBJECT PROPERTY																
127 CARBONE	3	3	2720	8	X	X	X		2	210	205	76	–	–	–	
SOLD																
806 SMITH	3	3	2800	9	X	X	X		2	220	210	75	64	–	12/1	
91 SOUTH	4	3	2750	8	X	X	2	X	2	225	219	80	78	OC 2nd	12/14	BEAUTIFUL POOL
230 ALTO	3	2	2600	6	X	X	X		2	220	193	74	29	–	12/30	
FOR SALE NOW																
1223 CARBONE	3	3	2840	8	X	X	X		2	212	–	75	41	–	–	VERY NICE
1380 CARBONE	4	3	2960	9	X	X	X		3	225	–	76	84	–	–	
8110 - 2ND	3	2	2500	8	X	X	X		2	185	–	74	74	–	–	WILL SELL QUICKLY
EXPIRED																
486 HOWARD	3	3	2900	8	X	X	X	X	2	232	–	80	180	–	–	RENTED
774 CAROL	3	3	2700	8	X	X	X		2	220	–	81	240	–	–	OFF MARKET

unrealistic. There is a very good chance that their home will not sell. Likely their home also will become a "stale listing"—one with which most buyers and almost all agents will refuse to work.

SETTING THE PRICE

If we use the home utilized in our Comparative Market Analysis (CMA) as an example, we have determined that the market value of that property is approximately $206,000.

Unless a very strong sellers' market exists and homes are selling as quickly as they are listed, most buyers are not going to offer full list price for a property. Therefore, sellers, when setting their list price, should leave some allowance for the negotiation process that almost every buyer will expect.

Understanding the history of pricing will help guide sellers with regard to their particular market condition. In the late 1970s, it was not uncommon for sellers to list a home at or slightly above market value and, within a few days, receive four or five offers, all at or very close to list price. In some cases offers were presented *above* the full list price.

Only a couple of years later, in the early 1980s, mortgage interest rates had risen to 16, 18, or even 21 percent in some areas. Buyers who could qualify for these high-interest loans were scarce; consequently, many properties sat on the market for six to 18 months. When these properties finally sold, the sellers seldom received the full market value. Also, many of these sales involved some type of owner carryback financing, and often sellers were forced to provide for the buyers special incentives. It was not uncommon for sellers to receive 10 to 15 percent below their listed or market value price. This very difficult time created a pure "willing buyer, willing seller market," and, for the first time in the history of real estate sales, comparable sales had little value for the purpose of pricing. Prices actually dropped 10 to 30 percent in some areas across the United States.

Toward the mid- to late 1980s and on into the 1990s, the market became more stabilized. In 1993 interest rates dropped to the lowest percentage rate in 30 years; nevertheless, for reasons that most economists could not understand, appreciation on properties remained minimal—1 to 3 percent per year in most areas.

In the past, when interest rates had fallen, prices of properties had risen dramatically due to the increase of qualified buyers and ultimately, higher demand for homes. In 1993, however, home sales rose only approximately 6 percent above the prior two years.

Several factors played a part in this unexpected limited increase, but the most prominent elements were:

1. More stringent qualification processes for potential borrowers —it just became harder to get a loan.
2. The insecurity on the part of the borrowing public with regard to the overall economy—people were afraid to buy or make a move.

Early in 1995, after seven consecutive increases in interest rates by the Federal Reserve Board, mortgage interest rates rose to over 10 percent in some areas and housing sales slumped dramatically again. Sale prices began to drop slightly, and once again it became a buyers' market.

During that time, comparable sales data was scrutinized very carefully and like for like homes had to be exactly that, with little deviation.

Buyers who could qualify at the higher interest rates were not afraid to make offers considerably below the listed prices, because they recognized the strong bargaining position in which this weak sellers' market had put them.

Consequently, active and progressive real estate agents began listing property at or just below market value and preprogrammed sellers to agree to reduce the price of the property no less than every 30 days during the listing period. Also, most of these agents asked sellers to reinstate the original listing period or term each time a price reduction occurred.

Although this type of pricing strategy may seem a bit radical to some sellers, it became recognized as an effective tactic to use during difficult sales periods. If a home has been marketed aggressively for 30 days and very few, if any, potential buyers have viewed the property, it should become apparent to the agent and the seller that price or lack of terms are probably the weak factor in the sales equation.

If, on the other hand, numerous potential buyers have viewed the property and no offer has been received, price or lack of terms still could be the deterring factor. However, other things, such as preparation or cleanliness of the home, also could be the problem.

The significance of this little history lesson is simply this: Home sale prices can rise and fall considerably within just a few weeks or months, due to local market conditions, Federal Reserve intervention, a rise or fall in interest rates, or other world events that might cause instability in the overall housing market.

Sellers must be able to analyze all of these factors properly when setting the price of their home. They also must be willing to recognize that, six months or a year earlier, homes comparable to their home actually may have sold for more than their home is now worth.

> **SMART TIP:**
> Sellers who truly want to sell their property must be willing to match their sales strategy to the sales market that exists at the time they are trying to sell. Furthermore, these sellers must recognize that the sales market may evolve or change dramatically even during the term of their listing.

Now, returning to the example property discussed at the beginning of this section, the market value was determined to be approximately $206,000. An acceptable beginning list price would be somewhere in the area of $209,900. The $3,900 above-the-market value is an acceptable cushion to allow potential buyers room to negotiate and feel as if they have received a bargain.

However, as explained previously, in a buyers' market there is a very good chance that buyers will start the offer process much lower, possibly somewhere in the range of $190,000, or anywhere from 6 to 15 percent or more below the actual comparative market value.

In this type of market, it is not uncommon to prepare and present four to six counteroffers during the negotiation process. Chapter 13, on the negotiation process, explains counteroffers and provides direction regarding the actual negotiation.

For now, recognize that it is most important for sellers to keep their listing price very near that of the determined market value. If you must sell quickly, you should be realistic enough to understand that you must list your home at or below the determined market value.

Even if you are not in a great hurry to complete the sale of your home but do want to sell, you should be aware of the many long-term, negative effects that pricing their home too high will create.

SHOULD YOU GET
AN APPRAISAL?

Some sellers feel uncomfortable using just market evaluation and comparable sales data to establish their listing price. Even after receiving an estimate of value from a real estate professional, they still believe they need more information before they determine their asking price.

Usually these types of sellers believe their property to be worth considerably more than the comparative market analysis has shown. In these cases, it may be necessary for sellers to order a professional appraisal from a reputable appraiser.

The Financial Institutions Recovery and Reform Act of 1989 detailed certain requirements that appraisers must meet. But most states require no licensing for people to call themselves appraisers. Therefore, if you order an appraisal on your property, you should do so from someone with the proper credentials to value the property correctly.

Over 20 designations are awarded by professional organizations or indicate the expertise of that particular real estate appraiser. The most recognized and accepted designations are the MAI (issued to an appraiser who is qualified to appraise any type of property) and the SRA (issued to an appraiser specializing in residential valuations). Both designations are used by the Appraisal Institute and require a considerable amount of course work and experience.

If you do decide to order an independent appraisal prior to the sale of the property, you should understand that the appraisal may or may not meet your expectations with regard to sales price. Also, with regard to disclosure, any problems, repairs, or special requirements you are made aware of in the appraisal would have to be disclosed to any potential buyer.

Another consideration is cost. You probably will spend between $300 and $500 for an appraisal. There is a very good chance that when the property sells and the buyer applies for a loan, the buyer's lender will require a new appraisal by their designated appraiser, which will cost you, the seller, another $300 to $500. Unless you are in a very big hurry to sell your home, a written appraisal on the property is not necessary or advisable until an offer has been written and accepted.

Most real estate professionals will recommend that sellers do *not* order an appraisal until a willing buyer has been procured.

HOW LONG DO YOU STICK TO YOUR PRICE?

As I indicated earlier, the overall market can change dramatically in just a few weeks.

If interest rates are high and buyers are at a premium, it becomes a buyers' market. Sellers who must sell urgently may be forced to begin price reductions immediately if potential buyers are not looking at their property.

If, on the other hand, there appears to be a great deal of interest in the property (i.e., many buyers looking at the property), you might be well served to stick with your initial listing price for 60 to 90 days.

If you or your agent has followed a competent and complete marketing campaign very closely and a buyer has not been produced in 60 days, you should begin price reductions and possibly step up the intensity of the marketing program.

If after 30 more days interest in the property is still weak or nonexistent, you should consider another price reduction. However, at that point, it may be in your best interest to try to increase buyer interest by offering valuable incentives.

THE "POWER OF FREE"

Ever since the difficult market of the early 1980s, it has become quite commonplace, especially in a buyers' market, for sellers to offer incentives to the buyer who purchases their property.

Some of the examples I have discussed already are: allowances made for carpet or other improvements, home warranties or appliances, or other personal property that might stay with the home. Other incentives that have been used are "free" home security systems, "free" housekeeping services for six months to a year, "free" utilities (gas and electric) for a year, or "free" expensive jewelry, boats, or cars.

One example of this type of incentive/giveaway involved a property that was originally listed for $1,100,000 in Beverly Hills, California. After sitting on the market for four months with practically no buyer interest, the agent asked for and received a price reduction to $999,000. After another three months the seller decided to reduce the price to $949,000, the figure that the agent had indicated was the proper price from the onset of the listing. Again, another two months passed and though some buyer interest was generated, no offers were written. At the end of nine months, the seller decided to order a professional appraisal, which, much to his surprise, came in at $948,650, only $350 below the price the agent had indicated was the proper market value.

It was apparent that the price or property condition was not the problem. Instead, homes in that price range were selling very slowly. Some homes, well prepared and well priced, had taken up to 18 months to sell; overpriced homes were still sitting after two to three years on the market.

At this point, the seller had to sell because he had already purchased another home 400 miles away. The seller was making two large house payments and trying to commute back and forth so neither home sat vacant.

The agent suggested an incentive giveaway to create buyer interest. The seller, having had no experience with such matters, decided to trust the agent and give it a try.

As outlandish as it sounded, the agent suggested that the seller give away his BMW to a buyer who purchased the property. At first the seller resisted; however, after he considered that the car was six years old and only had a true value of about $9,500, he agreed.

Remember, this home had sat on the market for nine months with very little buyer interest. Also, the seller had indicated to the agent that he was willing to let the property go for $800,000, nearly $150,000 below appraisal value.

The agent prepared the marketing card shown in Figure 8.3 and distributed 300 — yes, only 300 — to apartment and condo renters, in the same area, who were paying substantial rent, some as much as $3,000 per month.

FIGURE 8.3
ADVERTISEMENT CARD

FREE BMW FREE BMW FREE BMW FREE BMW

THAT'S RIGHT! IF YOU PURCHASE OUR HOME DURING THE MONTH OF SEPTEMBER AND THE SALE CLOSES BY NOVEMBER OF THIS YEAR . . . YOU KEEP OUR BEAUTIFUL BMW!

Park your BMW in the 3-car garage and stroll through the acre+, parklike grounds. Enjoy the unique pool, spa, and cabana. Prepare luscious meals in the large, recently remodeled kitchen. Lounge comfortably by the two fireplaces. Gaze tranquilly across the Canyon Creek greenbelt from the huge double-pane living room windows. Spread out in over 6,000 square feet of living space which includes 5 bedrooms and 4 baths, all exquisitely appointed. Only four minutes from shopping and the East Ridge Parkway. Experience living as it should be . . . and for much less than you expect.

Call today for a private showing: John Doe (000)123-4567

Remember, you keep the BMW!

The agent's telephone lit up and an offer was written and accepted in only four days! Most important, the home sold for $879,300, or $79,300 more than the seller had indicated he would be willing to accept. The transaction closed in 37 days.

The agent loves to tell the story. According to her, most of the calls went something like this:

> CALLER: Hello, are you the agent with the home for sale in Beverly Hills that comes with a free car?
>
> AGENT: Yes, that is correct.
>
> CALLER: Well, can you tell me about . . . ah . . . the BMW?

This was a $900,000 home and most of the potential buyers first wanted to know about the "free" car. Obviously, in the minds of buyers, expensive homes for sale are a dime a dozen. But a "free" BMW—now, that's worth looking into!

Each year hundreds of sales are made because a creative seller or agent utilizes the exceptional "Power of Free."

Of course, not every property will be as difficult to sell as that million-dollar home in Los Angeles. However, on a smaller scale, many sellers can utilize this same technique should they experience difficulty in getting their property sold in a reasonable period of time.

In some cases proper pricing may need to include special financing incentives. The different options that sellers may offer with regard to financing terms are discussed next.

CHAPTER NINE
Terms and Financing

ARE TERMS REALLY NECESSARY?

Most sellers would like to believe that the sale of their home will be a quick and easy process in which the home will sell at full market value. The buyer will apply for and receive the full loan amount requested. The transaction will close within the original closing period and the buyer will move in. The seller will walk away, cash in hand, and everyone involved in the transaction will be happy as clams.

In the perfect world, that is the way every transaction would occur. However, in the real world, all potential buyers have their own unique financial situation. A seller who will look only at purchase contracts from buyers who "cash out" the seller, either with a new loan or a substantial down payment that pays the seller all of his or her equity, is limiting the opportunity to reach many potential buyers.

WHAT OFFERS MIGHT YOU SEE?

Consider the following scenario involving a seller's decision to accept an offer whereby the seller agrees to carry back a second deed of trust for a buyer who has a good down payment and a very good job but cannot qualify for the entire loan amount necessary to cash out the seller.

Bill purchased his home in 1987 in Sacramento, California, and now he has decided to move to a rural area where he can have horses and a little more space. He contacts a very active real estate professional in the area and asks her to prepare a Comparative Market Analysis (CMA) on his property. The agent determined that Bill's home had a current market value of approximately $181,000. The agent further calculated that Bill's gross net proceeds from the sale of his home, using $180,000 for a sale price, would be approximately $104,000. Excluding sales costs, title fees, escrow charges, and commission, Bill would receive net proceeds of approximately $90,000. Bill listed the property for $182,500.

SHOULD YOU BUY BEFORE YOU SELL?

Armed with the information regarding his projected net proceeds, Bill began searching for his new country property.

In only two days he found a home on one acre that he felt would perfectly suit his needs. Bill made an offer on the new property of $220,000, conditioned upon the sale of his current home. The offer was accepted.

ALWAYS BE PREQUALIFIED

Before Bill had begun his search for his new property, he had made an appointment with a local mortgage company and had been prequalified for a loan amount up to $137,200. Assuming Bill received the full $90,000 in equity from the sale of his current home, his loan amount would be only $130,000 with payments of $1,093 per month.

Bill's agent marketed his current home very aggressively, but due to a rather slow economy in the area, not many potential buyers looked at the property. After 30 days, Bill became disappointed and started to worry about losing the new property, which was still being shown. If another, noncontingent buyer made an offer and Bill was unable to remove the condition of his current home selling, he might lose the new property. This is one problem with buying another home before your property has sold.

THE OFFER PROCESS BEGINS

On the thirty-second day of the listing, a young doctor and his wife viewed Bill's property and showed a great deal of interest. Bill's agent indicated that she felt this couple would make an offer, but she also did not think they could qualify for a new loan large enough to cash Bill out and, further, she was convinced that they were going to ask Bill to carry back a second.

DON'T BE TOO QUICK TO JUDGE

Bill immediately rejected this idea, saying he must cash out or he couldn't get his new loan.

As the agent had anticipated, the new doctor and his wife did make an offer with the terms as follows:

- $40,000 down payment
- Buyer to assume original mortgage of $76,000
- Seller to carry back a second deed of trust in the amount of $64,500, interest of 9.5%, monthly payments of $601, principal and interest and a balloon payment of $46,500, due in 10 years.

Bill could not see any way he could accept this offer, even though he felt this might be his one chance to get his home sold and get into his new property.

THE AGENT DID HER JOB WELL

Fortunately, Bill's agent was very competent in the area of financing and she had done her homework.

Prior to submitting this offer to Bill, she had run a credit report on the doctor. She also had obtained all of his and his wife's financial data, and she had determined that the only reason they could not qualify for a new loan in the amount necessary to cash Bill out was income. The doctor was a brand-new resident in a small hospital. Although he could anticipate major increases in his salary in the near future, currently he would not qualify. He did, however, have perfect credit and few bills.

Bill's agent also had called the lender through whom Bill had been prequalified and explained the dilemma Bill was facing. The lender examined the financial data as well as the doctor's credit report and advised the agent that, from the income Bill would be receiving, the second mortgage could be used to help qualify him for the higher loan amount necessary to get him into his new property. Although all of this sounds very complicated, it's not.

WHAT ARE THE CHOICES?

Here, in very simple terms, are the choices Bill had: He could simply reject the offer and hope another buyer would come along quickly before he lost his new property ... or he could accept the doctor's offer, which would, after all closing and sales costs, net him $26,000 to put down on his new property. Bill would obtain a loan of $194,000 with payments of $1,631 per month and he would use the $601 per month paid to him by the doctor to offset the additional monthly payments created by the larger loan amount. Bill was actually $63 per month ahead by accepting the doctor's offer, which is exactly what he did. It was a win-win situation for all parties.

FIGURE 9.1
CASH-OUT SALE VS. SELLER CARRY-BACK

	Down Payment	New Loan Amount	Monthly Payment	Additional Monthly Payment	Total Income Outlay	Positive/ Monthly
Cash Out	$90,000	$130,000	$1,093	—	$1,093	—
Seller Carry-Back	$26,000	$194,000	$1,631	$601	$1,030	+$63 per month

Figure 9.1 shows the difference to Bill as a buyer between the cash-out sale and the seller carry-back that he accepted.

When sellers consider any type of seller financing terms, many variables must be considered. It is advisable that sellers always have this type of transaction approved by professional counsel.

SMART TIP:

In my book *How to Buy the Home You Want, for the Best Price, in Any Market* I cover, in detail, many ways for a buyer to purchase a home using alternative purchase techniques. Check that book out to learn about all types of seller-assisted financing and many financing techniques used by professional investors.

THERE'S NO SUBSTITUTE FOR EXPERIENCE

As you can see, it was critically important to the success of the transaction that Bill's agent had a good working knowledge of seller carry-back financing and that she understood how this type of financing could work for Bill.

Most sellers will never have the desire or need to understand all of the nuances of specialty financing methods. But a buyer with special needs or constraints may need to look at some type of special government subsidized loan, an assumption, rollovers, buy-downs, land contracts, or even lease options.

Again, before sellers become involved in any of these types of transactions, an attorney or some other type of professional counsel should look at the transaction and the paperwork to make sure that the sellers have not put themselves in a vulnerable position.

CHAPTER TEN

Home.
Warranties

WHAT IS
A HOME WARRANTY?

A home warranty works exactly as warranties work on other products. When you receive a warranty or guarantee on a new stereo, the manufacturer or the store that sells the product is guaranteeing, for a period of time, that the product will not have defects and will work properly. If something should go wrong, the guarantor will fix the product at no cost or at a minimal predetermined service charge.

In the early 1970s, a man named David Smith and his company, American Home Shield, pioneered the home warranty business. Since that time, the home warranty business has flourished and numerous warranty companies now offer policies to hundreds of thousands of real estate buyers each year.

TYPES OF
HOME WARRANTIES

Like almost every product on the market, home warranties come in all shapes, sizes, and special coverages. Some warranties cost less and, as you might imagine, often cover less. Other warranties are more expensive and have much greater or more complete coverage.

Your real estate agent probably will have several brochures printed by home warranty companies available for you to examine. These brochures will explain the exact coverage of different warranties available in your area. The cost of each of these warranties also should be detailed in the brochures; if not, a quick call to the warranty company should answer any questions you may have.

WHAT IS COVERED?

Home warranties protect buyers or homeowners from having to pay the costs of repairing built-in appliances, structural problems, roof leaks, plumbing, and electrical or any other problems that may occur in the home if these items are specifically covered by the warranty.

Most home warranties are written for one year. Sometimes they may be extended at the mutual option of the warranty company and the homeowner.

Almost all buyers will look very favorably at a property on which a home warranty is offered and included in the sale of the home at no extra charge (remember, the "Power of Free").

As the general public has become more aware of the availability of home warranties, homes offered with warranties have become more common.

According to the National Home Warranty Association in St. Louis, Missouri, in 1995 alone over 801,000 home warranties were purchased by consumers and real estate professionals. Most important, it was reported that these member warranty companies processed over 1,292,000 claims.

Considering that the average cost of a home warranty is less than $360, I strongly recommend that sellers include a home warranty or guarantee with the sale of their home.

WHY SHOULD A WARRANTY
BE INCLUDED?

There are three main reasons to purchase and include a home warranty with the sale of the home.

1. It makes the home more salable. Most homes with warranties sell faster than those that are not covered.
2. It adds value to the home. Homes with warranties are worth more to potential buyers.
3. It will give the seller and buyer peace of mind after the transaction has closed. The seller will not have to be concerned with the buyer's after-close complaints.

HOW DO YOU CHOOSE
A WARRANTY?

Your real estate professional will be able to advise you on the different choices or warranty companies available in your area. If you are selling your home yourself, look in the telephone directory under Home Warranty Companies or in the real estate section of the newspaper.

Some home warranties cover only specific items and exclude others. For example, one warranty might cover structural defects; electrical, plumbing, heating, and cooling systems; and ventilation fans but would not cover appliances, fixtures, or built-in equipment.

Make sure that whatever warranty you choose to offer on your property covers a wide range of items. Some warranties specifically exclude swimming pools and spas or require an additional addendum or rider and fee if these items are to be covered. It is always in the best interest of both sellers and buyers for these items to be covered.

WHAT SHOULD THE WARRANTY
INCLUDE?

Every home warranty should include the following:

1. The name or names of the person who is warranteed.
2. An explanation as to if or how this warranty can be transferred.
3. The term of the warranty.
4. Exactly what is covered by the warranty and what items are specifically excluded.
5. An explanation of exactly how a claim must be filed.
6. A statement of who will make necessary repairs. Is there a service company or does the warranty company have repair people on staff?
7. How long will it take to have a service or repair person respond.

8. Any deductibles or service fees in addition to the original warranty policy cost, if applicable.
9. Any specific limitations as to what will or will not be covered as far as personal property items.

Like any other guarantee, sellers should check out the warranty they will offer.

CAN A BUYER PURCHASE THE WARRANTY?

While a buyer can purchase a home warranty, in most cases, the buyer will ask the seller to pay for it. In some cases the seller and the buyer might split the cost.

Every real estate professional, almost without exception, will encourage every seller to offer a warranty with the sale of a property, primarily because it makes the home more salable and gives the buyers the feeling they are buying a good product. It's peace of mind for the seller, the buyer, and the agent at a very reasonable cost.

CHAPTER ELEVEN

Getting the Buyers' Attention

HOW DO YOU DO IT?

Most sellers believe that the majority of buyers find the home in which they are interested by picking up a newspaper or a home magazine and browsing through the available properties until an ad or photograph catches their attention. However, in a survey conducted in 1994 by an independent research firm, it was determined that most buyers found the home that they ultimately purchased by first targeting a neighborhood. They then determined what homes were available in that neighborhood either by contacting a real estate agent or simply by driving around and writing down information on signs they saw in that area.

A successful marketing campaign should include contact with two types of potential buyers: those who know they are interested in purchasing a home and are actively looking for a property, and those who are capable of purchasing a home but have not yet made the decision to start looking.

Many potential buyers who are not actively searching for a property will buy if they are given enough reasons to do so.

In other words, if you cannot find buyers who are ready, willing, and able to purchase your property, with a proper marketing program you will create buyers who could be ready, willing, and able to buy your home. If you have listed your home with a real estate professional, that agent should have provided you with a complete performance or marketing campaign.

The agent should know the advertising and sales techniques that are effective in the marketing area and should have a detailed plan as to how to apply those techniques to your particular property.

WHERE DOES THE MARKETING START?

As explained earlier, you should understand that successful marketing of your property starts with the preparation of the home.

Knowing that many buyers find their properties merely by driving around a neighborhood, you should understand the importance of "curb appeal." "Curb appeal" is simply preparing your home in such a way that when potential buyers see it from the street, they will be compelled to see the inside of the property. "Curb appeal" is of critical importance to selling your home quickly and for the highest price.

IDEAS TO INCREASE "CURB APPEAL"

Some suggestions for increasing "curb appeal" were made in earlier chapters; however, I feel it is important to review some of the recommendations with regard to the exterior of your home.

- Have yard and shrubs manicured perfectly.
- Make sure all walkways, driveways, and entry areas are clean and uncluttered.
- See that cement areas are clean and free of grease or oil spots.
- Make sure cars, especially junkers that do not run, are not parked in the driveway, at the curb in front of the home, or in adjacent parking areas on the property.
- Provide color to the front yard and home in the form of flowers in the flower beds or in flower pots around the home.
- See that there are no dead plants or shrubs in the yard.
- Try to make the interior of the home visible from the exterior. Trim back shrubs and bushes from the doors and windows and make sure drapes and curtains are left open. Have the home bright and well lit, inside and out.
- Be sure the roof and gutters are free of leaves, pine needles, or other debris.
- Make sure all of the windows are crystal clean.
- See that the front, garage, or other doors visible from the front of the home are clean and well painted (no chipping or peeling).

- Be sure the entire front of the home is clean, well painted, and free from any discoloration from water or mud splash.
- Keep the grass well trimmed and edged.
- See that all gutters and downspouts are attached securely and not hanging from the eaves or roof.
- Make sure that all lights work properly, especially in the evening or night hours.
- Try to make the entryway feel warm and inviting, possibly by using potted plants or a porch swing or rocking chair.
- Try to make the home feel inviting and warm without being cluttered.
- Make sure there are no children's toys, games, or bicycles cluttering the yard or entryway.

Without a doubt, the best advertising dollars that you will spend are in giving your home the best "curb appeal" possible.

AFTER YOU HAVE "CURB APPEAL"

After you have effectively established your home's "curb appeal," the next step is to place the for sale sign in your yard.

Again, if you have listed with a real estate professional, he or she should be able to guide you with regard to placement of the sign. However, just a few suggestions would be:

- Make sure the sign is visible up and down the street from both directions.
- See that the sign is at the proper distance from the street and that it catches your eye even if you are not looking at the home.
- Be sure the sign is not too close to or does not hang over the sidewalk.

Figures 11.1 to 11.4 are examples of proper sign placement.

> **SMART TIP:**
> Make sure that the person who installs the yard sign is aware of any underground sprinklers or watering systems. It might be advisable for the agent and the seller to choose and mark the location or locations for the sign at the time the listing is taken. That way, there will be no questions as to where the sign is to be placed.

FIGURE 11.1 **SINGLE SIGN PLACEMENT**

This picture shows the best sign placement for a property on a standard thoroughfare.

FIGURE 11.2 **CUL-DE-SAC SIGN PLACEMENT**

If your home is at the end of a dead-end street or cul-de-sac, it would probably be more effective to place the sign where it can be viewed directly from the curb in front of the home.

FIGURE 11.3 **CORNER SIGN PLACEMENT—TWO SIGNS**

If your home is on a corner lot, usually it is best to place signs on both streets, making them visible from all four directions.

FIGURE 11.4 **CORNER SIGN PLACEMENT—ONE SIGN**

Another suggestion for a corner lot is to place the sign on the corner, making it visible from any of the four directions. Make sure that the sign is visible at all times of the day and is not hidden by shrubs, bushes, or trees.

Chapter 16, on selling the home yourself, covers color and verbiage with regard to For-Sale-by-Owner signs.

When selling a home with or without an agent, it is not a bad idea to state amenities in the home on the sign itself. This information can be included on the sign itself or on sign riders. Figure 11.5 shows two separate sign layouts that detail amenities included in the home or terms offered on the property.

Note that each sign has a box or holder for information brochures or cards. I discuss what these cards and brochures should say later in this chapter.

If your home is a condominium or co-op and there is no place to position a yard sign, place signs in windows visible from every walkway, driveway, or street that borders the property. Also, if it is not a violation of your homeowners' association rules, place a sign on the garage door or near the carport area.

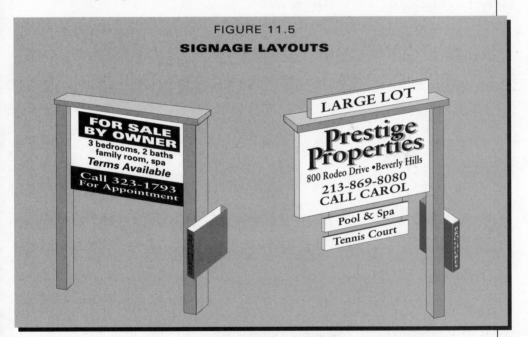

FIGURE 11.5

SIGNAGE LAYOUTS

MULTIPLE LISTING SERVICE (MLS)

The next method by which agents and buyers will be made aware of your home is the entry of your home into the Multiple Listing Service (MLS). The service, which is provided by and for the exclusive use of member agents and brokers, makes available information on all homes that are listed by any member broker. The advantage of this type of cooperative service is that every agent can show his or her buyers all of the homes in which they are interested.

MLS is one of the main reasons that you should consider using a sales professional to sell your home.

Figure 11.6 is an example of an MLS entry form. Although MLS services use different computer systems, the information included on the form is fairly consistent throughout the industry.

As you will note, the MLS entry form has space for comments. It is strongly suggested that sellers assist the agents in preparing in-

FIGURE 11.6 **MLS ENTRY FORM**

ABC REALTY			(800) 123-4567	01-01-95		TIMZIMMER
GLVAR			RESIDENTIAL	01-01-95		01:32 PM
ML# 75235 OFFC TODA PUBID 002246	STATUS A AREA 401	L/PRICE $169500			
ADDRESS 720 CHABOT		ZIP CODE 89107	FRTBUY MAP 3634K		
LEGAL	L*142	B*6	SUBDIV *CHARLESTON	EST #5		SUBDIV# *1600
COUNIY	CLARK TWN*20 RG*61 SECT*30		PARCEL# 139-30-711-032	ZN SINGLE	
BUILDER			MSTPLN	COMMUNITY	
MODEL CUSTOM			YR BUILT 1972/RE		
ELEM SCH FIFE – YR ROUND		N	6TH GRD GIBS	JR HI GIBS	HI SCH WEST

* * * GENERAL INFORMATION * * *

TYP/STYL 2 STORY/DETACHED	#BDRMS 4	#BATHS 1/2/0
GARAGE 3/ATTACHED/AIrlqODR/ENTRYHS/RV/BOAT	CONV N	CARPORT 0/
ARCHITECT	SF +/- 2700	#ACRES+/-
ROOF PITCHED/SHAKE	LOT DESC	
SPA N	LOTDIMEN +/-*	74 X* 109
PV POOL Y/INGRND/POOLEQP	POOL SIZE +/- 14X32	

D: I 95 TO VALLEY VIEW NORTH TO WASHINGTON TURN LEFT 3 STREETS CHABOT BEAUTIFUL NEIGHBORHOOD NEAR GOLF COURSE (PUBLIC) JUSTREDUCE S10.400 MODELHOME CONDITION

R: EXCELLENT CONDITION SHOWS BETTER THAN NEW HOME, VERY LARGE ROOMS, FORMAL LIVING AND DINING ROOM DON'T LET POODLE OUT THANKS. BDRMS UPSTAIRS CD/BE MSTERS NEW CARPET/NEW TEXTURED PAINT/NEW APPLIANCES, JENNAIR 6C FANS, WATERFILTER SYS, MATURE LANDSCAPING SURROUNDING POOL RV PARKING WRITE UP AN OFFER TODAY!!!

* * * FINANCIAL INFORMATION * * *

1ST BAL S /	PMT $	INCL	RATE	%		ASSUMP FEE 1 $
2ND BAL $ /	PMT $	INCL	RATE	%		ASSUMP FEE 2 $
DWN PAYMENT $ 169500		ANNUAL TAXES $* 1230		RENT S	POSSESS COE
CASH TO ASSM $ 169500		MP FEE/PMT $		ASSOC FEE $	ASSESSMENTS $
EARN DEPOSIT $ 5000 EXISTING FINANCE CONV					
FINANCE CONSID CASH/CONV/VA					

* * * LISTING INFORMATION * * *

L/AGENT ZIMMER, TI L/A PHONE 123-4567 OWNR LIC N		CSUB 3:008 EX N	
OFFICE ABC REALTY OFF PHONE 234-5678		BONUS SO	CBB 3:00~ VP N
RESIDENT M/M ADAMS	RES PHONE 345-6789		PHOTO 1
SHOWING KEY CALL/PETS	OWN OCCUPIED	POWER ON	

* * * APPROXIMATE ROOM SIZES AND DESCRIPTIONS * * *

LIV I9X13	2ND BEDR I9X12	DIN IIX10/FORMAL	DESC CEILIN/W CLOS KIT	
BRKBAR/PANTRY/TILFLE		3RD BEDR 13X13	FAM 20XI9/WETBAR	DESC CEILFN
MBR 17X13/CEILFN/DRESRM/WICLOS		4TH BEDR 12X9	MB BATH SHOWER	BED & BATH DOWN Y
REFRG N / DISPOS Y / COMPAC N / WASHR N / DRYR N /			OVEN/RANGE / E/BUILTIN/SELFCLN	
OTH APPLIANCES	CENTVAC/INTERCM/DRAPES/WINDWCOV	FLOORING CERAMIC/CAPPET	
FIREPL 1/EQPSTAY/WDBURN		FENCE F/BLOCK	FRTHIGH/REAR	SIDES	EQUEST
HSE FACE WEST	MISCEL HWO	EXTERIOR BI-BBQ	CVPATIO	LANDSCAP AUTOSPK/BUBDRIP/FLOWER/
LAWNFR/LAWNRR/MATCRE/SHRUBS/SPRKFR				

* * * UTILITIES INFORMATION * * *

HEAT SYS CENTRAL HT FUEL ELEC	WATER PUBLIC
COOL SYS CENTRAL CL FUEL ELEC	SEWER PUBLIC
UTIL INF CABLAVL	ENERGY SOLSCRN

formation that can be used for the MLS entry form as well as for ads and brochures prepared to assist in the sale of the home.

SELLER INFORMATION SHEET

The Seller Information Sheet depicted in Figure 11.7 will assist you in providing information for agents. If your agent does not provide you with a similar information sheet, use a copy of this form. Give the agent any information you feel may interest buyers and ultimately produce a buyer.

FIGURE 11.7

SELLER INFORMATION SHEET

Tell me about your home . . .

What makes your home different from others in the area/neighborhood? _
_____
_____

What improvements have you made? _____
_____
_____

What are the best features of your home?_____
_____
_____

Why is your home's location a benefit? _____
_____
_____

What is the neighborhood like? _____
_____
_____

How did you find your home (real estate agent, newspaper, yard sign, etc.)?
_____
_____

FIGURE 11.8

SAMPLE PROPERTY INFORMATION BROCHURE

Almost a Steal!

This is the home your buyers are searching for!

$206,000

Benefits for Your Buyer:

California-style, large kitchen made for entertaining, glass-enclosed breakfast nook, exposed beams in the kitchen and dining area, 3 fireplaces (including 1 in the very romantic master suite), 4 large bedrooms, 3 bathrooms, separate maid's quarters next to the kitchen, 30 x 28 great room over the garage, separate area (for storage or a shop) in the garage, indoor laundry facilities, professionally landscaped backyard, 3-car garage, and much more!

Call Jane Doe Today!
(000) 123-4567

ABC REALTY • 1234 Main Street • Anywhere, CA 00000

PROPERTY INFORMATION BROCHURE

The next method by which you will notify buyers and other agents about your property is a professional Property Information Brochure or Card.

This brochure should include a good photograph of the property. A black-and-white photo run off on a copy machine is not acceptable. A halftone or computer-scanned image is necessary for these brochures. Also include approximate square footage of the property; the number of bedrooms and baths; if there is a formal dining room; central heat and air; fireplace; number of cars that fit in the garage; appliances; specialty items such as garage door openers, professional landscaping, triple-pane windows; window coverings such as drapes or blinds; fencing; specialty cabinets; sprinkler systems, security systems; garden areas; television cable or satellite; wet bars; and any other pertinent information that may interest buyers or other agents.

Also, the brochure should include any terms you are willing to offer. The price needs to be prominently displayed, and the flyer must include whom to contact to see the home as well as the phone number. If there are any limitations as to seeing the home, these should also be stated. An example might be: Home available for showing only evenings after 6:00 P.M.

The brochure in Figure 11.8 is an example of the type of fact sheet brochure that should be readily available for all prospective buyers and agents. These brochures should be placed in the brochure boxes on the yard signs and should be available inside the home as well.

This type of brochure can be altered slightly to fit a large postcard ($5^1/_2$" x $8^1/_2$"), called a bonus postcard.

Some advantages to using this type of card as opposed to a full brochure are:

- Research has shown that readership and response rates are five to seven times greater with cards.
- Cards are easier to handle than brochures.
- Card can be used as a direct mail item without an envelope.

Figure 11.9 is an example of this type of information card.

FIGURE 11.9

SAMPLE PROPERTY INFORMATION CARD

Almost a Steal!
2456 Park Lane • Anywhere, CA

$206,000

California-style, large kitchen made for entertaining, glass enclosed breakfast nook, exposed beams in the kitchen and dining area, 3 fireplaces (including 1 in the very romantic master suite), 4 large bedrooms, 3 bathrooms, separate maid's quarters next to the kitchen, 30 x 28 great room over the garage, separate area (for storage or a shop) in the garage, indoor laundry facilities, professionally landscaped backyard, 3-car garage, and much more!

Call Jane Doe Today!
(000) 123-4567
ABC REALTY • 1234 Main Street • Anywhere, CA 00000

As the seller, you should assist the agent in every way possible by distributing flyers, brochures, cards, or other information. These advertising items should be given to coworkers and family members and can be posted on bulletin boards at grocery stores, dry cleaners, and restaurants. Don't be stingy with flyers and brochures; flood the market everywhere and in every way possible.

CONVENTIONAL ADVERTISING METHODS

When they list your property, most professional real estate agents will tell you what type of conventional newspaper and homes magazine advertising they intend to use. The agency may even provide a detailed advertising program, specifying the number of times a property will be advertised and in what magazines or newspapers.

Remember, your real estate professional probably has a good sense for what will work in the area for your particular property. That, coupled with expertise and experience in past sales, should give the professional the edge in getting your property sold.

Again, trust your agent but do not be afraid to make suggestions, especially if your home does not appear to be receiving a substantial amount of buyer attention within the first month of the listing.

There is an old adage in the real estate industry with regard to newspaper advertising that goes something like this:

Display ads get listings
Line ads sell homes!

There is a lot of truth to that statement. Figure 11.10 is an example of a display ad.

FIGURE 11.10

SAMPLE DISPLAY ADVERTISEMENT

John Doe
Your Personal Realtor® for Life

Call My 24-HOUR Property Information System Today! (800) 123-4567

Ad # 1234

1234 Mission Way — This brick masterpiece with 4 bedrooms, 2½ bathrooms, a covered patio with a built-in barbecue, and a large family room is located near great schools, freeways, and shopping. You couldn't find a better deal for this price.

Everybody who is selling their home ought to know that . . . *in a declining market, if you wait to sell your home, it's not a question of IF you'll lose money, it's only a matter of how much!* CALL TODAY FOR RESULTS!

Ad # 2345

3456 Valley Blvd. — This immaculate brick and wood home with four bedrooms, 3 bathrooms, a remodeled kitchen and bathroom and a formal dining room is on a large, gorgeous lot in one of the marina's finest neighborhoods. If there's a better value out there, we don't know about it.

Ad # 3456

23456 Park Lane — This unbelievable value provides country living at its very finest. This well-priced executive home has it all: 4 bedrooms, 3 bathrooms, a master suite, professional landscaping, plus much more.

You probably could tell by reading the information on the third property in this ad that this was the home previously depicted in the information brochures and cards in this chapter. However, if buyers had been looking for a property similar to the seller's property, they probably would have scanned right over this portion of this ad because it states very little about the property.

The two-line ads in Figure 11.11 depict the subject property quite differently. These ads have proven to be much more effective in attracting buyers.

FIGURE 11.11

SAMPLE LINE ADS

NEW LISTING	LOW DOWN!
Assumable Loan - Low Down Secluded - 4-Bdrm., 3-Bath 2-Story All Brick - 2 Fireplaces Fenced Yard $206,000 372-1396	Assumable - $30,000 move-in Country Elegance - 4-Bdrm., 3-Bath Master Suite - 2 Fireplaces Priced Below Appraisal! $206,000 372-1396

Ads that work must sell a particular home to many potential buyers who might be interested in that property. Figure 11.12 depicts examples of specialty ads that have proven to attract numerous buyers. These types of ads are used literally thousands of times everyday across the United States and Canada.

Brainstorm with your agent about advertising your property. Don't be afraid to throw out ideas. Remember, as I have said earlier, your agent is your partner in the sale of your home. You both get paid only when the property is sold.

The following list of "hot" words will help you or the agent write effective ads, brochures, advertising cards, and letters. The most effective marketing gets immediate response because the advertising item says what the reader wants or needs to hear. (See Table 11.1.)

FIGURE 11.12 **SPECIALTY ADS**

ONLY $1252 Per Month!

1214 Manhattan Drive
Anywhere Beach

★ ★ ★

Just steps to the beach, this ginger-bread charmer boasts 12-ft. ceilings, walk-in closets, hot tub, and an ocean view.

ALL FOR UNDER $300,000
Call John Doe
ABC Realty
(800) 123-4567

Payments calculated with a 20% down payment and an adjustable rate mortgage of 4.75%.

We'll miss those cozy evenings . . . we shared by the glowing fireplace and the early winter mornings when we jumped out of bed to see the snow-covered mountains, which are visible from the spacious kitchen windows.

We'll remember the many family summer gatherings on the covered patio and the delicious meals we prepared on the oversized, built-in brick barbecue. YES, we will miss all of these things and much more, but in five years our family has grown and the two large bedrooms are just not enough for the five of us.

If you appreciate a beautiful, professionally landscaped backyard, views of the mountains, and a cul-de-sac with very little traffic, you may want to buy our home at 231 Yipper Drive.

We hope so. We wouldn't want it to be empty and alone at Christmas.

For more information call:
Sally at (800) 999-0000

Need a Huge Home And Large Yard?

6 Bedrooms, 4 Bathrooms,
3 Fireplaces,
Gigantic Family Room
(Including Pool Table),
Huge Convenient Kitchen,
Enormous Closets,
and situated
on a ½-Acre Lot.

And most important . . .

Priced Right
$399,500
Call Sally Today
800-321-4567

TABLE 11.1

"HOT" WORDS FOR ADVERTISING

ENJOYMENT WORDS	STATUS WORDS	SECURITY WORDS	FINANCIALLY DESIRABLE WORDS
bright	castle	advantage	abundance
brilliant	elegant	benefit	advantage
calm	estate	certain	auction
clean	exquisite	credible	bargain
cute	fashionable	faithful	benefit
darling	gorgeous	guarantee	bonus
delightful	grandeur	opportunity	discount
enjoyment	lavish	protected	economical
faith	luxury	reliable	fortune
fresh	magnificent	secure	gain
friendly	majestic	snug	growth
frills	mansion	sound	guarantee
gentle	opulent	sure	improvement
healthy	palace	trustworthy	low down
home	prestigious		premium
love	prosperity		prize
lovable	quality		profit
mild	radiant		reward
nice	splendid		sale
outdoors	stately		save
peaceful			value
placid			warranty
pleasure			windfall
pure			
quiet			
relaxed			
restful			
rustic			
serene			
soft			
sunny			
tranquil			
wooded			

Many real estate professionals are trained and have significant experience in preparing all types of advertising. On the other hand, some agents have never developed expertise with regard to preparing ads and other advertising methods.

Although your general information or fact sheet brochure or

card will be your primary advertising item, many other advertising methods can be used to help sell a home quickly.

OTHER ADVERTISING ITEMS

The following advertising cards, brochures, letters, and door hangers have proven to be successful in almost every area across the United States and Canada. These types of advertising items can be sent or delivered to every potential buyer for a particular property. (See Figures 11.13, 11.14, and 11.15.)

FIGURE 11.13
SAMPLE BUYER CARDS

Would You Throw Away $45,000?

If you only pay $750 per month rent for 5 years, that's exactly what you

**Build Equity!
Save on Taxes!
BUY A HOME!**

Call John Doe Today!!

< Renters are shocked to realize how much rent they will pay in 5 years.

The perception of trading is easier than selling and buying a new home. This card is good for areas with first-time home buyers and renters. >

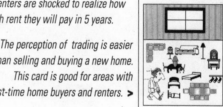

**Is there no way left to rearrange it?
TRADE UP TO A LARGER HOME.**

Call today for details:
John Doe
ABC Realty
(800) 123-4567

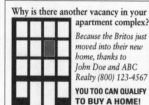

Why is there another vacancy in your apartment complex?

Because the Britos just moved into their new home, thanks to John Doe and ABC Realty (800) 123-4567

YOU TOO CAN QUALIFY TO BUY A HOME!

< Your agent can distribute this card in any apartment complexes where he or she previously sold a renter a home in the same price range as your home.

This card shows the advantages of condominium ownership. >

ADVANTAGES OF CONDOMINIUM OWNERSHIP

1. Tax benefits of homeownership.
2. Usually less expensive due to lower building costs.
3. You have a say in your neighborhood through the Homeowner's Association.
4. Minimal upkeep. Yard maintenance usually is handled by Homeowner's Association.
5. Possible lower energy costs.
6. Facilities you might not otherwise afford: swimming pools, weight rooms, tennis courts, etc.
7. Social atmosphere.
8. Possible better location. Because they can get more homes on one piece of real estate, builders often place them on their best lots.

**JOHN DOE SELLS HOMES
ABC REALTY (800) 123-4567**

2041 TYLER STREET
HAS JUST BEEN LISTED FOR SALE!
Don't miss your opportunity to own this lovely 3-bedroom, 1-bath custom home on 1 acre!
TURN YOUR DREAM INTO REALITY . . .
For details . . . call:

John Doe
ABC Realty
(800) 123-4567

< This card utilizes graphics to show a new listing. It also creates urgency.

This card explains that there are many ways to own a home and the agent has the answers. Also, it shows a happy family, who took advantage of homeownership. >

Did You Know There Are Over 50 Ways to Buy a Home?

With that many choices, it may be easier than you think for you to experience the joy and financial security of homeownership! John Doe examines every possible option and helps you make the right buying choices! If you want to own a home,
call John Doe today!
ABC Realty • (800) 123-4567

IT JUST DOESN'T FIT!

**Apartment
Sweet
Apartment!**

If you are looking for a "HOME SWEET HOME"

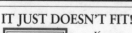

*Call John Doe
ABC Realty • (800) 123-4567*

< Renters will visualize and feel the awkwardness and temporary status of renting.

This simple puzzle catches readers' attention and invites them to an open house. >

You are invited to an . . . **OPEN HOUSE** we'll be . . .
. . . and showing
Don't Miss It!
2879 Squire Avenue
Sunday, July 7th • 12:00 - 4:00 p.m.

For more information call:
John Doe
ABC Realty
(800) 123-4567

FIGURE 11.14

SAMPLE BUYER LETTERS

January 1, 1997
The Johnson Family
2800 Harbor Lane
Fresno, California 90000

Dear Future Homeowner,

How much longer will you let your money fly out the window?

Paying only $750 per month rent, you will throw away $45,000 in only 5 years!

Owning a property may be much easier than you think. I can show you over 50 ways to buy a home! One of these ways may fit your needs.

Please call me today at (800) 123-4567 to learn all of the exciting ways you too can experience homeownership.

Sincerely,

John Doe
Realtor®
(800) 123-4567

January 1, 1997
The Johnson Family
2800 Harbor Lane
Fresno, California 90000

Dear Mr. and Mrs. Johnson,

Since You Own a Property in the Neighborhood . . .

I thought you might be interested in knowing that . . .

1212 Ardmore Avenue is available for purchase!

If you know of anyone who is looking for a home in this area, please call John Doe at (800) 123-4567.

Here's your chance to choose your own neighbor!

I can help you!

Sincerely,
John Doe
Realtor®
(800) 123-4567

FIGURE 11.15
SAMPLE BUYER DOOR HANGERS
(actual size 4" x 10")

You are Invited
to a Celebration!
2828 Elm Street

has just been listed for sale!

Saturday, July 2nd

12:00 pm

We would like you to attend an Open House Celebration. Come to see a terrific home . . . stay for the special refreshments.

Special evaluation forms will be available to assist you in determining the value of your home.

For more information call:
John Doe
(800) 123-4567

Almost A Steal!

$206,000

23456 Park Lane

California-style, large kitchen made for entertaining, glass-enclosed breakfast nook, exposed beams in the kitchen and dining area, 3 fireplaces (including 1 in the very romantic master suite), 4 large bedrooms, 3 bathrooms, separate maid's quarters next to the kitchen, 30 x 28 great room over the garage, separate area (for storage or a shop) in the garage, indoor laundry facilities, professionally landscaped backyard, 3-car garage, and much more!

Call John Doe Today!
(800) 123-4567

Your agent also should know the type of renters who might be interested in your property. By that I mean, if you are selling a $350,000 home, you probably would not send advertising material to apartments/renters where the average rent is $350 per month. You would instead target areas or potential buyers who probably would be able and desire to purchase a property in the price range of your home.

In some areas, real estate professionals have access to county records that provide information regarding property ownership. Also, in some areas, nonowner occupants or renters can be identified. Again, your real estate professional will be able to access this information if it is available.

A renter who pays substantial rent in a neighborhood would be a likely prospect to become a buyer for a property located in that same neighborhood.

Remember, when a seller or agent chooses to use an advertisement exclusively designed for a particular property, the percentage of response may not be exceptionally high. However, this type of advertising will generate numerous calls and potential buyers. If an agent hesitates to spend the money advertising your property, you should remind the agent of the enormous potential for buyers and sellers that will be generated not only for your property but for other properties and sales as well. Creating a strong buyer pool will greatly enhance the agent's success. Most important, sellers and agents must recognize that if buyers are not appearing, they must be created. Advertising cards, brochures, or letters, delivered to the proper potential buyer pool, will produce results.

Figure 11.16 is an advertising schedule prepared by a successful agent for a property she had listed. Note the frequency and numbers of the marketing items included in this specific marketing campaign.

As you can see this marketing campaign was INTENSIVE. However, you will also note that it was very effective. The home sold in 36 days. But what about the cost of this marketing program? If you are not sitting down, you better do so. (See Figure 11.17 on page 142.)

Let's examine the specifics of this listing and sale, because not

FIGURE 11.16

SAMPLE ADVERTISING AND MARKETING CAMPAIGN >

ADVERTISING AND MARKETING CAMPAIGN

Designed for: 2828 Monroe Way
Owner: Sheryl and John Carlisle

WEEK 1:

74 copies of MLS input sheet to all agents in my office
2400 Information/Fact brochures to every member of MLS
Submit for inclusion to office display ads for upcoming weekend
Submit 1/8 page for Homes Magazine for 1st of month (25th deadline)
1100 new listing Information/Fact cards mailed to surrounding neighborhood
200 Information/Fact cards to seller for sign and distribution
50 Information/Fact cards to relocation department

WEEK 2:

2 line ads, Tribune and Times newspapers - Sunday - Saturday
500 Information/Fact cards to all ad boxes (grocery store, dry cleaner, 2 local hotels)
30 Letters and Information/Fact cards to top-selling agents in area

WEEK 3:

2 new line ads - Tribune and Times newspapers
2400 Information/Fact cards to every member of MLS
Include in office display weekend ad

WEEK 4:

1000 Information/Fact cards to adjoining neighborhood area
1 3" Display ad, Weekly Journal
Replenish Information/Fact cards in all boxes

HOME SOLD IN 36 DAYS

WEEK 5:

1500 Specialty ad cards to potential buyers in apartments
30 follow-up calls to top agents in area
2 line ads - Tribune and Times newspapers
Include in office advertising for weekend

WEEK 6:

2400 new Information/Fact brochures to every member of MLS
1000 new Information/Fact cards to all rentals surrounding property
Replenish all Information/Fact cards in all boxes

Prepared by: Agent's name & phone number

every property can have the benefit of this type of massive exposure.

FIGURE 11.17
COST OF ADVERTISING
AND MARKETING CAMPAIGN

8,000 Information/Fact cards	$620
2,400 Information/Fact brochures	$100
5 Newspaper ads—5 days each	$650
1 Magazine ad—1 month	$45
30 letters and cards	$40
1 MLS submission	$40
Postage (mostly bulk mail)	$550
Delivery costs	$250
TOTAL	$2,295

The home was exceptionally well prepared and located in a very popular area. The seller was very motivated due to a job transfer and listed the home approximately $500 below the estimated value, at $317,000.

The agent, who sells approximately 60 homes per year, knew the home would sell quickly if marketed correctly. However, she was making a huge investment based on her expertise and belief that the home would sell within the first six weeks of the listing period. If she had not been able to sell the home in that period, her outlay would have exceeded $2,500.

You now begin to see why I have been so emphatic about the fact that sellers and agents become partner when a seller hires an agent to sell a home.

In this example, the agent, due to her extensive marketing campaign for one seller, created the following:

1. Seven buyers of whom two actually purchased another home within 60 days (two more commissions for the agent). The

other five were still looking but also may purchase a home through the agent.

2. Listed two more properties in the area of the original listing.
3. Received enormous area exposure for future listings and sales.

The agent profited greatly from doing the best possible job for her client. The seller, by spending the time and money necessary to prepare the home properly and, most important, by pricing the home correctly, got a quick sale that saved interest payments and the expense of supporting two homes.

OTHER METHODS
OF ADVERTISING

Professional sales agents may use other types of advertising, such as television programming on special advertising channels, radio ads, or other types of verbal or visual media communication.

Another avenue of advertising that has become popular with agents is the rolling advertisements on local TV channels, when there is no scheduled programming in certain time slots. While this type of advertising has not proven to generate a great number of buyers for particular properties, it does generate a substantial buyer and seller pool for real estate agents.

Your individual agent will know if these are effective methods of advertising in your area.

MORE IS BETTER

Keep in mind that the more advertising you do, the more opportunity you have to find that specific buyer who will be interested in your property. The one important fact to remember is:

If you do not advertise, something terrible happens
... Nothing!

CHAPTER TWELVE
Showing the Home

ARE YOU READY?

Professional sales agents will tell you that most times when a home is shown, the home was not prepared properly for the showing. Even though sellers have been cautioned to keep their homes clean, uncluttered, and prepared for a showing at almost a moment's notice, most homes are not prepared as they should be for an effective showing.

Sellers must cooperate with agents and keep their home in what is called "show ready" throughout the listing and sales period and into the closing.

LOCK BOXES

In most areas, lock boxes are placed on homes that are listed for sale. These lock boxes contain a key or keys to the home and give all of the agents who belong to the MLS access when you are not available to allow entry.

Many agents avoid homes that do not have boxes. In the time that it would take to call a listing agent, have the listing agent call the seller and stop by and pick up a key, that selling agent could have shown three other properties with lock boxes.

One of the major disadvantages of selling your home yourself is that the home is not for sale all day everyday. If you cannot arrange for access and showing of your property during the most common showing periods, 9 A.M. to 8 P.M., your home is only a part-time listing.

PREPARING THE HOME FOR SHOWING

As mentioned in Chapter 2, two separate preparations must occur when a home is shown: the preparation of the home itself and the preparation of the seller.

As discussed earlier, sellers have difficulty accepting criticism about their property, from both potential buyers and other agents. The best advice a seller can be given is:

> Objectively think about the criticism, ask yourself
> if it could have merit, and then GET OVER IT.

Not everyone will love your home, your colors, your drapes, your decorating, or the neighborhood you live in. Keep an open mind and don't take it personally. Everyone has an opinion, and those opinions are not always going to be the same as yours. If you think about it, you probably wouldn't like the homes that belong to the buyers who are being critical of your property and you might be just as quick to criticize their decorating.

The first fact that sellers must recognize is that showings will always seem to occur at the most inconvenient times. Just when your dinner guests arrive, you will get the call from an agent wanting to show the property. Or just as you climb into the bathtub to enjoy a nice, relaxing half hour, the phone will ring and guess what ... the agent and potential buyers have seen the sign and they are sitting outside, calling on their cellular phone.

Keep in mind that with this inconvenience comes the possibility of that one buyer who will purchase your home.

When the call comes for the showing, it should not be a huge task to get the home ready to show. If the property has been kept "show ready," a light dusting, light cleaning, and clutter collection should suffice.

Your agent will have asked you to have the home prepared in a certain manner. This may include things such as: lights turned on, fire burning in fireplace (if the proper season), have a light-scented potpourri simmering, have all of the curtains open to allow light in, candles burning on the mantel and, possibly, soft music playing.

Follow your agent's directions explicitly, but don't overdo it. Be realistic. If it's 80 degrees outside, don't light a fire. Or, on the other hand, if it's 30 degrees outside, don't leave all of the doors and windows open to "freshen up" the house.

Try to imagine how you would view your home if you were the potential buyer. What would make you feel warm and comfortable?

SPECIALTY SHOWING TECHNIQUES

Professional salespeople use a number of very effective techniques when showing a home.

Staging

"Staging" is simply preparing your home as if you were setting a stage for a play, making it feel very complete and comfortable for buyers as they tour the property.

You may want to refer back to Table 4.2 in Chapter 4, "50 Tips to Help Sell a Home."

Specific staging techniques include: setting the dining room table complete with dishes, utensils, serving trays, napkins, and candles or flowers. (Make the table look as if you are preparing for a Thanksgiving feast.) Staging a living room or family room might include a fire in the fireplace, pillows on the sofa, an open book on the coffee table with reading glasses lying on the book, a rocking chair with a knitting basket sitting beside it, quilts resting on or beside a sofa, or wind chimes hanging just outside a partially open window. For the bedroom, staging might include quilts or bedding folded back in a turn-down fashion (this does not mean unmade), pillows arranged near and around the headboard, candles burning, soft music playing, or a book and glasses on nightstand.

Staging has proven to be an effective showing technique and has become more popular and widely used in recent years. Have bread dough cooking in oven. Boil cinammon sticks. Have fresh coffee perking in the morning.

Model homes are often "staged" very carefully. If you have time, visit some decorated model homes to get ideas on showing or staging a home for sale.

As with anything else, don't overdo it. There is a fine line between comfort and clutter.

Descriptive Signing

Another specialty technique involves the use of small, professionally printed signs, approximately two inches high and two to four inches wide. The signs can be placed throughout the home pointing out specific highlights of the property.

Again, many of the new, model homes will have these signs and they have proven to be very effective.

The following graphics show examples of the type of signs that the seller should consider printing and using to show or better yet, "Show Off" their home.

Should You Be There?

Real estate professionals almost always suggest that you vacate your property while it is being shown.

Many potential buyers feel uncomfortable if you are in the home because they will want to look at the property very closely. That may mean looking in closets, storage areas, cabinets, refrigerators, under beds, and snooping around in the garage.

Remember, these potential buyers are making a major life decision as to whether they want to live in this house, possibly forever (or so they think). They certainly deserve to feel comfortable if they are going to make that decision.

Sometimes it will be impossible for you to leave the property while it is being shown. In those cases you should remember to dress nicely and make every effort to stay completely out of the way of the agent and potential buyer. If the weather is warm, you can go outside and sit in a

FIGURE 12.1
"SHOW OFF" SIGNS

ROSEWOOD MANTEL

TRIPLE-PANE WINDOWS

CLIMBING ROSES WILL COVER FENCE IN SPRING

GAS STARTER IN FIREPLACE

DOUBLE OVEN WITH MICROWAVE

Use signs like these sparingly for very special amenities.

lawn chair. Or, better yet, you can go visit a neighbor while the showing is occurring.

Many sellers try to sneak a peek at potential buyers; this often results in a very uncomfortable situation. The buyers feel they are being spied on, and the sellers are horribly embarrassed if they get caught. The agent showing the property also will feel uncomfortable. Sellers should allow agents to do their job and stay completely out of the way.

If an agent or potential buyer has questions, the seller should attempt to answer those questions honestly but should not over-elaborate or make conversation with the potential buyer.

Children and Pets

If children are present during the showing, you should make every effort to control them as much as possible. Keep them out of the different areas of the home while those portions of the property are being shown.

Buyers often bring their children to a showing. It may turn into a disaster if your children and the buyer's children become close, quick buddies and begin romping madly through the home.

Also, you need to take great care to make sure children's toys are not left strewn throughout the house, for two reasons. One is to avoid the general clutter factor. The second reason is the potential liability you would have if a buyer stepped on a roller skate and took an unplanned flight down the beautiful spiral staircase on which the attention sign had just been placed.

Also, as indicated earlier, if there are any animals in the home, they should be properly controlled and kept quiet during the showing. There is nothing more distracting than to have a barking dog or squawking parrot loudly expressing dissatisfaction with the intruders while the agent and buyer are discussing the amenities of the home.

Cards Left at Showings

As noted earlier, it is very important for you to provide the listing agent with all business cards that agents leave when they show the property. The listing agent should receive the information on the cards as soon as possible, to enable him or her to contact that agent and receive feedback on the showing.

If an agent shows the property but does not offer to leave a business card, you should ask for one.

Home Showing Checklist

Figure 12.2 should be used as a reminder just before your home is shown.

HOLDING AN OPEN HOUSE

Many sellers believe that holding an open house for the public is an absolute, certain way to sell their home. However, according to a report published by the National Association of Realtors®, only 1 to 2 percent of homeowners actually sell their home through an open house.

SMART TIP:
For obvious security reasons, do not allow entry to potential buyers who show up at the door, without an agent, wanting to see the property. Tell these people that they will need to contact your agent. Get their name and phone number and give this information to your agent. This also holds true for anyone who shows up at your door and claims to be an agent. If they had no appointment, ask for I.D. Most agents will have an I.D. card issued by their Board of Realtors® as well as business cards.

Like other sales activities discussed in this book, an open house creates potential buyers and sellers for the agent holding the open house.

In a survey conducted by an independent research firm, using exit interviews with people who had attended open houses, it was determined that over 70 percent of these people were not there with the intention of buying the homes. They were there to compare their home to the open house and decide if they wanted to sell their home.

Knowing these facts, do you just forget the open house? The answer is *no*. You should hold open houses.

However, you must recognize that the old "80–20 rule" applies just as much in real estate as it does in any other part of life. By that I mean, 80 percent of the people who see your home will probably not be interested in buying your home, but . . . 20 percent probably will have some interest and one of that 20 percent actually may be the buyer you need.

FIGURE 12.2

HOME SHOWING CHECKLIST

Item	OK	Work to Be Done	Comments
Floors mopped and vacuumed	_____	_____	_____
Windows cleaned	_____	_____	_____
Appliances cleaned	_____	_____	_____
Counters cleaned	_____	_____	_____
All lights on	_____	_____	_____
No odors—air out or freshen with potpourri or by baking bread	_____	_____	_____
Interior doors open	_____	_____	_____
Beds made	_____	_____	_____
Staging—set table, beds turned down, etc.	_____	_____	_____
Curtains open	_____	_____	_____
Mirrors and glass cleaned	_____	_____	_____
Bathrooms cleaned and smell fresh	_____	_____	_____
Tubs and sinks cleaned	_____	_____	_____
Fixtures cleaned and polished	_____	_____	_____
Towels neatly arranged	_____	_____	_____
Soft music playing	_____	_____	_____
Clothing put away	_____	_____	_____
Laundry area uncluttered	_____	_____	_____
Garage door closed	_____	_____	_____
Garage swept out	_____	_____	_____
Workbenches cleaned and uncluttered	_____	_____	_____
House at comfortable temperature	_____	_____	_____
Front entry cleaned and uncluttered	_____	_____	_____
Yard and exterior cleaned and uncluttered	_____	_____	_____
Animal droppings in yard picked up	_____	_____	_____
Leaves, etc., in yard picked up	_____	_____	_____
No cars in garage, driveway, or curb	_____	_____	_____
All clutter removed	_____	_____	_____

Of the homes that sell:

- 1 to 2 percent sell through open houses
- 7 to 8 percent sell through direct agent marketing
- 5 to 6 percent sell through media advertising
- 10 to 13 percent sell through agents in MLS participation
- 4 to 6 percent sell through brokers' open houses or caravans
- 6 to 7 percent sell through sign calls or neighborhood recognition
- 2 to 3 percent sell through word-of-mouth advertising

and on and on and on . . .

Are you starting to get the picture?

Each small technique used in the marketing of a home is an integral part of the entire selling puzzle that must be assembled if you want to "Sell Your Home Fast and for the Highest Price, in Any Market."

Figure 12.3 illustrates exactly what has just been demonstrated. Leave out one piece and the puzzle is incomplete. And that one missing part could be from where your buyer would have come.

PREPARING FOR AN OPEN HOUSE

Preparing for an open house is very much like preparing for a showing, but with a few additions. Reread the section on "Preparing the Home for Showing" and utilize your Home Showing Checklist. Then you should be able to prepare your home, comfortably and confidently, for an open house. Do every item on the Home Showing Checklist for an open house.

SMART TIP:

Be cautious of open-house "overkill". Hold no more than one public open house per month. Why? If potential buyers or agents see a home held open, time after time, week after week, they may come to believe that either:

A. There is something wrong with the property because it is not selling; or

B. The seller is desperate and may be a target for a low-ball offer.

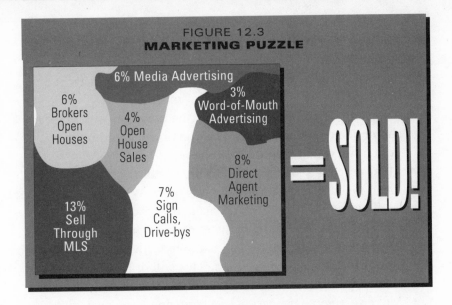

FIGURE 12.3
MARKETING PUZZLE

6% Media Advertising

6% Brokers Open Houses

4% Open House Sales

3% Word-of-Mouth Advertising

8% Direct Agent Marketing

7% Sign Calls, Drive-bys

13% Sell Through MLS

= SOLD!

PLANNING A SUCCESFUL
OPEN HOUSE

Your agent will advertise and draw potential buyers to your open house. However, in this area almost every agent can use all the help he or she can get. Consequently, share the following steps freely with your real estate professional.

- Ads should be placed in local papers giving information about the open house. Ads should run Thursday and Friday for a Saturday open house and Friday and Saturday for a Sunday event.
- Open house flyers or cards should be mailed or delivered to potential buyer areas such as apartments, condos, and non–owner-occupied homes surrounding the seller's property. (Make sure it is indicated that refreshments are being served and if any door prizes are being given away.)
- Information/fact sheets or cards must be available in the home and on the for sale sign.
- A loan officer should be available to prequalify any potential buyers who visit the property and may want this service. The

loan officer does not need to be on site but should at least be available by telephone or pager.

- A potential loan availability sheet should be available, showing two or three ways a buyer may be able to purchase the home. Figure 12.4 is an example of this sheet.

- Make the home smell great by baking bread or cookies, or by simmering cinnamon sticks (but don't burn them) or potpourri (very light scented, nothing heavy).

- Make sure the seller and all pets are out of the home for the open house. Place open house signs on every major corner leading into the property, and make it very easy to find the home. If possible, put the address on the signs.

- Tie three or four helium-filled balloons with five- to six-foot strings to each open house sign. This will draw even more attention from passing motorists.

- Make sure you have permission from any homeowners on properties where you have placed an open house sign. If signs are placed on city, county, or province property, be sure you are not violating any ordinances against this type of temporary signing.

- Post open house flyers or cards on all bulletin boards in the neighborhood. Places such as grocery stores, dry cleaners, health clubs, and churches have good readership.

- Send approximately 10 Open House Information Brochures or Cards to every real estate office in the area and ask that one of these items be posted.

- Send an Information/Fact Brochure plus an Open House flyer to the 50 top-selling agents in the area. Include a special cover letter inviting the agent to the open house.

FIGURE 12.4

LOAN AVAILABILITY SHEET

MODEL: DOLPHIN   BASE SALES PRICE: 139,990

LOAN AMOUNT: 125,990   90% LTV

1-year ARM with conversion option		30-Year Fixed		20-Year Fixed Rate Mortagage Loan		30-Year Fixed Rate Due in 7	
RATE	4.75%	RATE	8.875%	RATE	7.625%	RATE	7.875%
POINTS	.75%	POINTS	-0-%	POINTS	-0-%	POINTS	.25%
P&I	$ 657.22	P&I	$ 1002.43	P&I	$ 1024.62	P&I	$ 913.51
Taxes	$ 204.00	Taxes	$ 204.00	Taxes	$ 204.00	Taxes	$ 204.00
Haz/Flood	$ 50.00	Haz/Flood	$ 50.00	Haz/Flood	$ 50.00	Haz/Flood	$ 504.00
PMI	$ 51.00	PMI	$ 51.00	PMI	$ 51.00	PMI	$ 514.00
Totol PITI	$ 962.22	Totol PITI	$ 1307.43	Totol PITI	$ 1,329.62	Totol PITI	$ 1,285.00
Down payment	$ 14,000.00	Down payment	$ 14,000.00	Down payment	$ 14,000.00	Down payment	$ 14,000.00
Closing Costs	$ 5,035.00	Closing Costs	$ -0.00	Closing Costs	$ 5,035.00	Closing Costs	$ 5,305.00
Prepaids	$ 2,515.00	Prepaids	$ 2,515.00	Prepaids	$ 2,515.00	Prepaids	$ 2,515.00
Points	$ 944.93	Points	$ -0.00	Points	$ 1,259.90	Points	$ 314.98
TOTAL CASH TO CLOSE	$ 22,495.00	TOTAL CASH TO CLOSE	$ 16,515.00	TOTAL CASH TO CLOSE	$ 21,810.00	TOTAL CASH TO CLOSE	$ 21,865.00

For further information contact: John Doe, ABC Realty

(800)123-4567

Figure 12.5 presents an Open House Celebration Card and Figure 12.6, an Open House Celebration Brochure.

FIGURE 12.5
OPEN HOUSE CELEBRATION CARD

YOU ARE INVITED TO AN
Open House Celebration!

23456 Park Lane
Anywhere, CA

California style, large kitchen made for entertaining, glass-enclosed breakfast nook, exposed beams in the kitchen and dining area, 3 fireplaces (including 1 in the very romantic master suite), 4 large bedrooms, 3 bathrooms, separate maid's quarters next to the kitchen, 30 x 28 great room over the garage, separate area (for storage or a shop) in the garage, indoor laundry facilities, professionally landscaped backyard, 3-car garage, and much more!

Call John Doe Today!
(000) 123-4567

Making the Open House
an Event

The day of the open house, the home should be more than "show ready," it should be "show perfect"! It is very important that there are no cars, including the agent's car, in the garage, the driveway, adjacent parking areas, or at the curb in front of the house. Leave as much parking space as possible to make it very easy for buyers to look at your home.

FIGURE 12.6 OPEN HOUSE CELEBRATION BROCHURE >

You Are Invited to a Celebration!

2828 Elm Street has just been listed for sale!

Special evaluation forms will be available to assist you in determining the value of your home.

We would like you to attend an Open House Celebration. Come to see a terrific home . . . stay for the special refreshments.

1234 Main Street
Anywhere, CA 90000

For more information call
John Doe
(800) 123-4567

Have a large, descriptive open house sign in front of the property. The for-sale sign is not enough. As mentioned earlier, attach some helium-filled balloons to the open house sign to attract more attention.

You also can use these balloons to create a walkway effect up the driveway or the sidewalk, by driving small stakes into the grass and securing the balloons on these stakes.

Refreshments

For refreshments, provide foods that will not crumble or leave debris throughout the home. A good choice might be fruit, vegetable, or cheese trays—any foods that can be eaten with toothpicks off small paper plates. Bite-size items create less mess. Soft drinks or coffee should be served in small cups so people won't walk around with their drinks. Serve these refreshments in the kitchen area or, better yet, if it is nice weather, on the back patio or porch.

Because of the obvious liability problem, do not serve alcoholic beverages at an open house.

If the weather is warm, make sure all of the windows and doors are open if there are screens. Make the home seem as bright and airy as possible.

Be sure that all children and pets are removed from the property the day of the open house.

The house should be left completely to the agent on the day the property is held open.

After the Open House

All of the open house material—signs, brochures, balloons—must be removed immediately after the open house. If cards or brochures have been placed on bulletin boards, the items should be replaced with Information/Fact Brochures or Cards.

BROKERS' OPEN HOUSES OR AGENT CARAVANS

You should prepare your home for a broker's open house or agency caravan exactly the same way as for the public open house.

If you can get 40 to 100 agents through your property, each one of those agents probably knows at least five potential buyers, equating to 200 to 500 buyers. Very few public open houses will ever draw that much attention.

Have the Information/Fact Brochures and the Lender Information Sheets available for each agent who tours the home.

Again, serve refreshments for the brokers' open house or agent caravan, just as for the public open house.

> **SMART TIP:**
> Statistics have shown that the broker's open houses or agent caravans are much more important to the sale of most homes than public open houses.

DEALING WITH COMMENTS AND CRITICISMS

Your agent probably will receive a few comments and criticisms when a public open house is held.

However, when a brokers' open house is held, your agent will ask for and receive comments and criticisms from virtually every broker and agent who attends. Also, each agent may be asked to give an estimate of value of the property.

You and your agent should review the comments and criticisms and price recommendations as soon as possible after the open house. You do not need to know which agents made what comments. Carrying a grudge against an agent who may have made a derogatory comment about the home will serve no purpose. That same agent may, sometime in the future, have a buyer for that property.

You must remain objective, open-minded, and utilize those suggestions to improve the home and the potential for selling it.

CHAPTER THIRTEEN

Negotiating Offers

THE PROCESS
OF NEGOTIATING
AN OFFER

Throughout this book, I have reminded you that all of the preparation, the cleaning, the repairs, the showings, the open houses, the advertising, the brochures . . . everything is done to achieve one result—reaching a point where a buyer says "Yes, I want to make an offer on the property."

For everything they go through, sellers sometimes lose sight of the fact that this is what they have been working toward throughout the entire preparation and listing period: getting the property sold! But now, when the time has finally come, what should you expect and how should you respond to these offers?

If you have listed your home with a real estate agent, he or she probably gave you some guidance with regard to dealing with offers, at the time your property was listed. However, that may have been a month or three or even six months prior to actually receiving the offer. Therefore, when you do finally begin the offer process, it will be important for you to communicate effectively with your agent. Most important, do not be afraid to ask questions. Ask about any part of the offer you are unsure of. There is nothing more frustrating to an agent than to be 10 days away from closing a transaction and have a seller or buyer say, "I really didn't understand this portion of the contract and I do not want to close this transaction under these circumstances." All the time and work and expense goes right down the drain with these few words.

Also remember, once you sign that sale contract, it is, for the most part, the "point of no return." You have received what you wanted and your house is sold. All that will be left is to complete the closing process.

WHAT IS YOUR
AGENT'S JOB NOW?

When you listed your home with a real estate professional, the agent established what is known as a fiduciary relationship. You hired that agent to do a job for you, to work only for you, and to do everything in his or her power to get you the most money possible for the sale of your property.

Your agent also has a legal responsibility to deal fairly and honestly with all parties to the transaction, which includes all buyers. However, the seller's agent must work for the best interest of the seller. The primary factor that establishes this fiduciary relationship is that the seller is paying the agent's commission.

If another agent from another company is the one who procures or produces the buyer in this transaction and that buyer's agent brings an offer, there is a good chance that the buyer's agent will ask to share the commission the seller has agreed to pay to the listing agent. In essence, the buyer's agent becomes a subagent of the listing agent.

So, who would you guess the buyer's agent legally represents with regard to a fiduciary relationship?

You got it, the seller. Why? Because the seller is paying the commission and is actually the party who has hired these agents and subagents. Again, both the seller's and the buyer's agents have the responsibility to deal fairly and honestly with all parties to the transaction, but that buyer's agent actually has a responsibility to try to get the best deal possible . . . *for the seller.*

In some cases, a buyer's agent may collect a commission from the buyer and from the seller. If that is the case, the buyer's agent must disclose this fact to all parties.

I discuss fiduciary relationships because it is important for you to understand the responsibilities of agents and subagents. In some cases, it may become necessary to remind a buyer's agent who he or she actually represents. Who has actually employed the agent? Who is paying the agent's salary?

Get the point? Make sure the agents do.

WHAT CONSTITUTES
AN OFFER?

Most buyers will, with the help of the agent who has shown them the property, prepare a written deposit receipt or purchase contract for purchase of your property. In every state in the United States and every province in Canada, real estate contracts must be in writing. (This is not true for all other types of contracts.)

If a buyer's agent calls your agent and indicates that a buyer has made an offer, the first question should be "Do you have the offer signed by all of the buyers?" If the buyer or buyer's agent has any other answer than a simple "Yes," such as "Well, we haven't put it in writing yet, but this is what we were thinking of offering," tell the person to call back when there is an offer in writing signed by all parties.

Unless that offer is in writing and is accompanied by an earnest money deposit (called "consideration" in the world of contracts), there is actually no offer. If you have an agent, he or she will be sure that there is a legitimate offer before presenting any information to you.

Prior to the presentation of the offer, your agent should prepare a Net Proceeds Worksheet and have the offer presentation complete when the offer is actually presented. (See Figure 7.1 in Chapter 7.) You should have a copy of all the information that was discussed when the listing was taken, including estimated Net Proceeds Worksheet. That way, you will not have to try to remember exactly what figures were used when the listing was taken.

In some areas, it is customary for the buyer's agent to accompany the seller's agent when the offer is presented to the seller. In some cases, the agent who is acting on behalf of the buyer will present the offer to the seller (in the presence of the seller's agent, of course). When the buyer's agent accompanies your agent to present an offer, it is your responsibility to listen to the entire offer and to ask any questions you may have with regard to the offer or the buyer. However, before you make a decision on the offer, the buyer's agent should be excused from the meeting; that way you and your agent can discuss, in private, the merits and drawbacks of the offer.

In some cases, the seller takes a little time to evaluate the offer, if the terms are substantially different from what was requested in the listing contract. In other words, if it is a low offer and you must decide whether to accept this lesser price, you should take time to evaluate the offer and make sure this is a contract that you can live with.

You should be acutely aware of the importance of the words, "Time is of the essence," and should make a decision as soon as possible as to whether to accept the offer or prepare a counteroffer.

SMART TIP:
Offers usually are written for only a short time, either one or two days. That means that you must decide on that offer within one or two days or the offer is automatically rescinded. You also should be aware that if the buyer decides to withdraw the offer before you accept and the acceptance is communicated to the buyer, the contract can be null and void. That is why the following words are printed on every deposit receipt or purchase contract: *TIME IS OF THE ESSENCE.*

You should never totally reject an offer; you should always prepare a counteroffer.

Remember, everyone wants a "deal;" potential buyers are no different. They may not offer what they are willing to pay for the property in the initial purchase agreement. You must be willing to negotiate. As I indicated earlier, it may take five or six counteroffers before the purchase agreement finally takes place.

SPECIAL COUNTEROFFER TECHNIQUES

One method by which you may be able to get buyers to accept the first counteroffer is called "loading." In such cases, you actually load information that may influence buyers' decision and cause more urgency on their part.

In other words, give them so many reasons to say "yes," it seems ridiculous to say "no." As an example:

A buyer offers $205,000 on a property that was listed for $219,000. The sellers prepare a counteroffer for $212,000 indicating they will accept no less. Included with the counteroffer is:

- A list of all comparable sales showing that two comps have sold within the past six months for $212,500 and $212,900. Further, the comp sale sheet showed that at $212,000, the buyer has received approximately $1,000 of free equity at the close of the sale.

- A list of the special amenities that the home includes, such as a hot tub, walk-in closets, a new fence, new paint, new carpet, with a dollar value shown for each item.
- A list of five other homes with fewer amenities that are priced higher.
- A list of the neighborhood conveniences that will be of interest to the seller.
- A letter written from the seller to the buyer stating a commitment to make this sale a smooth and comfortable transaction for all parties.

More times than not the buyer will accept the first counteroffer. "Load" the counter. It works!

HOW WILL THE OFFER BE STRUCTURED?

A Deposit Receipt or Purchase Contract is a legal and binding document that contains numerous sections and subsections. This offer to purchase may include anywhere from one to 10 pages depending on which form the buyer or buyer's agent has used.

Figure A.4 in the appendix includes an example of a Real Estate Purchase Contract used in the real estate industry. This form should help you to understand each area that can be addressed when a buyer actually makes an offer to purchase.

These forms are copyrighted and cannot be reprinted. For information regarding the use of or to obtain these forms, please contact your local Board of Realtors®.

ACCEPTING THE OFFER OR WRITING A COUNTEROFFER

After you have completely evaluated the offer and have prepared a Net Proceeds Worksheet (showing approximately what you will receive if you accept this offer), it is decision time.

Do you accept the offer or prepare a counteroffer for the buyers?

If you accept, you will sign the agreement, keep your copy, and return the buyers' copy to them before the time allowed for acceptance has expired. (Your agent will handle this for you.)

IF YOU WRITE A COUNTEROFFER

If you decide to prepare a counteroffer, you and your agent will prepare another Net Proceeds Worksheet, using the sales figure of the counteroffer to determine if your net proceeds will be what you are expecting at the close of the transaction.

Just as the buyers make an offer to purchase under their terms and conditions, your counteroffer actually becomes your offer to sell under your terms and conditions.

If the buyers choose to accept your counteroffer to sell, you have a transaction and you will begin the closing process. Consequently, the preparation of that counteroffer is extremely important.

Figure 13.1 is an example of a counteroffer form. This form is copyrighted and is *for information only*. It is not meant for your use. Should you require more information or wish to obtain this form, contact your agent or possibly a local stationery store that handles forms.

Your counteroffer should be very specific with regard to any changes, alterations, or additions to the original purchase agreement. Remember, as I explained earlier, you can use special techniques to help your first counteroffer be accepted so you are not forced to go through the counteroffer process six or seven times. *Mention the method of "loading" to your agent.*

Once your counteroffer has been prepared, your agent or the buyer's agent will deliver this document and explain to the buyers what changes you have made on your "Counter to the Counter."

As I said earlier, don't become disappointed during the counteroffer process. As long as offers and counteroffers are being sent back and forth, there is still opportunity to put the transaction together.

FIGURE 13.1
COUNTEROFFER FORM

COUNTEROFFER

The offer made by _____

to purchase the real property commonly known as_____

_____

dated _____is not accepted in its present

form, but the following counter offer is hereby submitted:_____

_____

_____

_____

_____

_____

_____

_____

OTHER ITEMS: All terms to remain the same as original Offer and Acceptance.

RIGHT TO ACCEPT OTHER OFFERS: Seller reserves the right to accept any

other offer prior to purchaser's acceptance of this counteroffer and seller's agent

being so advised in writing.

EXPIRATION: This counteroffer shall expire unless a copy hereof with pur-

chaser's written acceptance is delivered to seller or his/her agent within ___days

from date.

Date_____   Seller _____

Time _____   Seller _____

The above undersigned purchaser accepts the above counteroffer.

Date_____   Purchaser_____

Time _____   Purchaser_____

ACCEPTING AN OFFER

Once buyers and sellers have reached agreement, in either an offer or a counteroffer, and all parties to the transaction have signed the same document, the home is sold (or at least the sale is pending).

Now it is time to move on to the last and most important step, the closing.

CHAPTER FOURTEEN

Closing the Sale

WHAT ARE THE SELLER'S RESPONSIBILITIES?

Even if sellers have used the services of a real estate professional to handle the sale of their home, sellers have certain responsibilities. These may include:

- As much as possible, keep your home "show ready" throughout the closing process. Remember, different inspectors will be viewing your home, the appraiser will be completing his or her valuation of the property, the buyers may be compelled to see the property again, or your agent may have other potential buyers who want to see the property (just in case the original transaction falls apart).
- At your listing agent's direction, there will be certain documents for you to sign at the title company, escrow office, or closing company during this process.

Figure 14.1 explains in some detail what is involved in an escrow/closing process. You should be aware of and willing to help with any portions of this closing process where your assistance is needed.

In most cases, it will be very important, at the beginning of the closing process, to see that escrow/closing instructions are signed and submitted to the escrow/closing agent.

In some states, the closing agent will be an attorney. However, in most states, attorneys do not have to participate in a standard real estate transaction. The closing/escrow process will be handled by an escrow company, a closing agent, an abstract company, or a title company.

These closing/escrow agents act as a third party to the transaction, to make sure that all required documents have been prepared and submitted properly, all loan papers are submitted correctly, all

FIGURE 14.1

THE ESCROW/CLOSING PROCESS

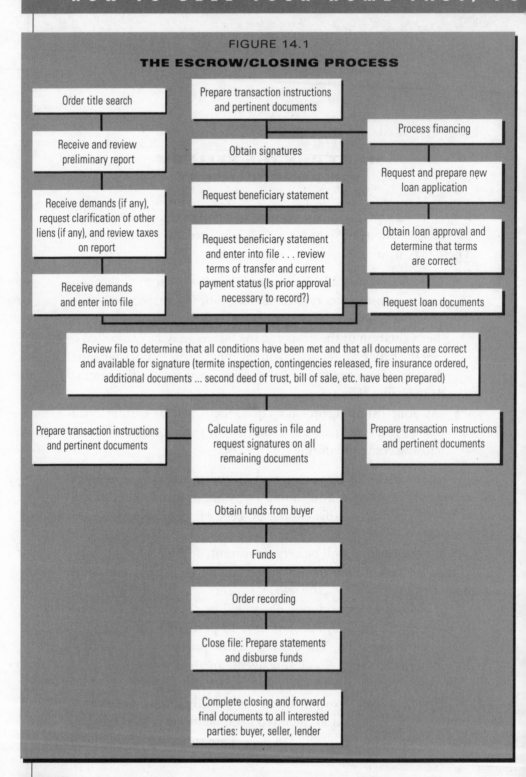

Order title search

Receive and review preliminary report

Receive demands (if any), request clarification of other liens (if any), and review taxes on report

Receive demands and enter into file

Prepare transaction instructions and pertinent documents

Obtain signatures

Request beneficiary statement

Request beneficiary statement and enter into file . . . review terms of transfer and current payment status (Is prior approval necessary to record?)

Process financing

Request and prepare new loan application

Obtain loan approval and determine that terms are correct

Request loan documents

Review file to determine that all conditions have been met and that all documents are correct and available for signature (termite inspection, contingencies released, fire insurance ordered, additional documents ... second deed of trust, bill of sale, etc. have been prepared)

Prepare transaction instructions and pertinent documents

Calculate figures in file and request signatures on all remaining documents

Prepare transaction instructions and pertinent documents

Obtain funds from buyer

Funds

Order recording

Close file: Prepare statements and disburse funds

Complete closing and forward final documents to all interested parties: buyer, seller, lender inspections have been completed, and all monies have been received.

Once all of these things have occurred, the escrow/closing is deemed to be "perfected." This means the closing process is complete, buyer and seller will sign the final closing documents, and the escrow/closing agent will see that all of the required documents, such as the Grant Deed, and Mortgage or Deed of Trust, are recorded with the county or province recorder's office. This recording process, in essence, gives public notice to this transaction.

Once this recording process has taken place, the escrow/closing agent will release the monies due to the seller, pay all fees that are to be paid out of the escrow/closing, and advise the agents and seller to release possession of the property to the new buyer.

All fees, commissions, prorations, charges, and recordings will be processed and/or paid by this escrow/closing agent and the transaction is complete.

Figure 14.2, an escrow/closing checklist, will assist sellers, buyers, and agents alike in making sure that nothing is missed during this very important closing process.

You will note that a "goal date" as well as the "actual date" are listed. All parties to the transaction should watch carefully to see that the target dates are met and that none of these important steps is forgotten.

ESCROW/CLOSING PROBLEM AREAS

If an agent, seller, or buyer sees that one or more of the target dates have passed without completion, the party responsible for seeing that the item is completed should be notified immediately.

Numerous problems can crop up during a closing process. Once such an obstacle is recognized, it should be brought to the attention of the parties of the transaction immediately!

Figure 14.3, a list of problem areas, will give you an idea of the time delays that can occur if certain difficulties arise. As you can see, it doesn't take much to slow up or kill a transaction. Every one of these potential problems could "blow the deal," so make sure all parties stay on top of the transaction.

FIGURE 14.2

CLOSING CHECKLIST

The following list is to confirm all the dates necessary to achieve a smooth closing. Please verify the dates with your clients and return a copy to me with your signature.

For Property at: _____	Goal Date	Actual Date
1. Contract acceptance with all decision makers present	_____	_____
2. Property inspection by buyer	_____	_____
3. Promissory note inspection and approval	_____	_____
4. Listing disclosure signed	_____	_____
5. Agency signed	_____	_____
6. Service contract approval	_____	_____
7. Income/expense approval	_____	_____
8. Permit approval	_____	_____
9. Inventory approval	_____	_____
10. Escrow instructions prepared	_____	_____
11. Escrow instructions signed	_____	_____
12. Deposit submitted	_____	_____
13. Deposit clears	_____	_____
14. Professional property inspection	_____	_____
15. Inspection accepted	_____	_____
16. Estoppel certificates approval	_____	_____
17. Termite inspection	_____	_____
18. Earthquake and flood zones	_____	_____
19. Deposit increase to escrow	_____	_____
20. Preliminary title report approval	_____	_____
21. City approvals obtained	_____	_____
22. Loan submitted complete to lender	_____	_____
23. Appraisal made	_____	_____
24. Appraisal done	_____	_____
25. Termite work finished	_____	_____
26. Obtain insurance	_____	_____
27. Reappraisal done	_____	_____
28. Other work finished	_____	_____
29. PMI approval	_____	_____
30. FIRPTA signed	_____	_____
31. Other contingencies cleared	_____	_____
A. _____	_____	_____
B. _____	_____	_____
C. _____	_____	_____
32. Formal written loan approval	_____	_____
33. Loan documents signed	_____	_____
34. Cleared funds submitted for down payment	_____	_____
35. Buyer's occupancy	_____	_____

Buyer's Agent _____ Date _____

Seller's Agent _____ Date _____

FIGURE 14.3

ESCROW/CLOSING PROBLEM CHECKLIST

1. Buyer and seller do not sign escrow/closing promptly.	5 days
2. Buyer's good-faith deposit check does not clear.	3 days
3. Buyer does not complete loan application in a timely manner.	10 days
4. Buyer or seller does not return calls of agent or lender.	10 days
5. Buyer or seller wants to change some terms of the transaction.	5 days
6. Buyer loses job.	30 days
7. Buyer lied on prequalification to lender.	10 days
8. Buyer cannot supply tax returns in timely manner.	10 days
9. Seller changes mind about selling.	5 days
10. Seller leaves town and does not leave a power of attorney with anyone.	5 days
11. Seller did not disclose all liens against him- or herself.	20 days
12. Unknown problems with home are discovered.	10–30 days
13. Low appraisal.	15 days
14. Slow appraisal.	15 days
15. Difficult appraisal.	5 days
16. Incorrect appraisal.	15 days
17. Lender made a mistake on prequalification.	5 days
18. Lender decides not to loan on property or borrower.	10–30 days
19. Borrower does not qualify for loan.	10 days
20. Lender requires repairs on property.	15 days
21. Agents do not return calls.	5 days
22. Agents go on vacation.	5 days
23. Buyer or seller does not sign final closing papers in a timely fashion.	5 days
24. Escrow/closer/lender loses file.	10 days
25. Escrow/closer/title company/lender very busy.	5–20 days
26. Seller or buyer wants to change closing date.	5 days
27. Inspection companies too busy or slow.	5–10 days
28. Many things required by the inspection process.	5 days
29. Additional inspections required by appraiser or lender.	5–10 days
30. Title company finds problems with the title.	5–15 days

Sellers and buyers will be asked to approve several documents during the closing process. Samples of several of these forms appear in Figures 14.4, 14.5, and 14.6.

FIGURE 14.4
GRANT DEED v

FIGURE 14.5

HUD STATEMENT>

RECORDING REQUESTED BY

And when recorded, mail this deed and, unless otherwise shown below, mail tax statement to:

Name

Address

SPACE ABOVE THIS LINE
RECORDER'S USE

Documentary Transfer Tax $ _____
_____ Computed on full value of property conveyed,
_____ or computed on full value less liens and
       encumbrances remaining at time of sale.

_____
Signature of Declarant or Agent determining tax. Firm Name

GRANT DEED

FOR A VALUABLE CONSIDERATION, receipt of which is hereby acknowledged,

hereby GRANT(s) to

the following described real property in the _____
County of _____ , State of _____

Assessor's Parcel No:

Dated _____   X _____

_____

State of _____
County of _____

On _____before me,
_____ personally appeared

_____

_____

personally known to me (or proved to me on the basis of satisfactory evidence) to be the person(s) whose name(s) is/are subscribed to the within instrument and acknowledged to me that he/she/they executed the same in his/her/their authorized capacity(ies), and that by his/her/their signature(s) on the instrument the person(s), or the entity upon behalf of which the person(s) acted, executed the instrument.

WITNESS my hand and official seal.

_____

(Space for official notarial seal)

MAIL TAX STATEMENTS TO PARTY SHOWN ON FOLLOWING LINE;
IF NO PARTY SHOWN, MAIL AS DIRECTED ABOVE.

OMB No. 2502-0265

U.S. DEPARTMENT OF HOUSING AND URBAN DEVELOPMENT

A. Settlement Statement

B. Type of Loan

1. ❑ VA 2. ❑ FmHA 3. ❑ Conv. Unins.	6. File Number	7. Loan Number	8. Mtg. Insurance Case Number
4. ❑ FHA 5. ❑ Conv. Ins.			

C. NOTE: This form is furnished to give you a statement of actual settlement costs. Amounts paid to and by the settlement agent are shown. Items marked "(p.o.c)" were paid outside the closing; they are shown here for informational purposes and are not included in the totals.

D. Name and Address of Borrower	E. Name and Address of Seller	F. Name and Address of Lender

G. Property Location	H. Settlement Agent	
	Place of Settlement	I. Settlement Date

J. Summary of Borrower's Transaction		K. Summary of Seller's Transaction	
100. Gross Amount Due From Borrower		**400. Gross Amount Due To Seller**	
101. Contract sales price		401. Contract sales price	
102. Personal property		402. Personal property	
103. Settlement charges to borrower (1400)		403.	
104.		404.	
105.		405.	
Adjustments for items paid by seller in advance		**Adjustments for items paid by seller in advance**	
106.		406.	
107. County taxes		407. County taxes	
108. Assessments		408. Assessments	
109.		409.	
110.		410.	
111.		411.	
112.		412.	
120. Gross Amount Due From Borrower		**420. Gross Amount Due To Seller**	
200. Amounts Paid By Or In Behalf of Borrower		**500. Reductions in Amount Due To Seller**	
201. Deposit or earnest money		501.	
202. Principal money of new loan(s)		502. Settlement charges to seller (1400)	
203. Existing loan(s) taken subject to		503. Existing loan(s) taken subject to	
204.		504. Payoff of first mortgage loan *	
205.		505. Payoff of second mortgage loan *	
206.		506. Mortgage loan to Borrower	
207.		507.	
208.		508.	
209.		509.	

U.S. DEPARTMENT OF HOUSING AND URBAN DEVELOPMENT - page 2

Adjustments for items unpaid by seller		Adjustments for items unpaid by seller	
210.		510.	
211. County taxes		511. County taxes	
212. Assessments		512. Assessments	
213.		513.	
214.		514.	
215.		515.	
216.		516.	
217.		517.	
218.		518.	
219.		519.	
220. Total Paid By/For Borrower		520. Total Reduction Amount Due Seller	
300. Cash At Settlement From/To Borrower		600. Cash At Settlement To/From Seller	
301. Gross amount due from borrower (120)		601. Gross amount due to seller (420)	
302. Less amounts paid by/for borrower (220)		602. Less reductions in amount due seller (520)	
303. Cash ❑ From ❑ To Borrower		603. Cash ❑ To ❑ From Seller	

L. Settlement

700. Total Sales/Broker's Commission based on price $　　@　% =		Paid from Borrower's Funds at Settlement	Paid from Seller's Funds at Settlement
Division of Commission (700) as follows			
701. $　　　　to			
702. $　　　　to			
703. Commission paid at Settlement			
704.			
800. Items Payable In Connection With Loan			
801. Loan Origination Fee　　　　%			
802. Loan Discount　　　　%			
803. Appraisal Fee　　　　to			
804. Credit Report　　　　to			
805. Lender's Inspection Fee			
806. Mortgage Insurance Application Fee　　to			
807. Assumption Fee			
808.			
809.			
810.			
811.			
900. Items Required By Lender To Be Paid In Advance			
901. Interest from　　　to　@$　　/day			
902. Hazard Insurance Premium for　　years to			
903. Flood Ins. Premium　　years to			
905.			
906.			
907.			
908.			

U.S. DEPARTMENT OF HOUSING AND URBAN DEVELOPMENT - page 3

1000. Reserves Deposited With Lender				
1001. Hazard Insurance	months @$	per month		
1004. County property taxes	months @$	per month		
1005. Annual assessments	months @$	per month		
1006.				
1007.				
1008.				
1100. Title Charges				
1101. Settlement or closing fee to				
1102. Abstract or title search to				
1103. Title examination to				
1104. Title insurance binder to				
1105. Document preparation to				
1106. Notary fees to				
1107. Attorney's fees to				
(includes above items numbers)				
1108. Title insurance to				
(includes above items numbers:1102, 1103, 1108, and endorsements, if any)				
1109. Lender's coverage	$			
1110. Owner's coverage	$			
1111.				
1112.				
1113.				
1114.				
1200. Government Recording and Transfer Charges				
1201. Recording fees: Deed $	; Mortgage $	; Release $		
1202. City/county tax/ stamps: Deed $	; Mortgage $			
1204.				
1205.				
1206.				
1300. Additional Settlement Charges				
1301. Survey/Inspection	to			
1302. Survey/Inspection	to			
1303.				
1304.				
1305.				
1306.				
1307.				
1308.				
1309.				
1310.				
1311.				

1400. Total Settlement Charges (enter on 103, Section J and 502, Section K)

To the best of my knowledge, the HUD-1 Settlement Statement which I have prepared is a true and accurate account of the funds which were received and have been or will be disbursed by the undersigned as part of the settlement of this transaction.

_____   _____
Escrow Officer   Date

FIGURE 14.6

ESCROW/CLOSING INSTRUCTIONS

Escrow #: _____

TO: ABC TITLE COMPANY   Date of Deposit Receipt: _____
     123 10th Street
     Anywhere, CA 90000

RE: Property Known As _____ Deposit Amount: $_____

Gentlemen:

You are advised that we have negotiated the purchase of real property referred to above.

We hereby hand you a check payable to ABC Title Company for the above deposit amount.

You are to deposit the check and hold the funds represented thereby and any additional funds deposited with you in your escrow trust account. You are instructed not to release any funds until mutually acceptable instructions are received by you from the undersigned Sellers and Buyers.

Any principal instructing you to cancel this escrow shall file notice of cancellation in your office, in writing, and so state the reason for cancellation. Upon receipt of such request, you shall prepare cancellation instructions for signatures of the principals and shall forward same to the principals. If no written objection is filed with you upon receipt of the mutually agreeable cancellation instructions signed by all principals and after payment of your cancellation charges, you are authorized to comply with such instruction and cancel your escrow. If, after 30 days from date of notice of cancellation, you have not received mutually agreeable cancellation instructions, the principals hereto expressly agree that you, as escrow holder, have the absolute right at your election to file an action in interpleader requiring the principals to answer and litigate their several claims and rights among themselves, and you are authorized to deposit with the clerk of the court all documents and funds held in this escrow. In the event such action is filed, the principals jointly and severally agree to pay your cancellation charges and costs, expenses, and reasonable attorney's fees which you are required to expend or incur in such interpleader action, the amount thereof to be fixed and judgment therefor to be rendered by the court. Upon the filing of such action, you shall thereupon be fully released and discharged from all obligations to further perform any duties or obligations otherwise imposed by the terms of this escrow.

We hereby apply for a California Land Title Association standard form policy of title insurance to be issued on closing the sale and request that a preliminary report be issued for the purpose of disclosing the terms and conditions upon which you are willing to provide such title insurance policy.

BUYER : _____   SELLER : _____

x _____   x _____

FIGURE 14.7

NET PROCEEDS STATEMENT

Escrow No.: _____ Filing Date:_____

Escrow Settlement	Debit	Credit
Total Consideration		
Deposit		
Deposit		
Deposit		
Paid Outside of Escrow to		
Principal Balance of First Trust Deed of Trust of Record		
Principal Balance of Second Trust Deed of Trust of Record		
Amount of New Loan		
Purchase Money Deed of Trust		
Taxes $ per from to		
Personal Property Tax		
Insurance on $ Premium $ per		
from to		
Interest on $ @ from to		
Interest on $ @ from to		
Impounded Funds Held by Lending Institution		
Rents		
# $ per from to		
# $ per from to		
Rental Deposits:		
#		
Deducted by Lender:		
Commission to		
Commission to		
Termite Company Paid		
Payment of Demand to		
Interest on $ @ from to		
Prepaymant		
Forwarding Fee		
County Tax Collector		
Title Policy/ATA Policy		
Revenue Stamps		
Recording		
Reconveyance Fee		
Tax Service		
Sub Escrow Fee		
Completing Documents		
Notary Fee		
Insurance Endorsement Fee		
Reconveyance Fee		
Loan Escrow Fee/Beneficiary/Demand Processing Fee		
Balance - Check Herewith		
TOTAL		

AFTER THE CLOSE

You will have agreed to deliver possession of the property usually at the closing or within two days after the close of the transaction. You must be prepared and ready to make this move and deliver possession as agreed.

Prior to the close, it is imperative that you have scheduled the packers, movers, cleaners, or any other party whose services will be necessary to complete the moving process. If possession is not delivered to buyers as agreed in the contract, there is a good chance that you will end up paying buyers a daily rental fee for staying in the home.

If you anticipate that you will need to maintain possession of the home longer than the initial contract allowed, this condition should be addressed immediately with the agents and the buyers, and an addendum should be added to the closing instructions. A per-day rental rate should be included in this agreement so there is no question as to when and how the final possession process will occur.

THE WHAT-IFS

What if the appraisal for the lender who is making the loan for the buyer comes in at an evaluation lower than the sale price and the loan amount is reduced?

A written appeal can be made to the lender for an increase in the appraisal and/or loan amount. The lender that is making the loan will be able to guide the borrower as to how this appeal process should be handled.

OR

A new appraisal could be ordered if it appears that the original appraisal is incorrect.

What if, even after the appeal, the lender refuses to raise the loan amount to that amount which the buyer needs to close the transaction?

The buyer could still complete the sale by adding the additional funds and agreeing to close the sale at above appraisal price (not likely).

OR

The seller could consider carrying a second mortgage for the buyer for the difference in the loan amount and the down payment (again, not likely because the buyer is still paying more than appraisal for the property).

OR

The seller will reduce the sale price of the property to match the appraised value (the most likely scenario).

What if the sale price is altered due to a low appraisal? Can sellers renegotiate fees or other costs they have agreed to pay such as repairs, inspections, loan fees or commissions?

Absolutely! When that sale price changes, it may become a free-for-all as to who will pay these fees and figures. As indicated earlier, if something changes in the contract, the seller may ask the lender and the title/escrow/closing company to reduce their fees; even real estate agents may be asked to reduce their commission, to keep this transaction together.

Don't try to penalize all parties to the transaction if the problem is created by one of the parties, even if that party is you. Try to place responsibility for the additional cost on the person or company that has caused the problem.

What if a buyer, though they were prequalified, does not ultimately qualify for the loan? (This can occur for any number of reasons.)

> **SMART TIP:**
>
> Remember, the agent has done his or her job; produced a buyer and put the transaction together. If you get a low appraisal, there is a good chance the agent warned you about this from the beginning and it's not his or her fault, it's yours. Or, if the lender is just being unreasonable and the agent has provided comparable sales data that supports the sale price, again, this is not the agent's fault. Before you change the price, you should have the buyer change lenders.

Try to have the buyer solve the problem for the nonqualification and have the lender resubmit the package.

OR

Have the buyer talk with several other potential lenders and determine if these other lenders might be able to make the loan.

OR

Look at alternative methods by which the buyer may be able to buy the property, such as seller carry-back or the buyer obtaining a private loan for the larger down payment and/or assuming the existing loan.

What if the buyer tries to continue to negotiate throughout the closing process? In other words, the buyer continually stops by the house asking the sellers or their agent things like "Do you suppose you could leave that wheelbarrow?" or "Would you throw in all the leftover chemicals for the pool?" or "Would you leave the children's swing set in the backyard?"

These types of buyers can create a great deal of frustration for all parties to the transaction and should be dealt with immediately. Have the buyer's agent advise these buyers that no more negotiation may be done until the transaction is closed. They have a contract that stipulates what goes and what stays, and any changes in that agreement must be in writing, to their agent. In other words, tell them, "Stop it . . . right now!"

For Sale by Owners often must deal with this type of buyer. Again, the problem must be handled immediately. Because there are no third-party negotiators, these buyers think even though the instructions have been given to the closing agent, they can continue to ask for more throughout the closing process.

What if the buyer, the buyer's agent, the lender, the title company, the escrow/closing agent, the appraiser, the different inspectors, or repairpeople are not doing their jobs within the time frames that were projected at the onset of the closing and it appears that these actions are going to delay the closing?

Your agent should be notified if it appears that these delays are occurring, especially if the delays appear to be a pattern of any particular party. It may take numerous and continual phone calls or written contacts to keep all parties on track and on schedule. All you will ask is that each party will do "as they agreed; when they agreed."

What if a buyer has a significant change in his or her life before the closing (i.e., loses job, divorce, or bankruptcy)?

In the purchase contract, there are usually conditions with regard to some of these contingencies, such as "Conditioned upon buyer qualifying for and receiving a loan in the amount of $____." Obviously, if buyers lose their jobs or have a major financial disaster, they probably won't qualify for the loan and that condition of the contract would give a way out. On the other hand, if the buyers split up and/or get a divorce during the closing process and decide not to close the transaction, they may have a problem legally retracting their offer. However, in the real world, the seller would probably choose not to litigate (which is almost always the best choice) and would probably just keep the good-faith deposit, exercise the liquidated damages clause of the contract, go back to square one, and find a new buyer.

What if sellers decide not to sell and a purchase contract is already in force?

If buyers are not willing to freely rescind the contract, sellers may face a lawsuit by the buyers, for damages or specific performance. Also, the agents involved in the transaction may have a possible action for the commission they are due.

What if the termite, home, roof, or other inspections turn up more work than the sellers anticipated and the expense for these repairs is much greater than expected?

Obviously, sellers can go ahead, bite the bullet, and make the repairs on the property. These damaged or problem areas are the sellers' responsibilities; let them handle and pay for it.

In some cases, however, sellers may not be financially able to make these repairs. If that is the case, buyers may offer to help with some of the repairs.

OR

Buyers may accept some of these problems with the home and make the repairs when they choose.

What if the home suffers major damage in an earthquake, flood, fire or other act of God?

Well . . . this is pretty much a transaction killer. There is a good chance that the buyers are not going to be willing to wait for the house to be rebuilt or repaired. Also, there is always the question as to whether the sellers have enough insurance to rebuild the property and bring it back to its original state. Many homeowners are severely underinsured.

What if liens or encumbrances are discovered that have been placed against the property? As an example, if sellers were slapped with a large tax lien against the property that had to be paid at or before the closing and the sellers would now not have enough money to purchase their new property—what could happen?

This, again, is the sellers' responsibility, and they should be willing to pay the lien and close the transaction. However, in the scenario just described, the sellers may choose not to close the transaction and "face the music" with any possible litigation. Another possibility will be that the sellers can negotiate a deal with the entity that placed the lien on the property. In any case, this should not become the buyers' problem and the sellers should not ask any of the parties to share in the responsibility of this lien.

What if the buyers change their minds at the last minute and decide not to close the transaction, for no apparent reason?

Both the buyers' and sellers' agents should make an effort to "resell" the buyers on closing the transaction.

OR

The sellers may want to hire an attorney to write a letter to the buyers explaining the possible consequences of their actions.

OR

Most commonly what happens is that the sellers keep the buyers' deposit, both parties agree to rescind the contract, and the sellers begin looking for a new "less flaky" buyer.

WHAT ABOUT THE TAXES?

If you have sold your home, decide to take the money from the sale and go off to Tahiti to live happily ever after, you may have some severe tax liability due to the "gain" that you have had on this sale.

It is fairly simple to calculate your actual gain by using a three-step process.

Step 1 Original Purchase Price + Cost of Improvements
     = Your Adjusted Basis

Although some of the closing costs when you purchased the home may be included with the cost of the home, not all of these costs are allowable. Some things such as insurance or tax impounds may not be included, but costs to obtain the loan can be. You should check with your tax preparer to determine which of these costs can be utilized.

Step 2 Costs of the Sale – Sales Price costs of the sale
     (commissions, fees, etc.)
     = Adjusted Sale Price

Step 3 Adjusted Basis – Adjusted Sale Price
     = Gain (what you have received from the sale)

The amount that you may owe in taxes depends on your individual tax position.

An example of the above explanation might be as follows:

Step 1 $260,000 Original Purchase Price of Home
     + $40,000 Cost of Improvement over ownership
     = $300,000 Adjusted Basis
Step 2 $330,000 Sale Price Home
     – $35,200 Cost of Sale
     = $294,800 Adjusted Sale Price
Step 3 $294,800 Adjusted Sale Price
     – $300,000 Adjusted Basis
     = $5,200 (No Gain)

If, on the other hand, you are buying a new home and you are using all of the gain for this purpose, you may "defer" the taxes as long as you purchase an existing home within 18 months after the close of the original sale, or you purchase a newly constructed home within 24 months after the close of the original sale. In other words, you are "rolling" your gain into your new property to become a part of the new home's adjusted basis, and you are legally telling the IRS "I'll owe you later."

WHEN WILL THE TAXES BECOME DUE?

If you sell a home and you do not purchase a home within the 18- or 24-month repurchase period, the gain on the sale of the last property that you sold will create a tax liability for that sale.

There is one very important exception of which sellers should be aware. The current IRS regulations allow a seller who is 55 years or older a one-time $125,000 exclusion to taxes owing on the gain accumulated throughout the sale of the properties. In other words, if a 55-year-old seller were to sell a property and come out with a gain of $124,999, he or she could choose to take a one-time exception and owe no taxes on this gain. Before a seller utilizes this one-time exclusion, the advice of a tax professional should be sought.

REPORTING THE SALE TO THE IRS

A seller is required to report the sale of a home to the IRS *in the year of the sale*. Although you probably will not be required to pay taxes on the gain if you are intending to or you have already purchased a new home, you must report the sale the year of the sale.

It is important that you closely track the costs of the purchase of your new home as you will use some of these costs to determine your new Adjusted Basis.

THE ACTUAL MOVE

Figure 14.8, the "Checklist for Moving," will assist you in ensuring that nothing is missed when the actual move occurs.

No doubt you may feel a little melancholy as you say "good-bye" to your neighbors and your house, but keep in mind, bigger and better memories are just over the horizon at your new home.

It is always a good idea to leave something to welcome the new buyers into the home. If they arrive and find a congratulations card and a small gift such as a plant, a chocolate cake, cookies, or a bottle of wine, chances are they will be less apt to feel twinges of that buyers' remorse we talked about earlier.

FIGURE 14.8
CHECKLIST FOR MOVING

ADDRESS CHANGE

- ❏ Give forwarding address to post office 2 to 3 weeks before moving.
- ❏ Charge accounts, credit cards.
- ❏ Subscriptions: Notice requires 6 to 8 weeks.
- ❏ Friends and relatives.

BANK

- ❏ Transfer funds, arrange check-cashing in new city.
- ❏ Arrange credit references.

INSURANCE

- ❏ Notify company of new location for coverages: life, health, fire and auto.

UTILITY COMPANIES

- ❏ Gas, light, water, telephone, fuel, garbage.
- ❏ Get refunds on any deposits made.
- ❏ Return cable boxes.

DELIVERY SERVICE

- ❏ Laundry, newspaper, changeover of service.

MEDICAL, DENTAL, PRESCRIPTION HISTORIES

- ❏ Ask doctor and dentist for referrals, transfer needed for prescriptions, eyeglasses, X-rays. Obtain birth records, medical records, etc.

PETS

- ❏ Ask about regulations for licenses, vaccinations, tags, etc.

FIGURE 14.8 **CHECKLIST FOR MOVING** (continued)

DON'T FORGET TO:

- ❑ Empty freezer, plan use of foods.
- ❑ Defrost freezer and clean refrigerator. Place charcoal inside to dispel odors.
- ❑ Have appliances serviced for moving.
- ❑ Clean rugs or clothing before moving. Have them wrapped.
- ❑ Check with your moving counselor, insurance coverage, packing and unpacking labor, arrival day, various shipping papers, method and time of expected payment.
- ❑ Plan for special care needs of infants or pets.
- ❑ Check with Agriculture Department of new area to see if they have restrictions on plants.

ON MOVING DAY:

- ❑ Carry enough cash or traveler's checks to cover cost of moving services and expenses until you make banking connections in new city.
- ❑ Carry jewelry and documents yourself, or use registered mail.
- ❑ Plan for transporting of pets; they are poor traveling companions if unhappy.
- ❑ Let close friends or relatives know the route and schedule you will be traveling, including overnight stops. Use them as message headquarters.
- ❑ Double-check closets, drawers, shelves to be sure they are empty.
- ❑ Leave old keys, garage door openers, broiler pans, landscape/house plans, and instruction manuals needed by new owner with real estate agent.

AT YOUR NEW ADDRESS:

- ❑ Obtain certified checks or cashier's checks necessary for closing real estate transaction (check transaction coordinator/title company for details).
- ❑ Check on service of telephone, gas, electricity, water, and garbage.
- ❑ Check pilot light or stove, for water heater and furnace.
- ❑ Ask mailcarrier for mail he or she may be holding for your arrival.
- ❑ Have new address recorded on driver's license.
- ❑ Visit city offices and register for voting.
- ❑ Register car within 5 days after arrival in state, or you may have to pay a penalty when getting new license plates.
- ❑ Obtain inspection sticker and transfer motor club membership.
- ❑ Apply for state driver's license.
- ❑ Register family in your new place of worship.
- ❑ Register children in school.
- ❑ Arrange for medical services: doctor, dentist, veterinarian, etc.

CHAPTER FIFTEEN

Saving Money When You Sell

MONEY-SAVING TECHNIQUES

There are some rules to follow when you are attempting to save money and get the best deal that you can. These rules are:

1. Always negotiate fairly and honestly and always be truthful in your statements.
2. Always try to negotiate any special discounts up front, before the deal is made. Never renege on any agreement you have made.
3. Don't try to get too much from any one person. A little discount from everyone will work wonders.
4. Try to put the agreements in writing.
5. Offer to give before you get. Make every situation "win-win" for all parties.
6. Don't get greedy.

COMMISSIONS AND FEES

The area of commissions and fees is very sensitive, especially to real estate agents, since they earn 100 percent of their income from commission. That means no salaries, no expense accounts, no bonuses . . . pure commission. Now, if they sell 30 or 40 homes a year, they can make a pretty good living. But if they sell five or six homes a year, they are barely paying expenses.

Real Estate Commission

The first way to save money when you sell your home is to sell it yourself. If your home sells for $100,000 and the customary commission in the area is 7 percent, you save $7,000. Well, or so it seems.

If you have read this book carefully, you know that marketing and selling a home can be expensive. Also, you have learned that it is "risky," at best, for sellers to believe they will ever get their home sold on their own. Remember, only one in 20 For Sale by Owners actually gets their property sold by themselves.

And most important, the whole idea is to "Sell Your Home Fast, for the Highest Price, in Any Market!" Isn't that what you really want? So, let's talk about ways you can utilize the services of a real estate professional and save money.

Remember, I said all commissions are negotiable. If agents tell you the fees are fixed or nonnegotiable, send them packing, because that is not true. If they would be untruthful about that, they may be untruthful about many things . . . and you don't need that from a person who is going to be your business partner for the next few weeks or months.

One choice you have is to just ask the agent to reduce the com-

FIGURE 15.1
BROKER WELCOME INFORMATION/FACT CARD

JUST LISTED

1258 MANHATTAN AVENUE

★ ★ ★

$3\frac{1}{2}$ %

to Selling Broker

★ ★ ★

- 3 bedrooms
- 2½ bathrooms
- Large living room
- Remodeled kitchen
- Pool and Jacuzzi
- 2-car attached garage
- Cozy country living

For more information call:

John & Susie Doe at (800) 123-4567

mission. If it is customary to pay 7 percent for selling a home, you could ask to pay only 6 percent. *However, there is a problem with this.* If agents out in the market have a choice of showing similar homes and one home has $7,000 commission and the other home has $6,000 commission, which one will they show first and sell the most? You got it, it's human nature. If you have a choice of doing one of two jobs and one pays $1,000 more, which would you choose?

Another way you may utilize an agent to sell your home without actually listing the property is to remain a For Sale by Owner. Then send out Information/Fact Brochures or Cards to all of the real estate agents, just as another agent would do, detailing the property and the commission that you are willing to pay the selling agent. (See Figure 15.1).

So what is the answer? Give before you ask to receive.

In Chapter 7 you read about the "Sellers' Action Plan" (Figure 7.6), which details the things you are going to do to make the listing agent's job easier. Very few sellers will cooperate and help like this! Also, you are going to follow the steps in this book and have your home "show perfect." Not many sellers will do that either.

Here is a suggested dialogue for you to use:

Mr./Ms. Anderson, I am interested in using your services to sell my home. I think you will do a good job for me selling my home and I believe that you are an above-average sales agent. However, I want you to understand that I am also an above-average seller, which will make your job easier.

(Pull out the Sellers' Action Plan and hand it to the agent.)
Here is the commitment I will make to you, if I become one of your clients tonight. Would you please read these two pages.

(Wait until the agent finishes.)
As you can see by the way I have prepared my home for sale and by the commitment I am making to help sell the home, I am serious about selling. I have agreed to price the home correctly and maintain the property "show ready" at all times.

Now, because I am a very well-informed and prepared seller, I am going to ask that you reward my efforts and re-

duce your commission only slightly. I know there are agents who, although the customary rate in the area is 7 percent, will take my listing as low as 5 percent, but I do not want that. I would ask that you take my listing at the customary 7 percent less $500 from the listing side because:

1. I am an above-average seller who will make your job much easier.
2. My home is well prepared and priced so that it will sell easily.

Also, I would ask that should you sell the home yourself, the commission be reduced to a flat 4 percent. (Have the figures prepared in your home and hand the sheet to the listing agent.)

> *$229,000 Sales Price x 7% commission*
> *= $17,030 total commission*
>
> *$17,030 total commission ÷ 2*
> *= $8,515 commission to your office*
>
> *$8,515 commission to your office*
> *– $500 less commission*
> *= $8,015 net commission to your office*

If you sell the home yourself the figures would be

> *$229,000 x 4% commission rate*
> *= $9160 net commission to office*

The agent may say, "If you think, as you said, that I am an above-average agent, why should you penalize me $500?"

Your answer would be:

Mr./Ms. Anderson, you and I both know a home priced well and prepared properly will sell in any market. You will not have to spend as much money or take as much time selling my home. My efforts and my commitment to assisting in the sale are certainly worth considerably more to you than the $500 I am asking. Every agent would recognize that. Will this commission arrangement be acceptable to you?

Be firm, and most times getting what you want will not be a problem. In some cases the agent will need to get approval from a manager or broker, so you will wait only one day for the answer. You want your home listed and sold *now*.

Will the agent accept? Absolutely! That is, absolutely with some "ifs."

- If your home is absolutely perfectly prepared as described in this book.
- If you will absolutely follow every item as you have detailed it in the Sellers' Action Plan.
- If you have absolutely priced your home correctly.
- If you are absolutely truthful in your commitment.

Only seldom will an agent say no. If an agent decides not to accept your offer, thank the person and call the next agent on your list of acceptable agents.

Remember, do not ask for too much. If you start asking for 1 percent or 2 percent off the overall commission, you may as well try to sell the home yourself. As I said earlier, the "selling" agents should have a full commission to work on. You are only asking your listing agent to reward you for your efforts. If you are not making the 100 percent effort, don't ask for the discount because the agent will have no reason to reward you.

> **SMART TIP:**
> Keep in mind that the commission for selling your home is a tax-deductible selling cost.

Title Insurance Fees

In most areas, it is customary for a seller to pay the cost of a title insurance policy, which guarantees for the buyer that the title to the property will be free of liens and encumbrances. This type of coverage is risk elimination insurance as opposed to most other types of policies, which are more risk anticipation.

Most states require title insurance companies to "post" their rates with the Insurance Commission or the Corporations Commission of their particular state, which means that rates, once they are established, are not to be altered unless another rate filing is submitted to the state. However, most of the general public is unaware of the fact that within these filed rates are sometimes hundreds of allowable discounts that are filed and approved. Sometimes, unless you ask for a discount, the title company can legally charge the consumer (the seller in most cases) a 100 percent full rate, even when a discount could be applicable.

As an example, most title companies have posted, with their filed rates, a discount for homes that have been insured within the two, three, or five years previous to the current sale. These are called short-term rates, and usually their discounts are 10 to 20 percent off the standard rate.

How much of a discount would this mean to seller?

If a standard rate title policy on a $180,000 home was $800 and a 20 percent short-term rate applied, the savings would be $160.

How do you get these discounts? Ask, ask, and ask again! Ask your sales agent to make sure you are given the best rate. Call the title company and ask if there are any other discounts available. Also, if the new lender for the buyer of your property is going to require a separate lender's title policy, make sure the buyers pay the cost of this policy. It is the buyers' lender and their policy, so they should pay for it. Often all of the title fees are passed on to the sellers, with the sellers not being aware of the different policies that are actually being issued.

At the end of this chapter is an example of the sale of a home utilizing many of the money-saving techniques described in this book. You will note that, upon request, the sellers were given a 20 percent short-term discount rate on their title policy, the buyers were asked to pay their own ALTA lender's policy, and the charges for an endorsement and a servicing fee were waived. Also, a fee known as a subescrow fee can be waived. (This is a fee charged to make the payoffs necessary for loans, leasing, etc.) These changes in the billing saved the sellers $411.

Escrow/Closing Fees

In some states, closings are handled by escrow/closing officers who are actually employed by title companies. In other areas, separate escrow/closing companies handle these duties; in still other areas, attorneys handle the closing activities.

In some states, such as New Jersey, closings have historically been handled by attorneys who charged anywhere from $250 to $1,000 or more for the closing process. More recently, title companies have begun to take over these closing activities, and their fees have been dramatically less. If you are in a state that does not require a closing to be done by an attorney, you may want to choose a less expensive alternative.

In states where closing/escrow officers actually handle the closings, their fees are usually minimal and there is not much room to negotiate for their services. If, however, the escrow/closing is being handled by the title company, there is a good chance their fees will already be low by comparison to an outside closing entity. Some companies may throw in typing fees, processing fees, holding fees, and other costs. Often these fees, referred to as "garbage fees," can be waived.

In any of these closing processes, make sure you look very closely at the Net Proceeds Statement, which details all of the fees being charged. If you see fees that you don't understand, ask why they are being charged. If it sounds like a garbage fee, smells like a garbage fee, then maybe it *is* a garbage fee. Don't be afraid to ask for the fee to be waived or discounted.

Some fees, such as notary fees (fees for the services of verifying you are who you say you are) and recording fees (fees paid to the county, city, or province for recording of documents) most probably will not be waived.

Inspection Fees

Several inspections may be required on your home when you sell it. These inspections may be requested by the buyers or the lender who will be making the new loan on the property. For the most part, these inspection fees are minimal, and asking for reductions is not feasible. Some examples of these fees charged by companies in Las Vegas, Nevada, are:

Roof Inspection:	$150–$200
Termite Inspection:	$60–$75
Home Inspection:	$200–$300

Now, saving money on the inspections and any subsequent work that is required by these inspections can get a little tricky. Here are some inside secrets: Many of these companies that make inspections also either do the work they call themselves or are associated with an affiliate company. In other words, a roofing company may make a roof inspection, specify the work that needs to be done and actually do the work (new roof or repairs), and finally give the sellers the approved certificate for the property.

In that example, sellers should:

1. Get an estimate of the cost of the necessary repairs from the company that made the inspection.
2. Get an estimate from two other roofers on making these repairs. Check whether either of these other roofers can give you the "approved certificate" at no extra charge if you select that company to do the work. (If the roofing company is not a state-licensed roof inspector, it may not be able to give you the required certificate and another inspection might need to be ordered.)
3. Next, take the lowest estimate you have received back to the original inspecting company and ask it to match the charges. In most cases, the estimates will be very close. Again, in most cases, the original company will match the low estimate to get the job.
4. After the original company agrees to do the work for the lower estimate, ask it to waive the original inspection fee. In many cases, it will do so.

Some inspection companies are independent and only make inspections, they do not make any of the repairs that they identify as needing to be made. In these cases, their fees are fairly fixed and will not be reduced.

Do not become greedy and ask for too much. You want this work done properly and these construction or repairpeople must make a living. Remember the old Golden Rule.

IMPROVEMENTS AND REPAIRS

Carpet or Floor Cleaning

Almost every area has numerous carpet cleaning companies that will steam clean your carpets at a very reasonable cost, usually $10 to $20 per room. (This cost can vary if furniture must be moved.) It is always best to have your carpets cleaned by a professional.

However, if you must save on the carpet cleaning, you can rent commercial steam cleaners and do the work yourself. Understand, these are not the two-bristle-brush carpet cleaners that merely smear the dirt around. These are full-fledged steam cleaners that steam the dirt out of the material, then suck the goop out of the carpet. Sound pretty gross? Well, it is, and if you have never done this, it's hard work, heavy lifting, and sometimes the results are not all that satisfactory. If you fail to mix the chemicals properly, you do not vacuum well enough, or you walk on the carpet too soon, your efforts and money spent may be wasted and it's back to square one with the professional.

Get estimates and negotiate the best price possible with the professional from the beginning and you will be much better off financially and emotionally.

Carpet or Floor Replacements or Repairs

When it comes to carpet or flooring replacements, it is a different story. There is lots of money to be saved. Here is the inside trick:

Go to three local floor covering companies and negotiate the best price for the floor covering (carpet, tile, or linoleum), excluding the installation. Then ask the same companies for a complete price, including the installation.

Most floor covering companies utilize services of independent contractor installers. Often these installers work for numerous companies and are not busy 100 percent of the time. Often the companies also make money on the installers' work. Many times installers may charge the company $20 to $30 an hour (or so much per square yard) and complete a four-hour job for $120, and the company charges the consumer an extra $400 above the cost of the carpet. Seldom, if ever, will these companies tell the consumer, "The job cost us less than expected, so here's the $280 back that we saved." Not likely!

Next, call these or other local floor covering companies and ask if you can obtain the name of an independent carpet installer who does work for them on a contract basis. They may try to sell you installation services. Decline, thank them, and simply say you would prefer to talk directly with an installer before you make any decisions. Again, ask if you can get a name and telephone number of the installer. You may have to call several companies, but eventually you will find someone who will be kind enough to give you a name and number. Make sure you thank that person.

At that point, call the installer direct. You will probably need to leave your name and number, as most of these contract workers put in long hours. (That's what you are hoping to find.)

When the installer calls back, ask what he or she will charge to do your installation. Try to have the following information: number of square yards in the job, number of rooms, and type of material and pad (carpet or tile). Make sure you ask if the installer will work by the hour or the job. You will probably get a better rate by the yard or the hour rather than by the job. Get a maximum estimate cost on any job you have done. Now compare the prices quoted by the floor covering companies and choose the highest quality carpet, in your range, at the least cost. Compare the installed cost quote with the quote of the most expensive floor covering only, installed by the least expensive installer you contacted. Here is an example of one home seller's research.

1ST FLOOR COVERING COMPANY

Carpet and pad alone:	$1,323
Carpet, pad, and installation:	$1,965

2ND FLOOR COVERING COMPANY

Carpet and pad alone:	$1,245
Carpet, pad, and installation:	$1,890

3RD FLOOR COVERING COMPANY

Carpet and pad alone:	$1,680
Carpet, pad, and installation:	$2,060

Three installers quoted the following for the installation:

Installer 1:	$295
Installer 2:	$185
Installer 3:	$200

The home seller went with the carpet from the first floor covering company and installer number 3.

Total cost:	$1,523
Saving:	$442 = 22.5%

The seller saved $367 from the lowest bid that included installation, and $537 from the most expensive bid.

All of these estimates were done on essentially the same carpet and pad.

Other Repairs

Most important, for any work that needs to be done, negotiate everything. You want the job done right, so don't be unrealistic. But make sure you ask for the best price you can get.

> **SMART TIP:**
>
> If a service person such as an installer does a great job, maybe works you into his or her schedule to meet your time frame, and just generally makes the job a pleasure to have done, don't be afraid to kick in a little extra bonus, say $25 or $50. It will be greatly appreciated and you will have a friend that you may want to use again in the future.

Another thought: Do you know anyone who can do any of the work that you need to have completed? Maybe you have a family member or friend who is a painter, electrician, carpenter, or general handyperson who would be willing to do the work for you. If he or she can do quality work, see if you can get a deal.

Also, if you decide to do some of the work yourself, you may do well to pick up a book at the library or the bookstore that details the best way to accomplish the tasks you are taking on.

OPTIONS: REPAIR OR REPLACEMENT

Always consider your options for repairs or replacements. Some examples might be: If you have miniblinds that were expensive when they were originally purchased but now are in need of replacement, you may be better off financially replacing the window coverings with sheer curtains and drapes. The buyer may not like the blinds anyway. They are definitely a personal taste item.

Another example would be if a ceiling is in need of being reblown with acoustic. If it is a large area, you would be better to just reblow the areas that are in the worst shape and simply repaint (usually with a small air compressor) the entire ceiling.

What if kitchen or bathroom cabinets need to be refinished? Again, you may be better off financially repainting the cabinets rather than having the wood refinished. Refinishing the enclosures is much more costly and time consuming. However, refinishing usually produces a higher-quality result.

Storage

Another great suggestion to help you save money is to store furniture with a friend or relative if you need to make your home more accessible while it is being shown and sold. Maybe they have a garage or extra room you can "stuff" for a few weeks. This could save you from $50 to $150 per month.

Painting

If you are not going to repaint your home yourself, you can save a considerable amount of money on this repair by:

1. Getting two or three estimates on the job—ask if your estimate can be made for the complete job, but also ask if they'll give you a per-hour fee. Most painters will be willing to do so. Ask if they will do the job for whichever is less. Most likely they will agree.
2. Buying and getting a deal on quality paint at a discount store. Sears, Kmart, or other stores are okay as long as you buy their "good stuff." You don't need the best, but don't buy the low-quality paint.
3. Having the home ready to paint by removing the electrical outlets and switch plates, removing all drapes and curtains from the windows, and having all furniture moved into the center of the rooms and away from the walls.

Remember, you have a choice of whichever estimate is less. Chances are you will find the per-hour basis, with you buying the paint, about 30-40 percent less than the price quoted for the entire job.

Plants and Shrubs

If you need to replace plants and shrubs, avoid buying these items from expensive nurseries. Instead, buy them from Target, Kmart, or other discount stores. Remember, buy good-quality items, with a lot of color, for the least price.

EXAMPLE OF SAVINGS

The following scenario explains how much one seller saved by utilizing many of the techniques explained in this chapter.

ITEM	SAVINGS
Real Estate commission	$500
Title insurance	$189
Lenders' required title policy	$162
Waiver of service fees	$ 94
Roof inspection	$ 50
Home inspection	$ 50
Roof work	$180
Carpet installation	$442
Painting labor	$155
Paint	$ 70
3 months storage for excess furniture	$240
TOTAL SAVINGS	**$2,132**

Selling
For Sale
by Owner

SELLING THE HOME
YOURSELF

Now, the big decision. You have read the book. You have examined all of the material. You have looked at all of your options. Now you must make the decision. Are you going to try to sell the home yourself, or are you going to list with a real estate professional?

You may remember from Chapter 1 that only one in six homes sell without the services of a real estate professional. You may be thinking that you are that one in six that could accomplish a by-owner sale. However, remember that the true statistics showed that when you removed from those sales attorney transactions, direct bank transactions for bank-owned properties, family sales, and other non-arm's length transactions, the true for-sale-by-owner figure was actually only about one in 20 homes that sell without the services of a real estate professional.

Again, you may be that one person that can accomplish that sale.

Refer back to the "Should I Sell My Home Myself" Checklist in Chapter 5 and review those questions. Understand that selling your home yourself is not easy, but you may very well be that one in 20 who can do it.

PUTTING TOGETHER
A SALES STRATEGY

Okay, you have decided to try to sell the home yourself. You need to put together a plan, start to finish, on everything that needs to be done to get the property sold, fast and for the highest price. So, let's take it step by step.

PREPARING THE HOME
FOR SALE

Chapters 3 and 4 cover everything in detail that must be done to prepare your home for sale. Using the home inspection sheets that are provided in those chapters, make a complete inspection of your home, and plan how your cleaning process will take place and what repairs or improvements you are going to make.

Then go to work. Complete the entire process for the preparation of your home for sale. Do not place any ads, put up signs, print any flyers . . . do nothing else until the entire preparation is complete.

ESTABLISHING
YOUR LISTING PRICE

As indicated in Chapter 1, contact three real estate professionals. Advise each of them that you are going to attempt to sell your home yourself. Further, let them know that after a certain amount of time, if the property does not sell, you will be willing to interview them with regard to listing the property if they will assist you with some information. Under those circumstances, ask the professionals if they would be willing to provide you with comparable sale information on homes in your neighborhood.

Most agents will be willing to do this knowing they may have a sales opportunity with you, and they know that the success rate of For Sale by Owners is very low.

If you do not want to use the real estate people to help you set the price of your home, you may want to order a professional appraisal, prior to putting the house on the market. However, remember, this is not recommended; historically, it is easier to receive the appraisal you want when you have a willing buyer in hand and an accepted offer on the property.

Remember, a particular buyer may choose a lender that will not accept the appraisal ordered by the seller. If another appraisal is required, you could be out another $200 or $300 for this additional valuation.

STRUCTURING
A MARKETING PLAN

As you have seen, structuring a marketing campaign that is both effective and works in a timely fashion can be very costly. Don't forget: The whole reason to sell your home yourself is to see if you can save the cost of the commission. If you are going to be successful selling your home yourself, you must be willing to spend some money to save some money.

Refer to Chapters 7, 11, and 12, which discussed advertising and marketing methods that have proven to be successful in any market or area. Many of the items shown in these chapters can and should be used by sellers who are attempting to sell their own property.

Here is an example:

Have a local printer print the Information/Fact Brochure or Card.

Take a photograph of your home (a good-quality, black-and-white glossy will be the easiest to work with). Take the photograph and the example Information/Fact Brochure or Card to your printer of choice. Make sure you have complete information on this brochure/card including any terms you may be offering.

Tell the printer how many to print. (The more you print, the cheaper per item.) Refer to the sample marketing strategies in Chapters 7 and 11 to decide on this number. Try to print everything at the same time to reduce the cost.

Distribute, mail, and post these advertising items exactly as indicated in Chapters 7 and 11. Distribute these brochures or cards to everyone you know who might know anyone interested in your home.

Don't forget, "Most every person you know knows 100 people they don't know they know." But if you say "Give these brochures/cards to every person in this area that you would invite to a wedding," suddenly there are a lot of names running through their heads.

SMART TIP:

If you have decided that you will pay a portion of a commission should an agent bring a buyer on your property, be sure to include that information in the card or brochure. Figure 16.1 includes in bold letters . . . "Brokers Welcome at 3 ½%."

FIGURE 16.1
BROKER WELCOME INFORMATION/FACT CARD

JUST LISTED

1258 MANHATTAN AVENUE

★ ★ ★

$3\frac{1}{2}$ %
to Selling Broker

★ ★ ★

- 3 bedrooms
- 2½ bathrooms
- Large living room
- Remodeled kitchen
- Pool and Jacuzzi
- 2-car attached garage
- Cozy country living

For more information call:
John & Susie Doe at (800) 123-4567

If the standard commission in your area is 7% and an agent does bring an offer that you accept, you have saved 3½% on a normal commission. For a $100,000 sale your savings would equate to $3,500.

However, you must be realistic. Few agents will actually work on this type of open listing because they do not feel that the seller is truly serious. Also, with no listing in effect, agents are afraid that a seller may obtain personal information from a buyer, then attempt to contact the buyer directly, circumventing the agent completely, thereby avoiding the commission altogether. Or the buyer may try to go back to the seller directly and buy the property for less, without the agent.

Don't be surprised if an agent asks for a "one person listing" before showing your home. This is a listing for one buyer. If you sell your home to that one person, the agent has earned a commission. This type of listing is for a certain period of time and has a protection period after the listing term has expired.

Also included in your marketing strategy should be a certain amount of newspaper advertising. As discussed and shown in Chapter 11, use line ads and specialty ads. Choose your wording carefully and utilize the ad techniques shown.

The most important marketing item with regard to marketing your own home will be your yard sign. Figure 16.2 presents two examples of acceptable For Sale by Owner signs that will get attention and encourage buyers to call.

FIGURE 16.2

FOR-SALE-BY-OWNER SIGNS

Do not have signs constructed until you check city, county, or province restrictions for size, color, and so on. These signs should be professionally painted. As far as color, your signs should have a light background—white or beige—and dark lettering.

In most areas, a local sign company can construct and/or paint the signs for you.

Make sure that you check your brochure box every day. At times neighborhood marauders will pirate your advertising items;

you never want the box empty, especially if you are not home 24 hours a day.

Refer to Chapter 11 for the proper placement of your yard sign. Make sure this most important marketing item is visible from all directions when approaching the home.

Note: Some communities have limitations and restrictions with regard to signing. Homeowners' associations or area governing organizations often have regulations that control this aspect of your advertising.

ONCE YOU BEGIN MARKETING

Once your sign is up, your brochures are out, and you begin running ads, be prepared for the onslaught of real estate agents. You may receive dozens of calls. Every one of these salespeople will have:

SMART TIP:
Make sure that a brochure box is attached to your signs. Anyone interested in the details about your home should be able to obtain that information at all hours of the day, whether you are home or not.

SMART TIP:
Before you install any yard sign, inquire as to local ordinances concerning regulations, restrictions, conditions, or covenants that affect the placement of yard signs.

SMART TIP:
Never use a hand-printed, nonprofessional sign. This is a critical advertising item and it must be done properly, both for the aesthetic value and so that any potential buyer will view you, the seller, as well prepared and informed. You want no indication or invitation that you are unprofessional or an easy target.

- A horror story about a For Sale by Owner who "blew" the sale of a home.
- Every reason imaginable why you should list with that agent.
- Every horrible statistic about For-Sale-by-Owner sales.
- A "better way" for you to sell your home, if, of course, you will list with that agent.

There will be a virtual parade of licensees from every company, so be ready, be direct, and be firm. Explain that you are going to try to sell your home yourself, before you consider listing your home.

An easy way to dissuade overly aggressive agents is to say "I am going to attempt to sell myself. If you will call me in (pick a number) days, I will consider talking with you at that time. However, if you bother me before then, I will definitely not consider your services." Most agents will get the hint and leave you alone.

One common ploy by agents is to ask you to sign an Exclusive Agency Listing Agreement. Under this agreement, you can sell your home yourself and pay no commission; however, any agent who sells your property must sell through the listing agent, and you would owe a full commission. If, on the other hand, you had not listed the property and that other agent brought a buyer, you would only owe the portion of the listing fee that you had agreed to pay if an agent brought a buyer.

The advantage to the Exclusive Agency is that you have your property accessed through the local Multiple Listing Service and you can still sell yourself and pay no commission.

> **SMART TIP:**
> If you are going to cooperate with agents and pay a portion of a commission, make sure you provide each agent who calls with your Information Brochures/Cards and point out that you are willing to cooperate, but you will not sign a listing.

WHO WILL TAKE THE CALLS?

Make sure that there is always someone at home to take the calls or that you have an answering machine with information and the ability to take messages from prospective buyers.

You may want to consider having an additional phone line installed during the sales period, to handle the buyer calls and to screen the numerous agent calls you will receive. In many areas, this additional telephone line may cost only $10 to $15 per month. The main advantage to having this additional line is that every time the phone rings, you know it is someone who is interested in your home or a real estate agent.

The following is a sample acceptable answering machine message.

Hello. If you are calling about the home for sale located at 2121 Valderas Drive, it is a four-bedroom, three-bath, two-

story home on a large lot in the Clear Creek area of Reno. The kitchen and all three bathrooms were recently remodeled, and the entire home has been repainted. There is a formal dining room. All of the bedrooms are large, and there is a master suite that includes a dressing area with an expansive walk-in closet. The home has a patio with a built-in gas barbecue. The central heat and air have been serviced recently. There is a three-car garage, and the home is close to shopping, churches and schools of the Clear Creek District.

The home is priced at $137,000 and there is an assumable First Deed of Trust if the buyer qualifies. If you would like to see the home, please leave your name, telephone number, and the best day and time to reach you. We will return all calls promptly and will set up a personal viewing at your convenience. Thank you for calling.

HOW TO GIVE INFORMATION

Always keep a fact sheet by the phone so you will not fumble for details when a caller is on the line.

Copy and keep by each telephone where "sale" calls may be answered the following fact sheet.

Be ready to screen out a number of flakes, time wasters, looky-lous (a real estate industry term for people who are looking with no intention of buying), and rip-off artists.

SMART TIP:
Make sure you establish rules in your home as to who will take the calls. Children should not be allowed to give out information or set up appointments with buyers or agents. It is even better if you restrict children from answering the "selling line" if you have a separate line. Caution children from saying things like "My parents are not home now" or "My parents won't be home for two hours" or "I am here by myself and I'm not allowed to show the home."

One major inconvenience will be the fact that potential buyers and agents will knock on your door at all times of the day and night. Even if you have specified "By Appointment Only!" you will still have numerous uninvited visitors. Be sure that every member of the family knows the procedure to be followed should anyone come to the door. You certainly don't want your six-year-old to take it upon himself to invite in potential buyers and start showing them the home before you have questioned these guests.

The prequalification worksheet in Figure 16.4 will assist you in

FIGURE 16.3:

HOME SALE FACT SHEET

HOME INFORMATION

Bedrooms _____	If assumption is option
Bathrooms _____	
Garage _____	
Interior Features	1st Loan
_____	$ _____
_____	
_____	2nd Loan
_____	$ _____
_____	
Exterior Features	Current Payments
_____	$ _____
_____	
_____	Interest Rate
_____	_____ %
_____	
Square Footage __	Amount down
Special Features	needed to assume
_____	% _____
_____	
Price $ _____	Current Lenders
Available Terms	
_____	_____
_____	_____
	_____

CALLER INFORMATION

Name _____
Address _____
_____
_____
Phone Home _____
Phone Work _____
Other Information (Take Notes)
_____
_____
_____
_____
_____
_____
_____
_____
_____
_____
_____
_____
_____
_____
_____
_____
_____
_____
_____
_____

HOME INFORMATION

Elementary School _____
Middle School _____
High School _____
Colleges _____
_____
Shopping _____
_____
Parks _____
_____
Library _____
When would you like to see the home? _____

qualifying potential buyers. You may want to make copies of this form and ask each potential buyer to complete it for security as well as for qualification purposes. You will provide this information to a loan broker or bank to help with prequalification.

Also, it would be a good idea to have loan information forms available for these potential buyers. Local loan brokers will be happy to provide the forms for you.

Figure 16.5 presents a sample loan availability form to give you an idea of what you should provide potential buyers. If buyers show interest, ask that they consider the lender that has supplied you with this information. Ask buyers to become prequalified as soon as possible.

WHAT ABOUT CRITICISM?

As a For Sale by Owner, be prepared for criticism. Potential buyers often feel that the more they can find wrong with the home, the better chance they will have to negotiate a better deal with the sellers should they decide to purchase the property.

> **SMART TIP:**
> Have available Information/Fact Brochures or Cards and a Loan Information Sheet that details at least three loans that might be utilized to purchase your home.

As indicated earlier, stay focused and don't take the criticism personally. You are trying to sell your home fast and for the highest price. That is what matters. If the buyers don't like your home's decorating or color schemes, they can buy it and change it.

SHOWING THE HOME

With regard to showing the home, make sure you review Chapter 12. Also, here are a few reminder suggestions:

❑ Make sure the home is "show perfect."
❑ Do a clutter patrol right before each showing.
❑ Be sure all kids and pets are either "caged" or sent off to the neighbor's house. (I'm kidding about caging the kids.)

FIGURE 16.4

PREQUALIFICATION WORKSHEET

BORROWER

Name:	Home Phone:
Age: Soc. Sec.#:	Dependents: Ages:
Marital Status: ❑ Married ❑ Separated ❑ Unmarried (include single, divorced, widowed)	

Residence	**If less than 2 years with current address:**
Current Address:	Prior Address:
City/State/Zip:	City/State/Zip:
Own or Rent: Years at address:	Own or Rent: Years at address:

Employment	**If less than 2 years with current employer:**
Employer:	Previous Employer:
Position:	Position:
Contact:	Contact:
Address:	Address:
City/State/Zip:	City/State/Zip:
Phone:	Phone:
Start Date:	From: To:
Years in this line of work:	Years in this line of work:
Monthly Income:	Monthly Income:

CO-BORROWER

Name:	Home Phone:
Age: Soc. Sec.#:	Dependents: Ages:
Marital Status: ❑ Married ❑ Separated ❑ Unmarried (include single, divorced, widowed)	

Residence	**If less than 2 years with current address:**
Current Address:	Prior Address:
City/State/Zip:	City/State/Zip:
Own or Rent: Years at address:	Own or Rent: Years at address:

Employment	**If less than 2 years with current employer:**
Employer:	Previous Employer:
Position:	Position:
Contact:	Contact:
Address:	Address:
City/State/Zip:	City/State/Zip:
Phone:	Phone:
Start Date:	From: To:
Years in this line of work:	Years in this line of work:
Monthly Income:	Monthly Income:

PURCHASE INFORMATION

Property Address:	Purchase Price:
City/State/Zip:	Mortgage Amount:
Estimated closing date:	
Real Estate Agent:	Phone Number:

PREQUALIFICATION WORKSHEET (continued)

ASSETS
Checking Accounts

Institution	Address	Account #	Balance

Savings Accounts, CD's, Money Market Funds, 401K, IRA

Institution	Address	Account #	Balance

Securities

Type	Broker Name/Address	# Shares/Bonds	Market Value

Life Insurance Policy

Face Value: $	Cash Value: $

Real Estate

Address	Type	Market Value	Mtg. Balance

Other Assets

Description	Est. Value	Description	Est. Value

LIABILITY
Loans, Revolving Credit Cards, Charge Accounts and Other Debts

Creditor	Address	Account #	Pmt./Balance

Mortgages

Lender	Address	Account #	Pmt./Balance

Additional Assets, Liabilities:

- ❏ Try to air out your home. If it is very cold or very hot outside, don't get carried away with "airing out."
- ❏ You may want to have potpourri simmering for a very light fragrance.
- ❏ Make sure the entire home is cool in the summer and warm in the winter. That includes attic and basement if these rooms are part of the actual living quarters. In other words, if it is 100 degrees outside, don't close off the bonus room from the air conditioning just to save on your power bill. If potential buyers enter that bonus room, they will immediately think there is something wrong with the cooling system for that part of the house and nothing you can say will convince them differently.
- ❏ Make sure all of the lights are on and the home appears bright and cheery.
- ❏ Be sure there are no cars in the driveway, the garage, or at the curb in front of the home.
- ❏ Have your information binder available so buyers may look at any utility bills, tax statements, etc., in which they may be interested.
- ❏ Have your Information/Fact Brochures or Card available.
- ❏ Have your Loan Availability Sheets available (see Figure 16.5).
- ❏ You may want to offer potential buyers cookies or other treats and soft drinks or coffee.
- ❏ View and treat every person who enters your home as an acquaintance you invited to an open house.
- ❏ Do not lead potential buyers through the home. Direct them into areas with comments such as, "Through these doors is the kitchen." Allow them to enter and make sure you stand back and allow viewers to look freely.
- ❏ Make sure you tell them to feel free to look anywhere they please, including cupboards, closets, appliances, or any nook and cranny.
- ❏ Be sure to mention a time or two before and during the tour that potential buyers should feel free to ask questions at any time.
- ❏ Don't make comments such as "This is the kitchen" or "This

FIGURE 16.5

LOAN AVAILABILITY SHEET

MODEL: DOLPHIN　　　　**BASE SALES PRICE: 139,990**
LOAN AMOUNT: 125,990　　**90% LTV**

1-year ARM with conversion option	30-Year Fixed	20-Year Fixed Rate Mortagage Loan	30-Year Fixed Rate Due in 7
RATE 4.75%	**RATE** 8.875%	**RATE** 7.625%	**RATE** 7.875%
POINTS .75%	**POINTS** -0-%	**POINTS** -0-%	**POINTS** .25%
P&I $ 657.22	P&I $ 1002.43	P&I $ 1024.62	P&I $ 913.51
Taxes $ 204.00	Taxes $ 204.00	Taxes $ 204.00	Taxes $ 204.00
Haz/Flood $ 50.00	Haz/Flood $ 50.00	Haz/Flood $ 50.00	Haz/Flood $ 504.00
PMI $ 51.00	PMI $ 51.00	PMI $ 51.00	PMI $ 514.00
Totol PITI $ 962.22	Totol PITI $ 1307.43	Totol PITI $ 1,329.62	Totol PITI $ 1,285.00
Down payment $14,000.00	Down payment $ 14,000.00	Down payment $ 14,000.00	Down payment$ 14,000.00
Closing Costs $ 5,035.00	Closing Costs $ -0.00	Closing Costs $ 5,035.00	Closing Costs $ 5,305.00
Prepaids $ 2,515.00	Prepaids $ 2,515.00	Prepaids $ 2,515.00	Prepaids $ 2,515.00
Points $ 944.93	Points $ -0.00	Points $ 1,259.90	Points $ 314.98
TOTAL CASH	TOTAL CASH	TOTAL CASH	TOTAL CASH
TO CLOSE $ 22,495.00	TO CLOSE $ 16,515.00	TO CLOSE $ 21,810.00	TO CLOSE $ 21,865.00

For further information contact: John Doe, ABC Realty
(800)123-4567

is a closet." If it is fairly obvious what the room is, don't insult the buyer's intelligence with an unnecessary explanation.

- ❑ Be friendly. Treat the buyers as guests.
- ❑ Don't oversell! If your home has been prepared properly, it will, for the most part, sell itself. If buyers have a question, they will ask. Just show the highlights.
- ❑ If your telephone rings during the tour, let the answering machine pick up the call. Don't leave the buyers and don't be interrupted.
- ❑ Stay back from the buyers so they do not feel crowded.
- ❑ Allow the buyers to tour the home at their pace. Do not rush them.
- ❑ Try to finish the tour in the kitchen area where you can offer the buyer refreshments and ask if they would like to sit down and talk more about the property.

Again, make sure the buyer has an Information/Fact Brochure or Card and a Loan Availability Sheet.

Be very patient and thorough in answering the buyers' questions, but do not talk too much. Remember, these buyers are considering a life-changing decision and they deserve your utmost attention and consideration. Allow potential buyers to do most of the talking. Learn to be a good listener and to answer questions well.

Ask "soft sell" questions after it appears that you have answered all of the buyer's questions. Some examples of "soft sell" questions would be:

- Is this the size of home you were looking for?
- Were you interested in a home with five bedrooms?
- Is this the type of neighborhood you think you may like?
- If you were to find the right home, are you ready to buy at this time?

Watch their responses. Don't just listen to what they say, watch how they react. Their reactions and expressions will be more indicative than their words.

If they appear to be uncomfortable, don't press the issue. When they begin to squirm, let them go.

If they appear comfortable and want to continue talking, be patient.

If after talking, they want to see the home again, patiently and hospitably do the entire tour again.

If the buyers attack your property unmercifully, berating everything about it, from color, to decorating, to style, there is a good chance they have read one of the many buyers' books available. These books detail an attack method of purchasing a property; the sellers are made to feel so badly about their property that, in disgrace, they beg buyers to purchase the property . . . at any price.

Bear in mind that these buyers are making these derogatory comments because they are interested in purchasing the property but want it at the lowest possible price. Don't react! Don't take the comments as a personal attack on you.

If buyers become belligerent or too overbearing, simply ask them to leave by saying something like "This probably is not the home that meets your needs or desires, so it might be best if you looked at some of the many other available properties."

WHAT IF BUYERS
ARE INTERESTED?

You must have a predesignated plan as to what you will do if buyers do want to purchase the home. There are several choices you can consider.

If you are very good with contracts and you understand all of the legal implications with regard to deposit receipts or purchase contracts, you may fill out one of these agreements. Take a good-faith deposit from the buyers and proceed to the title, escrow/closing company that will handle the closing.

If you don't feel comfortable filling out a purchase contract, you can simply write out, in longhand, everything to which the buyers have agreed: purchase price, deposit, term of closing, who pays for what inspections and the work that will need to be done to clear these reports, what kind of repairs and improvements are to be made by the sellers, and all of the "what-ifs" about which buyers and sellers are concerned. Refer to Chapter 13, which discussed many of these items of concern.

After a written statement of the agreements has been prepared between sellers and buyers, both parties should read and sign the document. If possible, both parties should receive a copy of what they have signed. Also, it is important that buyers give some kind of good-faith deposit, either when the agreement is signed or when the escrow/closing is opened.

All of this information should be taken to the escrow/closing or title company. Both buyers and sellers should be present to provide this company with the closing instructions.

The third choice, and probably the best of the three, is for buyers and sellers, once they have reached agreement, to go to an attorney and have the proper paperwork completed. Make sure that the attorney chosen is well versed in real estate transactions. Also, be sure the attorney specifies exactly what his or her fees will be to handle the transaction.

Understand that it is not absolutely necessary to draw up a formal purchase agreement between buyers and sellers at the time you reach agreement. However, the quicker the details are on paper and signed by all parties, the better. Don't forget, some buyers start developing "buyer's remorse" immediately after they agree to purchase. It is important to get their signatures as quickly as possible.

If you read and understand Chapter 13, where I discussed most of the nuances of the purchase contracts, you should have a basic understanding of what is necessary to prepare an acceptable contract purchase. However, in any owner sale, unless you are an attorney or a licensed real estate agent or broker, you should be very cautious in preparing any type of contract.

THE CLOSING PROCESS

Once the escrow/closing has been opened at the title, escrow/closing company, it will take anywhere from three to six weeks to complete the transaction.

The new buyers probably will be obtaining a new loan; the title will be searched and insured; all liens, encumbrances, accessed right of ways and the like that affect the property will be disclosed to the buyer; insurance will be ordered; inspection reports will be ordered and required work completed; an appraisal will be completed.

As you see, many actions must be taken to complete the transaction.

Both sellers and buyers should monitor this closing process. As the seller, you should use the Closing Checklist (Figure 14.2) from Chapter 14 to make sure that all of the contract requirements are met and completed in a timely fashion.

The final step will occur when all documents and monies have been delivered to the escrow/closing company. At this time, both buyers and sellers will sign the final closing instructions and the escrow/closing will be "perfected."

DO YOU NEED AN ATTORNEY?

If you do not use the services of a real estate professional, I highly recommend that you hire an attorney who is well acquainted with real estate contracts to guide you through your For-Sale-by-Owner transaction. An attorney will ensure that the transaction has been done legally and that both buyers' and sellers' interests and legal rights have been protected.

If your property is located in a state that requires an attorney to close the transaction, this may be all the counsel needed.

Sellers are sometimes surprised when they are billed by the hour by an attorney, and they receive a bill resembling the national debt. Remember to check the attorney's fees before hiring him or her.

> **SMART TIP:**
> Before sellers decide to sell their home themselves, they should definitely compare the cost of attorney fees to the services of a real estate professional. Often sellers can utilize a real estate agent to handle the entire listing, marketing, sale, and close for the cost of what an attorney will charge just to close the transaction.

AFTER THE CLOSE

If you are fortunate and turn out to be that one in 20 who actually close your For-Sale-by-Owner transaction, you may have some tax consequences. Review the tax section in Chapter 14, regarding the reporting of the sale.

CHAPTER SEVENTEEN

Now You're Ready to Sell

As you can see, selling your home can be a very complex and rather arduous task. However, whether you list your home with a real estate agent professional or sell your home yourself, by now you should have a fairly thorough knowledge of the process, start to finish.

Remember that your local market condition may have some influence on how quickly and for how much your home will sell. You must control as many of the selling factors as possible. Some suggestions to accomplish this are to:

- Properly prepare your home for sale in every possible way. Don't forget, your home will be competing with many other properties on the market. If your property "stands out" it will make it easier to sell.
- Price your home right. Use the factual sales data, following methods explained in this book. Make your price decision based on prices of comparable homes that have sold. Don't forget to separate your emotions from the facts when pricing your home.
- Utilize all available resources to get your home sold. Have a structured sales strategy and stick to the plan until the transaction has closed.
- If you use the services of a real estate agent or broker, make sure the salesperson has a reputation for success. Don't use a "loser" just to help the person out.
- Stay on top of all aspects of the transaction from advertising, home showings, agent follow-ups, inspections . . . to every possible part of the sale. See that every party to the transaction is fulfilling his or her responsibilities.
- Utilize the services of the best professionals in all areas of the transaction — brokers, lenders, title officers, escrow/closing people, accountants, attorneys, and even the state department

of real estate (when needed) to assure that you receive the most competent and effective advice and direction possible.

- Deal fairly and honestly with all parties to the transaction. Always create win-win situations.

Most important, remember to always be ready for the unexpected because no two transactions are ever the same. If you are patient, reasonable, and ready to negotiate, your transaction will go smoothly and comfortably with little stress or frustration.

Now, go out and sell your home quickly, for the highest price . . . in any market.

A P P E N D I X
FORMS AND
WORKSHEETS

PERFORMANCE CAMPAIGN

Prior to Listing:

- Research ownership
- Research legal description
- Research all comparable currently listed properties
- Research previous sales activity
- Order property profile from title company (if applicable)
- Review property profile (if applicable)
- Order assessors' tax information
- Review assessors' tax information
- Names of owners listed on title
- Prepare complete market study (CMA)
- Design marketing plan for seller
- Prepare effective marketing plan
- Plan goals of marketing campaign
- Create plan of action
- Suggest financing alternatives
- Prelisting checklist completed

During Listing Period:

- Review current title information
- Order plat map
- Confirm lot size
- Receive owner's house plans, if applicable
- Review house plans
- Organize file in proper order
- Order mailing list labels for advertisements
- Call owner to schedule caravan
- Prepare flyers for caravan
- Write newspaper ad
- Measure interior room sizes
- Plot exterior home dimensions
- Research year home was built
- Deliver property disclosure
- Prepare property data sheet for office
- Prepare showing instruction; notify office

- Seller provides loan company and loan number
- Lender verifies current loan information
- Research loan assumption requirements
- Seller provides second loan company and loan number
- Lender verifies second loan information
- Review current appraisal if available
- Research lot information for size and dimensions
- Research land use
- Research zoning
- Research required elementary school
- Research required junior high school
- Research required high school
- Contact homeowner's association manager (if condo)
- Research homeowner's association fee (if condo)
- Order copy of by-laws (if condo)
- Obtain list of services provided by the homeowner association (if condo)
- Copy of complex layout (if condo)
- Have extra key for lock box
- Install lock box
- Order sign
- Install brochure box
- Research available electricity
- Research average utilities
- Research sewer/septic system
- Research water availability
- Research natural gas availability
- Verify propane tank lease term and rate
- Note property inclusions and amenities
- Note property inclusions
- Ads written with seller's input
- Take color photo
- Review and file power of attorney
- Research and note all prorations

- Verify all rents and deposits
- Provide copy of leases
- Coordinate showings with tenant
- Repairs and maintenance completed
- Homeowner warranty made available
- Complete homeowner warranty application
- Mail homeowner warranty application
- Receive homeowner warranty
- File homeowner warranty
- Note all unrecorded property liens or agreements
- Enter new listing into MLS system
- Add property to active listed inventory list
- Confirm owner has a copy of the listing agreement
- Proof MLS computer printout
- Prepare marketing brochure
- Add to other home brochures around the area
- Mail marketing brochure to seller for review
- Deliver marketing brochure to brochure box
- Put marketing brochures in all agent mail boxes at all board offices
- Mail brochure to top-10% agents
- Schedule broker's caravan
- Promote at board of Realtors meeting
- Mail out "just-listed" announcements to neighborhood
- Advise referral network
- Submit listing information to "hot sheet"
- Provide marketing data to incoming referral buyers
- Provide marketing data to international relocation buyers
- Advertise in paper on rotating basis
- Mail copy of newspaper ad to seller
- Write ad for home magazines
- Advertise in home magazines when necessary

- Mail copy of home magazines to seller
- Review and file loan information
- Update loan information, if necessary, in MLS
- Send feedback letter to agents after showings
- Convey showing feedback to sellers weekly
- Review weekly market study
- Make regular calls to sellers to discuss marketing and pricing
- Prequalify all buyers when possible
- Enter price change into MLS computer
- Announce price change to all agents
- Change price on brochures
- Deliver new brochures as needed
- Refer seller to one of the best agents at his/her destination (if applicable)

Making the Offer:
- Contact selling agents to discuss buyers' qualifications and offer
- Review offer with seller
- Review all responses
- Present all needed forms to complete the sale
- Offer is accepted, amended, or countered
- Deliver signed offer to selling agent
- All parties sign contract

While in Closing Process:
- Deliver copies of contract to seller
- Deliver copies of contract to selling agent
- Place copies of contract in office file
- File original documents with agent obtaining offer
- Complete sale in progress checklist
- Record earnest money
- Deposit earnest money in escrow account
- Update closing file forms and files
- Restrict showings as seller requests

- Coordinate with selling agent and lender
- Fax copies of contract and addendum to lender
- Confirm purchaser prequalifications
- Review credit report results
- Provide credit information to seller if transaction involves an owner carry
- Assist in arranging financing
- Coordinate discount points being locked with dates
- Provide comparable sales for appraiser
- Schedule appraisal
- Follow-up on appraisal
- Appeal for increase if appraisal is low
- Relay results of CRV or appraisal to seller
- Confirm verification of deposits and employment have been returned
- Follow loan processing through to the underwriter
- Contact lender weekly to track processing
- Relay loan approval to the seller
- Fax copies of contract and addendum to the title company
- Fax closing and control form to the title company
- Confirm loan payoff statement created
- Confirm loan assumption statement ordered
- Contact existing lender for assumption requirements
- Compile all required items for assumption
- Submit all required items for assumption
- Order title insurance commitment
- Review title insurance commitment
- Confirm purchaser received title insurance commitment
- Confirm selling agent received title insurance commitment
- Note title insurance requirements
- Coordinate meeting all title insurance requirements
- Have buyers' hazard insurance delivered
- Provide homeowners warranty for closing
- Coordinate home inspection
- Review home inspection results
- Negotiate the payment and completion of all required repairs
- Inspection clause requirements completed
- Deliver unrecorded property information to buyer
- Order septic inspection (if applicable)
- Receive and review septic report (if applicable)
- Deliver copy of septic inspection report to lender and buyer (if applicable)
- File copy of septic inspection report (if applicable)
- Order water potability test (if applicable)
- Receive and review water potability test (if applicable)
- Deliver copy of water potability test to lender and buyer (if applicable)
- File copy of water potability test (if applicable)
- Loan approved
- Select closing location
- Confirm closing date
- Schedule closing time with seller
- Schedule closing time with title company
- Schedule closing time with lender
- Schedule closing time with selling agent
- Schedule closing time with buyer
- Schedule final walk-through for buyer
- Request closing figures from title company
- Receive and review closing figures
- Forward closing figures to selling agent
- Forward closing figures to buyer

- Request closing documents
- Review closing documents
- Forward closing documents to seller as requested
- Confer and review documents with seller's attorney
- Provide earnest money check for escrow
- Oversee the entire closing process
- Coordinate this closing with seller's next home purchase
- Present seller with a check at closing

After Closing:

- Make follow-up call to client
- Make follow-up call to buyer
- File entire closed package
- Place copy of seller's settlement statement in February 1 tax file
- Place copy of buyer's settlement statement in February 1 tax file
- February 1 of following year: mail settlement statements to buyers and sellers
- Remove property from property roster

FIGURE A.1 **PERFORMANCE CAMPAIGN** *(continued)*

FIGURE A.2

HOME INSPECTION FORM

AREA OR ITEM	OK	WORK TO BE DONE	COMMENTS
Floors (Check each room for the following)			
Carpets clean and in good repair	_____	_____	_____
No spots or discoloration	_____	_____	_____
Wood or tiling floors polished	_____	_____	_____
Baseboards clean and in good repair	_____	_____	_____
Floor electrical sockets clean and working	_____	_____	_____
Tile or linoleum no cracks or breaks	_____	_____	_____
No bubbles or sloping	_____	_____	_____
Walls (Check each room for the following)			
Walls clean with no spots	_____	_____	_____
Holes patched and painted	_____	_____	_____
Discoloration repaired and repainted	_____	_____	_____
Light fixtures clean and repaired	_____	_____	_____
Switch plates clean and repaired	_____	_____	_____
Socket plates clean and repaired	_____	_____	_____
No offensive wall hangings	_____	_____	_____
Mirrors and glass polished	_____	_____	_____
Doors (Check each room for the following)			
Paint or finish in good repair	_____	_____	_____
No dirt or discoloration	_____	_____	_____
No chipping or loose panels	_____	_____	_____
No cobwebs	_____	_____	_____
Doors move smoothly and no dragging	_____	_____	_____
Handles, hinges, and locks working well	_____	_____	_____
No squeaks	_____	_____	_____
Windows and Window Coverings			
No broken glass	_____	_____	_____
No cracks in frames	_____	_____	_____
Open and close easily	_____	_____	_____
Hinges in good shape	_____	_____	_____
Latches, handles, and cranks in good shape	_____	_____	_____
Slide smoothly and tracks clean	_____	_____	_____

Area or Item	OK	Work to be done	Comments
All locks working well			
Drapes and curtains clean and in good repair			
Blinds in good shape and working well			
Pull cords in good shape			
Drapes operating smoothly			
Curtain rods straight and attached well			
No discoloration on walls or coverings			
Ceilings (Check each room for the following)			
No stains or discoloration			
No damage			
Paint or finish in good repair			
No cobwebs			
Corners (top and bottom) cleaned			
Light fixtures clean with no dead bugs			
Light bulbs working and bright			
Track lighting directed properly			
Kitchen			
Refrigerator clean and in good repair			
Dishwasher clean and in good repair			
Stoves and ovens clean and in good repair			
Stove drip pans clean or replaced			
Switches and buttons in good shape			
Oven drip pans clean or replaced			
Sink clean and empty			
Cupboards clean and organized			
Faucets clean and shining			
Faucets, sinks, and pipes no leaks or drips			
Curtains clean and pressed			
Plants in good shape			
Garbage disposal working properly			
Living Room			
Good traffic flow			
Furniture clean and in good repair			
Good lighting			
Fireplace, hearth, and mantel clean			
No stacking of furniture, TVs, etc.			
Drapes and curtains clean and pressed			

FIGURE A.2 **HOME INSPECTION FORM** (continued)

Area or Item	OK	Work to be done	Comments
Blinds clean and in good repair	_____	_____	_____
Shelves not cluttered	_____	_____	_____

Bathrooms

Area or Item	OK	Work to be done	Comments
Bathtub clean with no spots or chips	_____	_____	_____
Soap holders clean and shining	_____	_____	_____
Tile walls clean and polished	_____	_____	_____
Grout scrubbed and clean	_____	_____	_____
No mildew	_____	_____	_____
Shower curtains or shower doors clean	_____	_____	_____
No water spots	_____	_____	_____
Faucets and handles polished	_____	_____	_____
Cabinets and cupboards clean and organized	_____	_____	_____
Fixtures clean and organized	_____	_____	_____
Toilet and toilet seat clean and in good repair	_____	_____	_____
Towels clean and arranged neatly	_____	_____	_____
Air freshener installed	_____	_____	_____
Colored water in toilet	_____	_____	_____

Bedrooms

Area or Item	OK	Work to be done	Comments
Dressers and cabinets clean and neatly arranged	_____	_____	_____
No offensive wall hangings	_____	_____	_____
Beds made neatly and clean underneath	_____	_____	_____
Window sills clean	_____	_____	_____
Curtains and drapes clean and pressed	_____	_____	_____
Personal items stored safely	_____	_____	_____
Valuables stored	_____	_____	_____
No excessive furniture	_____	_____	_____
Blinds clean and in good repair	_____	_____	_____

Closets

Area or Item	OK	Work to be done	Comments
Neatly arranged and not crowded	_____	_____	_____
Not jammed with shoes or sports equipment	_____	_____	_____
Belts and ties neatly hung	_____	_____	_____
Well lit	_____	_____	_____
Hanging bars secure and straight	_____	_____	_____
Walls clean with no spots	_____	_____	_____
No odor (use air freshener or cedar chips)	_____	_____	_____

FIGURE A.2 **HOME INSPECTION FORM** (continued)

Area or Item	OK	Work to be done	Comments

Laundry Area

No odor

Well lit

Very clean with no lint

Exhaust vents clear and clean

No piles of clothes

Cabinet and shelves neatly arranged

Staircases

Handrails, top and bottom posts secure

Stairs tight and no squeaks

Tile, carpets or other covering secure

No rails protruding

Side slats and vertical rail secure

Decorative knobs and pieces secure

Good lighting on entire staircase

Plenty of head room; if not, may need a sign

Pull-down staircase working smoothly

Shelves, Bookcases, and Drawers

Clean, not cluttered, level and secure

Finish or covering in good shape

Drawers move easily

Handles and knobs are tight

Fireplaces

Chimney clean

Inside clean with no excessive burn marks

Grate in place and in good shape

Mantel and hearth clean and in good shape

Screens or doors working well

Gas lighters and fans working properly

Electrical

Outlets working

Switches operative

Dimmers working properly

Wall plates clean and in good repair

Pull cords in good shape

FIGURE A.2 **HOME INSPECTION FORM** *(continued)*

Area or Item	OK	Work to be done	Comments
Heating and Cooling			
Units and thermostats working properly and recently serviced	____	_____	_____
Vent covers in place and working properly	____	_____	_____
Window units secure and sealed	____	_____	_____
Exposed ducting clean	____	_____	_____
Pilot lights stay lit	____	_____	_____
Basement			
Well lit	____	_____	_____
No odor	____	_____	_____
Dry	____	_____	_____
No excessive storage	____	_____	_____
Neatly arranged	____	_____	_____
Easy entry and exit	____	_____	_____
Attic			
No odor and well ventilated	____	_____	_____
Neatly arranged, not crowded if used for storage	____	_____	_____
Easy entry and exit	____	_____	_____
Well lit	____	_____	_____
Porches, Patios, and Entryways			
No clutter and neatly arranged	____	_____	_____
Coat racks empty	____	_____	_____
No shoes, clothing, or toys stored	____	_____	_____
Well lit	____	_____	_____
No odor			
Garage	____	_____	_____
Garage doors and openers working properly	____	_____	_____
Neatly arranged with no excessive storage	____	_____	_____
Rafter area neatly arranged and not overcrowded	____	_____	_____
Stains and spots removed from garage floor	____	_____	_____
Tools and yard equipment neatly stored	____	_____	_____
Workbenches clean and not cluttered	____	_____	_____

Area or Item	OK	Work to be done	Comments
Pools, Spas, and Saunas			
Clean and decks clean and organized			
Proper chemical balance in the water			
All pumps, heating, and drains in good repair			
Skimmers, hoses, cleaners operative			
Ladders, slides, diving boards in good order			
Pool furniture well maintained			
Safety equipment and signs in place			
Gates lock properly			
Lighting works properly			
Heating unit and timers working properly			
Door closes and seals well			
Sports equipment stored			
Walkways neat and well trimmed			
Home Exterior			
Exterior finishes in good shape with no chipping, peeling, cracks, or holes			
No discoloration from water splashes, drains, or the sun			
Eaves: no peeling, chipping, or molding			
Window frames caulked well			
Crawl spaces covered and accessible			
Vents and eave vents opened and screened			
Area around heating and cooling units clean			
Exterior doors (including garage door) clean, finished, and working well			
Roof			
Clean			
No missing tiles or shakes			
No leaks			
Gutters secure and clean			
Caulking in good shape			
No trees or bushes scraping the roof			
Yard			
Grass, bushes, and trees cut and trimmed neatly			
Leaves raked and picked up			
Sprinkler system working properly			
Driveways and walkways clean with no spots			

FIGURE A.2 **HOME INSPECTION FORM** (continued)

FIGURE A.3

EXCLUSIVE RIGHT TO SELL FORM (Copyrighted—do not copy)

EXCLUSIVE RIGHT TO SELL AGREEMENT

EXCLUSIVE RIGHT TO SELL, EXCHANGE OR LEASE CONTRACT
(This is a legally binding contract. If not understood, seek legal advice.)

For value received, I/We, the undersigned, hereinafter referred as to OWNER, do hereby irrevocably employ and give _____ ,
hereinafter referred to as REALTOR®, the exclusive right to sell exchange or lease the real property situated at _____ , city
of _____ , County of _____ , _____ described as follows: _____

_____

List price_____ Financing Available: _____

Commencing on _____ 19 _____ , and terminating at midnight _____ , 19 ____ , subject to the following terms and conditions:

A. The parties understand and agree that this is an exclusive right to sell, exchange or lease listing, and REALTOR® shall be entitled to the
commission hereinafter established if, (1) the property is sold, exchanged or leased by any person, including the OWNER, to any person during the term of this contract or any renewal or extension thereof, (2) OWNER or any member of the Multiple Listing Service
of the Anywhere Association of REALTORS® secures a buyer or lessee ready, willing and able to purchase, exchange or lease during
the period of this agreement said property for the price and terms as specified, or such other price or terms as OWNER may accept; or
(3) a contract is entered into to sell, exchange or lease and ultimately completed after the termination of this contract; (4) the property is sold, leased or exchanged by OWNER or any other person within __ days after termination of this listing to any person that commences or continues negotiations with OWNER during the term of this contract and of which REALTOR® has knowledge or notice
thereof or to whom the property was shown during the listing period; or(5) REALTOR® is the procuring cause of a sale, exchange or
lease of this property. In the event property is relisted with another licensed real estate broker, the protection period stated above shall
be waived so seller is not liable for dual commission.

B. It is understood that REALTOR® is a member of the AAR. It is agreed that REALTOR® shall file this listing with the Multiple Listing
Service to be referred to by AAR's members. It is agreed such members may act as SUB-AGENTS or BUYER'S BROKER in procuring
or attempting to procure a purchase in accordance with this agreement. If a sale, exchange or lease shall be made through any such
SUB-AGENT or BUYER'S BROKER, all terms of this agreement shall apply to such transaction, provided, however, that payment of
commission or compensation made hereunder shall be made by OWNER only to REALTOR®. In the event an offer and acceptance
has been executed, the REALTOR® shall have the affirmative obligation to immediately change the status of the listing to "sale pending" In the event an offer and acceptance has been executed but contains contingencies, the REALTOR® shall have the affirmative
obligation to immediately change the status of the listing to "contingency sale."

C. REALTOR® is herein authorized to accept a deposit for any part of the purchase price and hold it in a trust account or place it in an
escrow established for the sale of this subject property.

D. OWNER agrees to pay in cash to REALTOR® for his services a total commission:

__ % of selling price of the property, or
__ fixed amount
__ % of the total rental agreed to be paid by lessee, or
__ fixed amount
__ REALTOR® is authorized by Owner to offer and cooperate and compensate Buyer's Broker and Sub-Agents.

_____

The amount or rate of real estate commission is not fixed by law. They are set by each broker individually and may be negotiable
between seller and broker.

E. The following is a list of personal property items included in the list price, which are free of liens or encumbrances:

_____

Owner further agrees to deliver said personal property, if any, by a valid bill of sale.

F. The parties understand and agree that REALTOR®'S undertaking pursuant to this listing is limited to the procurement of a purchaser,
ready, willing and able to buy the property on the terms and conditions specified, and that the commission established herein shall be
due and payable immediately on such procurement.

G. OWNER hereby warrants that no options to purchase the property have been extended to any third party by OWNER. In the event
OWNER is unable to convey title as herein provided, OWNER shall be liable for all costs of escrow and for REALTOR®'S full commission. Additionally, all deposits made by the prospective purchaser may be returned without liability on behalf of the REALTOR®.

H. In the event of default by the prospective purchaser and/or forfeiture by him of any deposit and/or down payment, REALTOR® shall
retain one-half (½) of any such defaulted or forfeited sum up to the total commission figure established herein and distribute the balance, if any, to OWNER.

I. OWNER hereby warrants that the information given on the data input form is true correct and that OWNER is the OWNER in fact of the subject property (or that he/she is the authorized agent(s) of the true OWNER with complete and full authority to act on behalf of the OWNER). The OWNER hereby agrees to indemnify, actively defend and hold REALTOR® harmless from any damages, loss, liability and/or expenses arising from incorrect information or failure to supply material information regarding the subject property, including, but not limited to, the condition of appliances, heating, plumbing, wiring, sewage, location or property lines (habitability and/or merchantability, public and/or private restrictions of the use of the property, any loss of liability in conjunction with this Agreement or with REALTOR® or other members showing the property including but not limited to injuries suffered by other members and/or prospective purchasers.

J. OWNER warrants that he/she knows of no legal actions or special studies affecting the property.

K. OWNER has __ has not __ completed the Seller's Real Property information sheet (initial appropriate space).

L. FAIR HOUSING. REALTOR® shall offer said property without regard to race, color, sex, creed, religion, national origin, handicap or familial status. A copy of a current fair housing disclosure on back side of last page.

M. AGREEMENT TO MEDIATE: OWNER and REALTOR® do _____ do not _____ agree that any dispute or claim involving the undersigned and arising out of or relating to this contract shall be submitted to the Anywhere Association of REALTORS® for mediation in accordance with the Code of Ethics and Arbitration Manual of the National Association of REALTORS® and that neither party shall commence litigation without first participating or offering in good faith to participate in the mediation process.

N. In case of exchange, OWNER has no objection to REALTORS® representing and accepting compensation as disclosed from any other party to the exchange, as well from OWNER.

O. In the event suit is brought by either party to enforce this contract, the prevailing party is entitled to court costs and reasonable attorney's fees.

P. OWNER is aware that a photograph of the listed property may be taken by an authorized representative for publication in the MLS book.

OWNER'S initials _____

KEYSAFE AUTHORIZATION

OWNER hereby authorizes REALTOR®, to use keysafe holder in connection with the showing of the above property. In connection with such consent, OWNER acknowledges that he has been advised:

1. That the purpose and function of a keysafe is to permit access to the interior of said premises by all of the members of the Multiple Listing Service (MLS) of AAR.

2. That OWNER and REALTOR® have discussed the safeguarding of personal property and valuables located within said premises.

3. That it is not a requirement of the AAR's MLS that an OWNER allow use of a keysafe holder.

4. Where a tenant/lessee occupies the property, the tenant/lessee's consent is also required as evidenced by the attached Keysafe authorization form. OWNER further acknowledges that neither the REALTOR® nor AAR is an insurer against the loss of personal property. OWNER hereby releases REALTORS® and AAR from any responsibility therefor and any other REALTOR® members of AAR.

KEYSAFE AUTHORIZATION; YES _____ NO _____ (OWNER(S) initials)

TENANT: The undersigned approves the above provisions for a keysafe, and joins in the above release

_____	_____
TENANT SIGNATURE	TENANT SIGNATURE
_____	_____
COMPANY'S SIGNATURE	COMPANY'S ADDRESS
_____ BY	_____
BROKER'S INITIALS	AUTHORIZATION AGENT

In consideration of the above listing and authorization, REALTOR® and/or his representatives agree to use diligence in their efforts to bring about a sale, lease, or exchange of subject property OWNER HEREWITH ACKNOWLEDGES HAVING READ THIS ENTIRE CONTRACT AND AGREES TO THE TERMS AND CONDITIONS HEREIN. Receipt of a copy of this contract is hereby acknowledged.

Date _____ 19_____ OWNER _____ OWNER _____

TIME _____ A.M./P.M. ADDRESS _____

CITY, STATE, ZIP _____ PHONE _____

FIGURE A.4

REAL ESTATE PURCHASE CONTRACT (Sample—do not copy)

REAL ESTATE PURCHASE CONTRACT AND RECEIPT FOR DEPOSIT

THIS IS MORE THAN A RECEIPT FOR MONEY. IT IS INTENDED TO BE A LEGALLY BINDING CONTRACT. READ IT CAREFULLY.

DATE: _____ , 19 _____ AT _____ .

RECEIVED FROM _____ ("Buyer")

THE SUM OF _____ Dollars $ _____

as a deposit to be applied toward the

PURCHASE PRICE OF _____ Dollars $ _____

FOR PURCHASED OF PROPERTY SITUATED IN _____ , COUNTY OF _____ ,

DESCRIBED AS _____ ("Property").

1. FINANCING: THE OBTAINING OF THE LOAN(S) BELOW IS A CONTINGENCY OF THIS AGREEMENT. Buyer shall act diligent-ly and in good faith to obtain all applicable financing.

   A. FINANCING CONTINGENCY shall remain in effect until (Check ONLY ONE of the following):

      1. ❏ (If checked). The designated loan(s) is/are funded and/or the assumption of existing financing is approved by Lender.

      OR 2. ❏ (If checked). _____calendar days after acceptance of the offer. Buyer shall remove the financing contingency in writing within this time. If Buyer fails to do so, then Seller may cancel this agreement by giving written notice of cancellation to Buyer.

   B. OBTAINING OF DEPOSIT AND DOWN PAYMENT by the Buyer is NOT a contingency, unless otherwise agreed in writing.

   C. DEPOSIT to be deposited ❏ with Escrow Holder, ❏ into Broker's trust account, or ❏ _____

      BY ❏ Personal check, ❏ Cashier's check, ❏ Cash, or ❏ PAYABLE TO _____

      TO BE HELD UNCASHED UNTIL the next business day after acceptance of the offer, or ❏ _____ .

   D. INCREASED DEPOSIT, within _____ calendar days after acceptance of the offer, to be deposited ❏ with Escrow Holder, ❏ into Broker's trust account, or ❏ _____

   E. BALANCE OF DOWN PAYMENT to be deposited with Escrow Holder on demand of Escrow Holder.

   F. FIRST LOAN IN THE AMOUNT OF

      ❏ NEW First Deed of Trust in favor of ❏ LENDER, ❏ SELLER; or ❏ ASSUMPTION of existing First Deed of Trust; or ❏ _____ ; encumbering the Property, securing a note payable at approximately $ _____ per month (❏ or more), to include ❏ principal and interest, ❏ only, at maximum interest of _____ % ❏ fixed rate, ❏ initial adjustable rate with a maximum lifetime interest rate increase of _____ % over the initial rate, balance due in _____ years. Buyer shall pay loan fees/points not to exceed _____ .

   G. SECOND LOAN IN THE AMOUNT OF

      ❏ NEW Second Deed of Trust in favor of ❏ LENDER, ❏ SELLER; or _____ .

      ❏ ASSUMPTION of Existing Second Deed of Trust: or ❏ _____ ; encumbering the Property, securing a note payable at approximately $ _____ per month (❏ or more), to include ❏ principal and interest, ❏ interest only, at maximum interest _____ % ❏ fixed rate, ❏ initial adjustable rate, with a maximum lifetime interest rate increase of _____ % over the initial rate, balance due in _____ years. Buyer shall pay loan fees/points not to exceed _____ .

   H. TOTAL PURCHASE PRICE, not including costs of obtaining loans and other closing costs.

   I. LOAN APPLICATIONS: Buyer shall, within the time specified, submit to lender(s) (or to Seller for applicable Seller financing), a com-pleted loan or assumption application(s), and provide to Seller written acknowledgment of Buyer's compliance. For Seller financing: (1) Buyer shall submit a completed loan application on FNMA Form 1003; (2) Buyer authorizes Seller and/or Broker(s) to obtain, at Buyer's expense, a copy of Buyer's credit report; and (3) Seller may cancel this purchase and sale agreement upon disapproval of either the application or the credit report, by providing to Buyer written notice within 7 (or ❏ _____) calendar days after receipt of those documents.

   J. EXISTING LOANS: For existing loans to be taken over by Buyer, Seller shall promptly request and upon receipt provide to Buyer copies of all applicable notes and deeds of trust, loan balances, and current interest rates. Buyer may give Seller written notice of disapproval within the time specified. Differences between estimated and actual loan balance(s) shall be adjusted at close of escrow by:

      ❏ Cash down payment, or ❏ _____ .

      Impound account(s), if any, shall be: ❏ Charged to Buyer and credited to Seller, or ❏ _____ .

   K. LOAN FEATURES: LOANS/DOCUMENTS CONTAIN A NUMBER OF IMPORTANT FEATURES AFFECTING THE RIGHTS OF THE BORROWER AND LENDER. READ ALL LOAN DOCUMENTS CAREFULLY.

L. ADDITIONAL SELLER FINANCING TERMS: The following terms apply ONLY to financing extended by Seller under this agreement. The rate specified as the maximum interest rate in F or G above, as applicable, shall be the actual fixed interest rate for seller financing. Any promissory note and/or deed of trust given by Buyer and Seller shall contain, but not be limited to, the following additional terms:

1. REQUEST FOR NOTICE OF DEFAULT on senior loans.

2. Buyer shall execute and pay for a REQUEST FOR NOTICE OF DELINQUENCY in escrow and at any future time if requested by Seller.

3. Acceleration clause making the loan due, when permitted by law, at Seller's option, upon the sale or transfer of the Property or any interest in it.

4. A late charge or 6.0 % of the installment due, or $5.00, whichever is greater, if the installment is not received within 10 days of the date it is due.

5. Title insurance coverage in the form of a joint protection policy shall be provided insuring Seller's deed of trust interest in the Property.

6. Tax Service shall be obtained and paid for by Buyer to notify Seller if property taxes have not been paid.

7. Buyer shall provide fire and extended coverage insurance during the period of the Seller financing, in an amount sufficient to replace all improvements on the Property, or the total encumbrances against the Property, whichever is less, with a loss payable endorsement in favor of Seller.

8. The addition, deletion, or substitution of any person or entity under this agreement, or to title prior to close of escrow, shall require Seller's written consent. Seller may grant or withhold consent in Seller's sole discretion. Any additional or substituted person or entity shall, if requested by Seller, submit to Seller the same documentation as required for the original named Buyer. Seller and/or Broker(s) may obtain a credit report on any such person or entity.

9. If the Property contains 1 to 4 dwelling units, Buyer and Seller shall execute a Seller Financing Disclosure Statement, if applicable, as provided by arranger of credit, as soon as practicable prior to execution of security documents.

M. ADDITIONAL FINANCING TERMS: _____
_____

2. CONDITION OF PROPERTY: (Initial ONLY paragraph A or B; DO NOT initial both.)

Buyer's initials _____ Seller's initials _____ **A. SELLER WARRANTY:** (If A is initialled, DO NOT initial B.) Seller warrants that on the date possession is made available to Buyer: (1) Roof shall be free of KNOWN leaks; (2) built-in appliances (including free-standing oven and range, if included in sale), plumbing, heating, air conditioning, electrical, water, sewer/septic, and pool/spa systems, if any, shall be operative; (3) plumbing systems, shower pan(s), and shower enclosure(s) shall be free of leaks; (4) all broken or cracked glass shall be replaced; (5) Property, including pool/spa, landscaping, and grounds, shall be maintained in substantially the same condition as on the date of acceptance of the offer; (6) all debris and all personal property not included in the sale shall be removed; (7) _____
_____

NOTE TO BUYER: This warranty is limited to items specified in this paragraph A.

NOTE TO SELLER: Disclosures in the Real Estate Transfer Disclosure Statement and items discovered in Buyer's inspection do NOT eliminate Seller's obligations under this warranty unless specifically agreed in writing.

OR

Buyer's initials _____ Seller's initials _____ **B. "AS-IS" CONDITION:** (If B is initialled, DO NOT initial A.) Property is sold "AS-IS," in its present condition, without warranty. Seller shall not be responsible for making corrections or repairs of any nature except: (1) Structural pest control repairs, if applicable under paragraph 19, and (2) _____.

Buyer retains the right to disapprove the condition of the Property based upon items discovered in Buyer's Inspections under paragraph 9. **SELLER REMAINS OBLIGATED TO DISCLOSE ADVERSE MATERIAL FACTS WHICH ARE KNOWN TO SELLER AND TO MAKE OTHER DISCLOSURES REQUIRED BY LAW.**

3. TRANSFER DISCLOSURE STATEMENT: Unless exempt, a Real Estate Transfer Disclosure Statement ("TDS") (CAR FORM TDS-14) shall be completed by Seller and delivered to Buyer (Civil Code 1102-110.15). Buyer shall sign and return a copy of the TDS to Seller or Seller's agent: (a) ❑ Buyer has received a TDS prior to execution of the offer, OR (b) ❑ Buyer shall be provided a TDS within _____ calendar days after acceptance of the offer. If the TDS is delivered to Buyer after the offer is executed, Buyer shall have the right to terminate this agreement within three (3) days after delivery in person, or five (5) days after delivery by deposit in the mail by giving written notice of termination to Seller or Seller's agent.

4. PROPERTY DISCLOSURES: When applicable to the Property and required by law, Seller shall provide to Buyer, at Seller's expense, the following disclosures and information. Buyer shall then, within the time specified, investigate the disclosures and information and provide written notice to Seller of any item disapproved pursuant to A-C and E1(b) below.

A. GEOLOGIC-SEISMIC HAZARD ZONES DISCLOSURE: If the Property is located in a Special Studies Zone (SSZ), or in a locally designated geological, seismic, or other hazard zone(s) or area(s) where disclosure is required by law, Seller shall, within the time specified in paragraph 26B(7), disclose in writing to Buyer this fact(s) and any other information required by law. (GEOLOGIC, SEISMIC AND FLOOD HAZARD DISCLOSURE SHALL SATISFY THIS REQUIREMENT.) Construction or development of any structure may be restricted.

REAL ESTATE PURCHASE CONTRACT AND RECEIPT FOR DEPOSIT – page 3

Disclosure of SSZ and SHZs is required only where the maps, or information contained in the maps, are "reasonably available."

B. **SPECIAL FLOOD HAZARD AREAS:** If the Property is located in a Special Flood Hazard Area designated by the Federal Emergency Management Agency (FEMA), Seller shall, within the time specified, disclose this fact in writing to Buyer. (GEOLOGIC, SEISMIC AND FLOOD HAZARD DISCLOSURE SHALL SATISFY THIS REQUIREMENT.) Government regulations may impose building restrictions and requirements which may substantially impact and limit construction and remodeling of improvements. Flood insurance may be required by lender.

C. **STATE FIRE RESPONSIBILITY AREAS:** If the Property is located in a State Fire Responsibility Area, Seller shall, within the time specified in paragraph 26B(7), disclose this fact in writing to Buyer (Public Resources Code 4136). Disclosure may be made in the Real Estate Transfer Disclosure Statement. Government regulations may impose building restrictions and requirements which may substantially impact and limit construction and remodeling improvements. Disclosure of these areas is required only if the Seller has actual knowledge that the Property is located in such an area or if maps of such areas have been provided to the county assessor's office.

D. **MELLO-ROOS:** Seller shall make a good faith effort to obtain a disclosure notice from any local agencies which levy on the Property a special tax pursuant to the Mello-Roos Community Facilities Act, and shall deliver to Buyer any such notice made available by those agencies.

E. **EARTHQUAKE SAFETY:**

　1. **PRE-1960 PROPERTIES:** If the Property was built prior to 1960, and contains ONE-TO-FOUR DWELLING UNITS of conventional light frame construction, Seller shall, unless exempt, within the time specified, provide to Buyer: (a) a copy of "The Homeowner's Guide To Earthquake Safety" and (b) written disclosure of known seismic deficiencies (Government Code 8897-8897.5).

　2. **PRE-1975 PROPERTIES:** If the Property was built prior to 1975, and contains RESIDENTIAL, COMMERCIAL, OR OTHER STRUCTURES constructed of masonry or precast concrete, with wood frame floors or roofs, Seller shall, unless exempt, within the time specified, provide to the Buyer a copy of "The Commercial Property Owner's Guide to Earthquake Safety" (Government Code 8893-8893.5).

　3. **ALL PROPERTIES:** If the booklets described in paragraph E1 and E2 are not required, Buyer is advised that they are available and contain important information that may be useful for ALL TYPES OF PROPERTY.

F. **SMOKE DETECTOR(S):** State law requires that residences be equipped with operable smoke detector(s). Local ordinances may have additional requirements. Unless exempt, Seller shall, prior to close of escrow, provide to Buyer a written statement of compliance and any other documents required, in accordance with applicable state and local law. (SMOKE DETECTOR STATEMENT OF COMPLIANCE SHALL SATISFY THE STATE PORTION OF THIS REQUIREMENT.) Additional smoke detector(s), if required shall be installed by Seller at Seller's expense prior to close of escrow.

G. **LEAD BASED PAINT:** Buyers obtaining new FHA-insured financing on residential properties constructed prior to 1978 are required to sign a lead paint disclosure form. (NOTICE TO PURCHASERS OF HOUSING CONSTRUCTED BEFORE 1978 SHALL SATISFY THIS REQUIREMENT).

H. **OTHER:** _____ .

5. **GOVERNMENTAL COMPLIANCE:** Seller shall promptly disclose to Buyer any improvements, additions, alterations, or repairs ("Improvements") made by Seller or known to Seller to have been made without required governmental permits, final inspections, and approvals. In addition, Seller represents that Seller has no knowledge of any notice of violations of City, County, State, or Federal building, zoning, fire, or health laws, codes, statutes, ordinances, regulations, or rules filed or issued against the Property. If Seller receives notice or is made aware of any of the above violations prior to close of escrow, Seller shall immediately notify Buyer in writing. Buyer shall, within the time specified, provide written notice to Seller of any items disapproved.

6. **RETROFIT:** Compliance with any minimum mandatory government retrofit standards, including but not limited to energy and utility efficiency requirements and proof of compliance, shall be paid for by ❑ Buyer, ❑ Seller.

7. **FIXTURES:** All existing fixtures and fittings that are attached to the Property or for which special openings have been made are INCLUDED IN THE PURCHASE PRICE (unless excluded below) and are to be transferred free of liens. These include, but are not limited to, electrical, lighting, plumbing and heating fixtures, fireplace inserts, solar systems, built-in appliances, screens, awnings, shutters, window coverings, attached floor coverings, television antennas/satellite dishes and related equipment, private integrated telephone systems, air coolers/conditioners, pool/spa equipment, water softeners (if owned by Seller), security systems/alarms (if owned by Seller), garage door openers/remote controls, attached fireplace equipment, mailbox, in-ground landscaping including trees/shrubs, and _____.
ITEMS EXCLUDED:_____

8. **PERSONAL PROPERTY:** The following items of personal property, free of liens and without warranty of condition (unless provided in paragraph 10A) or fitness for use, are included: _____
_____
_____

9. **HOME WARRANTY PLANS:** Buyer and Seller are informed that home warranty plans are available. These plans may provide additional protection and benefit to Buyer and Seller. Broker(s) do not endorse, approve, or recommend any particular company or program. Buyer and Seller elect (Check ONLY ONE):

FIGURE A.4 **REAL ESTATE PURCHASE CONTRACT** *(continued)*　　253

❏ To purchase a home warranty plan with the following optional coverage _____, at a cost not to exceed $ _____, to be paid by _____, and to be issued by _____ Company,

OR

❏ Buyer and Seller elect NOT to purchase a home warranty plan.

10. SEPTIC SYSTEM: (If initialled by all parties.)

Buyer's initials _____ Seller's initials _____

❏ Buyer, ❏ Seller shall pay to have septic system pumped and certified. Evidence of compliance shall be provided to the other party before close of escrow.

❏ Buyer, ❏ Seller to pay for sewer connection if required by local ordinance.

11. PEST CONTROL: (If initialled by all parties.)

Buyer's initials _____ Seller's initials _____

A. Seller shall, within the time specified, provide to Buyer a current written Wood Destroying Pests and Organisms Inspection Report. Report shall be at the expense of ❏ Buyer, ❏ Seller, to be performed by _____, a registered Structural Pest Control Company, covering the main building and (If checked):

❏ detached garage(s) or carport(s); ❏ the following other structures on the Property: _____.

B. If requested by Buyer or Seller, the report shall separately identify each recommendation for corrective work as follows:

"Section 1": Infestation or infection which is evident.

"Section 2": Conditions that are present which are deemed likely to lead to infestation or infection.

C. If no infestation or infection by wood destroying pests or organisms is found, the report shall include a written Certification that on the inspection date no evidence of active infestation was found.

D. Work recommended to correct conditions shall be at the expense of ❏ Buyer, ❏ Seller.

E. Work recommended to correct conditions, if requested by Buyer, shall be at the expense of ❏ Buyer, ❏ Seller.

F. Work to be performed at Seller's expense may be performed by Seller or through others, provided that: (a) all required permits and final inspections are obtained, and (b) upon completion of repairs a written Certification is issued by a registered Structural Pest Control Company showing that the inspected property "is now free of evidence of active infestation or infection."

G. If inspection of inaccessible areas is recommended in the report, Buyer has the option to accept and approve the report, or request in writing within 5 (or ❏ _____) calendar days of receipt of the report that further inspection be made. BUYER'S FAILURE TO NOTIFY SELLER IN WRITING OF SUCH REQUEST SHALL CONCLUSIVELY BE CONSIDERED APPROVAL OF THE REPORT. If further inspection recommends corrective work, such work, and the inspection, entry, and closing of the inaccessible areas, shall be at the expense of the respective party designated in paragraphs (A), (D) and/or (E). If no infestation or infection is found, the inspection, entry, and closing of the inaccessible areas shall be at the expense of Buyer.

H. Inspections, corrective work, and certification under this paragraph shall not include roof coverings. Read paragraph 9A concerning inspection of roof coverings.

I. Work shall be performed in a skillful manner with materials of comparable quality, and shall include repair of leaking shower stalls and pans and replacement of tiles and other materials removed for repair. It is understood that exact restoration of appearance or cosmetic items following all such work is not included.

J. Funds for work agreed in writing to be performed after close of escrow shall be held in escrow and disbursed upon receipt of a written Certification that the inspected property "is now free of evidence of active infestation or infection."

K. Other: _____.

12. SALE OF BUYER'S PROPERTY: (If initialled by all parties.)

Buyer's initials _____ Seller's initials _____

This agreement is contingent upon the close of escrow of Buyer's property described as _____ situated in _____. Buyer's property is: ❏ Listed with _____ Company,

❏ In escrow No. _____ with _____ Company, scheduled to close escrow on _____, 19 _____.

A. (Check ONE:) ❏ Seller shall have the right to continue to offer the Property for sale, ❏ Seller shall NOT have the right to continue to offer the Property for sale (other than for back-up offers), ❏ Seller shall not have the right to continue to offer for sale (other than for back-up offers) until _____ calendar days after acceptance of the offer.

B. If Seller has the right to continue to offer the Property for sale (other than for back-up offers) and Seller accepts another offer, Seller shall give Buyer written notice to (1) remove this contingency in writing and (2) comply with the following additional requirements _____

_____.

If Buyer fails to complete those actions within _____ hours or _____ calendar days after receipt of such Notice from Seller, then this agreement and any escrow shall terminate and the deposit (less costs incurred) shall returned to Buyer.

C. If Seller does not give the Notice above the Buyer's property does not close escrow by the date specified in paragraph 3 for close of escrow of this Property, then either Seller or Buyer may cancel this agreement and any escrow by giving the other party written notice of cancellation, and the Buyer's deposit (less cost incurred) shall be returned to Buyer.

13. CANCELLATION OF PRIOR SALE/BACK-UP OFFER: (If initialled by all parties.)

Buyer's initials _____ Seller's initials _____

Buyer understands that Seller has entered into one or more contracts to sell the Property to a different buyer(s). The parties to any prior sale may mutually agree to modify or amend the terms of that sale(s). This agreement is contingent upon the written cancellation of the previous purchase and sale agreement(s) and any relate escrow(s).

(Check ONLY ONE of the following.)

❏ CANCELLATION OF PRIOR SALE: If written cancellation of the previous agreement(s) is not received on or before _____ , 19_____ , then either Buyer or Seller may cancel this agreement and any escrow by giving the other party to this agreement written notice of cancellation. Buyer's deposit, less cost incurred, shall then be returned to Buyer.

❏ BACK-UP OFFER: This is a back-up offer in back-up position No. _____ , BUYER'S DEPOSIT CHECK SHALL BE HELD UNCASHED until a copy of the written cancellation(s) signed by all parties to the prior sale(s) is provided to Buyer. Until Buyer receives a copy of such cancellation(s), Buyer may cancel this agreement by providing written notice to Seller. Buyer's deposit shall then be returned to Buyer. AS RELATES TO BACK-UP OFFER, TIME PERIODS IN THIS AGREEMENT WHICH ARE STATED AS A NUMBER OF DAYS SHALL BEGIN ON THE DATES SELLER GIVES TO BUYER WRITTEN NOTICE THAT THAT ANY PRIOR CONTRACT(S) HAS BEEN CANCELLED. IF CLOSE OF ESCROW OR ANY OTHER EVENT IS SHOWN AS A APECITIC DATE THAT DATE SHALL BE EXTENDED UNLESS BUYER AND SELLER SPECIFICALLY AGREE IN WRITING.

14. COURT CONFIRMATION: (If initialled by all parties)

Buyer's initials_____ Seller's initials

This agreement is contingent upon court confirmation on or before _____ , 19___. The court may allow open, comjpetitive bidding, resulting in the Property being sold to tha highest bidder. Buyer had been advised to be in court when the offer is considered for confirmation. Court confirmation may be required in a probate, conservatorship, guardianship, receivership, bankuptcy, or other proceeding. Buyer understands that the Property may continue to be marked by Broker(s) and others may represent other competitive bidders prior to and at the court confirmation. If court confirmation is not obtained by date shown above, Buyer may cancel this agreement by giving written notice of cancellation to Seller.

15. NOTICES: Notices given pursuant to this agreement shall, unless otherwise required by law, be deemed delivered to Buyer when personally received by Buyer _____, who is authorized to receive it for Buyer, or to Seller when personally received by Seller or _____, who is authorized to receive it for Seller. Delivery may be in person, by mail, or facsimile.

16. TAXWITHHOLDING:

A. Under the Foreign Investment in Real Propery Tax Act(FIRPTA), IRC 1445, every Buyer must, unless an exemption applies, deduct and withhold 10% of the gross sales price from Seller's proceeds and sent it to the Internal Revenue Service, if the Seller is a "foreign Person" under that statute.

B. Penalties may be imposed on a responsible party for non-compliance with the requirements of these statutes and related regulations. Seller and Buyer agree to execute and deliver any instrument, affidavit, statement, or instruction reasonably necessary to carry out these requirements, and to withholding of tax under those statutes if required.

17. RISK OF LOSS: Except as otherwise provided in this agreement, all risk of loss to the Property which occurs after the offer is accepted shall be borne by Seller until either the title has been transferred, possession has been given to Buyer, whichever occurs first. Any damage totalling 1.0 (one)% or less of the purchase price shall be repaired by Seller in accordance with paragraph 10, if applicable. If the land or improvements to the Property are destroyed or materially damaged prior to transfer of title in an amount exceeding 1.0 (one)% of the purchase price, then Buyer shall have the option to either terminate this agreement and recover the full deposit or purchase the Property in its then present condition. Any expenses paid by Buyer or Seller for credit reports, appraisals, title examination, or Inspections of any kind shall remain that party's responsibility. If Buyer elects to purchase the Property and the loss is covered by insurance, Seller shall assign to Buyer all insurance proceeds covering the loss. If transfer of title and possession do not occur at the same time, BUYER AND SELLER ARE ADVISED TO SEEK ADVICE OF THEIR INSURANCE ADVISORS as to the insurance consequences thereof.

18. CONTINGENCIES/COVENANTS: METHODS OF SATISFACTION/REMOVAL, TIME FRAMES, DISAPPROVAL/APPROVAL:

A. METHOD OF SATISFYING/REMOVING CONTINGENCIES: Contingencies are to be satisfied or removed by one of the following methods:

(1) **PASSIVE METHOD:** IF BUYER FAILS TO GIVE WRITTEN NOTICE OF DISAPPROVAL OF ITEMS OR OF CANCELLATION OF THIS AGREEMENT WITHIN THE STRICT TIME-PERIODS SPECIFIED IN THIS AGREEMENT (except financing contingency, if paragraph 1A(2) is checked), THEN BUYER SHALL CONCLUSIVELY BE DEEMED TO HAVE COMPLETED ALL INSPECTIONS AND REVIEW OF APPLICABLE DOCUMENTS AND DISCLOSURES AND TO HAVE MADE AN ELECTION TO PROCEED WITH THE TRANSACTION WITHOUT CORRECTION OF ANY ITEMS WHICH THE SELLER HAS NOTOTHERWISE AGREED TO CORRECT.

OR

(2) **ACTIVE METHOD:** IF BUYER AND SELLER INITIAL THIS PARAGRAPH, THEN PARAGRAPH A(1) SHALL NOT APPLY.

Buyer's initials _____ Seller's initials _____ BUYER'S DISAPPROVAL OF ITEMS OR REMOVAL OF CONTINGENCIES SHALL

BE IN WRITING (except financing contingency, if paragraph 1(A)(1) is checked). IF BUYER FAILS TO REMOVE OR WAIVE ALL CONTINGENCIES IN WRITING WITHIN THE STRICT TIME PERIODS SPECIFIED IN THIS AGREEMENT, THEN SELLER MAY CANCEL THIS AGREEMENT BY GIVING WRITTEN NOTICE OF CANCELLATION TO BUYER.

B. **TIME FRAMES:** Buyer and Seller agree to be bound by the following time periods:

BUYER has the following number of calendar days to take the action specified, BEGINNING ON THE DATE OF ACCEPTANCE OF THE OFFER:

1. _____ Loan Application(s) submit to lender(s) for new loan(s) and assumption(s), submit to Seller for seller financing), submit written acknowledgment to Seller

2. _____ Buyer Inspections of Property (complete inspections, except GEOLOGIC, and give notice of disapproval)

3. _____ Buyer Inspections of Property (complete GEOLOGIC inspections and give notice of disapproval)

4. _____

BUYER has the following number of calendar days to DISAPPROVE the items listed below, BEGINNING ON THE DATE OF BUYER'S RECEIPT OF EACH ITEM:

5. _____ Existing Loans Documents,

    Preliminary (Title) Report),

    Condominium/Planned Development Documents,

    Geological/Seismic/Flood/State Fire Zones/Areas,

    Governmental Notices Disclosure

6. _____

SELLER has the following number of calendar days to PROVIDE to Buyer, as applicable, the information listed below, BEGINNING ON THE DATE OF ACCEPTANCE OF THE OFFER:

7. _____ Geologic/Seismic/Flood/State Fire Zones/Areas Disclosures, if applicable, Homeowner's Guide to Earthquake Safety and/or Commercial Property Owner's Guide to Earthquake Safety

8. _____ Pest Control Report

9. _____

The items listed below, as applicable, shall promptly be requested and upon receipt provided to Buyer:

10. Existing Loan Documents,

    Preliminary (Title) Report,

    Condominium/Planned Development Documents,

    Mello-Roos Disclosure

11. _____

C. **DISAPPROVAL/APPROVAL OF ITEMS:** (1) If, within the time specified, Buyer provides written reasonable disapproval to Seller of any item for which Buyer has a disapproval right, Seller shall respond in writing within _____ calendar days after receipt of Buyer's notice. If Seller is unwilling or unable to correct the items disapproved by Buyer, then Buyer may cancel this agreement by giving written notice of cancellation to Seller within _____ calendar days (after receipt of Seller's response, or after expiration of the time for Seller's response, whichever occurs first), in which case Buyer's deposit shall be returned to Buyer. If paragraph A2 is initialled, then Buyer shall provide Seller with a written notice of either cancellation or election to proceed. If Buyer elects to proceed with the transaction without Seller's correction of items, Buyer shall assume all liability, responsibility, and expense for repairs or corrections, including the expense of compliance with governmental agency requirements. This does not, however, relieve the Seller of any contractual obligations to repair or correct items otherwise agreed upon. (2) If a MELLO-ROOS DISCLOSURE notice is delivered to Buyer after the offer is executed, Buyer shall have three (3) days after delivery in person or five (5) days after delivery by deposit in the mail to give written notice of termination to Seller.

D. **FOR ALL TIME PERIODS:**

1. Buyer and Seller understand that time periods can be changed only by mutual written agreement.

2. If this is a back-up offer (paragraph 21), time periods which are shown as a number of days beginning on the date of acceptance of the offer shall instead begin on the date Seller gives to Buyer written notice that any prior contract(s) has been cancelled.

19. **FINAL VERIFICATION OF CONDITION:** Buyer shall have the right to make a final inspection of the Property approximately 5 (or ☐ _____) calendar days prior to close escrow, NOT AS A CONTINGENCY OF THE SALE, but solely to confirm that: (a) Seller has completed alterations, repairs, replacements, or modifications ("Repairs") as agreed in writing by Buyer and Seller, and has complied with warranty obligations, if any, in paragraph 10, and (b) the Property is otherwise in substantially the same condition as on the date of acceptance of the offer. Repair under this agreement shall be completed prior to close of escrow unless otherwise agreed in writing, and shall comply with applicable building code and permit requirements. Materials used shall be of comparable quality to existing materials.

20. **MEDIATION OF DISPUTES:** BUYER AND SELLER AGREE TO MEDIATE ANY DISPUTE OR CLAIM BETWEEN THEM ARISING OUT OF THIS CONTRACT OR ANY RESULTING TRANSACTION BEFORE RESORTING TO ARBITRATION OR COURT ACTION. Mediation is a process in which parties attempt to resolve a dispute by submitting it an impartial, neutral mediator who is author-

ized to facilitate the resolution of the dispute but who is not empowered to impose a settlement on the parties. Mediation fee, if any, shall be divided equally among the parties involved. Before the mediation begins, the parties agree to sign a document limiting the admissibility in arbitration or any civil action of anything said, any admission made, and any documents prepared, in the course of the mediation. In addition, if paragraph 30 is initialled by Broker(s), Buyer and Seller agree to mediate disputes or claims involving an initialling Broker, as defined by that paragraph, consistent with this provision. The election by Broker(s) to initial not initial paragraph 30 shall not affect the applicability of this mediation provision between Buyer and Seller and shall not result in the Broker(s) being deemed parties to the purchase and sale agreement. IF ANY PARTY COMMENCES AN ARBITRATION OR COURT ACTION BASED ON A DISPUTE OR CLAIM TO WHICH THIS PARAGRAPH APPLIES WITHOUT FIRST ATTEMPTING TO RESOLVE THE MATTER THROUGH MEDIATION, THEN IN THE DISCRETION OF THE ARBITRATOR(S) OR JUDGE, THAT PARTY SHALL NOT BE ENTITLED TO RECOVER ATTORNEY'S FEES EVEN IF THEY WOULD OTHERWISE BE AVAILABLE TO THAT PARTY IN ANY SUCH ARBITRATION OR COURT ACTION.

However, the filing of a judicial action to enable the recording of a notice of pending action, for order of attachment, receivership, injunction, or other provisional remedies, shall not in itself constitute a loss of the right to recover attorney's fees under this provision. The following matters are excluded from the requirement of mediation hereunder: (a) a judicial or non-judicial foreclosure or other action or proceeding to enforce a deed of trust, mortgage, or installment land sale contract, (b) an unlawful detainer action, (c) the filing or enforcement of a mechanic's lien, and (d) any matter which is within the jurisdiction of a probate court.

21. ARBITRATION OF DISPUTES: Any dispute or claim in law or equity between Buyer and Seller arising out of this contract or any resulting transaction which is not settled through mediation shall be decided by neutral, binding arbitration and not by court action, except as provided by California law for judicial review or arbitration proceedings. In addition, if paragraph 30 is initialled by Broker(s), Buyer and seller agree to arbitrate disputes or claims involving an initialling Broker, as defined by that paragraph, consistent with this provision. The election by Broker(s) to initial or not initial paragraph 30 shall not affect the applicability of the arbitration provision between Buyer and Seller, and shall not result in the Broker(s) being deemed parties to the purchase and sale agreement.

The arbitration shall be conducted in accordance with the rules of either the American Arbitration Association (AAA) or Judicial Arbitration and Mediation Services, Inc. (JAMS). The selection between AAA and JAMS rules shall be made by the claimant first filing for the arbitration. The parties to an arbitration may agree in writing to use different rules and/or arbitrator(s). Judgment upon the award rendered by the arbitrator(s) may be entered in any court having jurisdiction thereof.

"NOTICE: BY INITIALLING IN THE SPACE BELOW YOU ARE AGREEING TO HAVE ANY DISPUTE ARISING OUT OF THE MATTERS INCLUDED IN THE ARBITRATION OF DISPUTES PROVISION DECIDED BY NEUTRAL ARBITRATION AS PROVIDED BY CALIFORNIA LAW AND YOU ARE GIVING UP ANY RIGHTS YOU MIGHT POSSESS TO HAVE THE DISPUTES LITIGATED IN A COURT OR JURY TRIAL. BY INITIALLING IN THE SPACE BELOW YOU ARE GIVING UP YOUR JUDICIAL RIGHTS TO DISCOVERY AND APPEAL, UNLESS THOSE RIGHTS ARE SPECIFICALLY INCLUDED IN THE ARBITRATION OF DISPUTES PROVISION. IF YOU REFUSE TO SUBMIT TO ARBITRATION AFTER AGREEING TO THIS PROVISION, YOU MAY BE COMPELLED TO ARBITRATE. YOUR AGREEMENT TO THIS ARBITRATION PROVISION IS VOLUNTARY."

"WE HAVE READ AND UNDERSTAND THE FOREGOING AND AGREE TO SUBMIT DISPUTES ARISING OUT OF THE MATTERS INCLUDED IN THE 'ARBITRATION OF DISPUTES' PROVISION TO NEUTRAL ARBITRATION."

22. BROKERS: (initialled.) Any Broker who initials below agrees to (a) mediate any dispute or claim with Buyer, Seller, or other initialling Broker, arising out of this contract or any resulting transaction, consistent with paragraph 28, and (b) arbitrate any dispute or claim with Buyer, Seller or other initialling Broker arising out of this contract or any resulting transaction, consistent with paragraph 29. However, if the dispute is solely between the Brokers, it shall instead be submitted for mediation and arbitration in accordance with the Board/Association of REALTORS® or MLS rules. If those entities decline to handle the matter, it shall be submitted pursuant to paragraphs 28 and 29. The initialling of this paragraph shall not result in any Broker being deemed a party to the purchase and sale agreement. As used in this paragraph, "Broker" means a brokerage firm and any licensed persons affiliated with that brokerage firm.

Selling Broker By: _____ Listing Broker By: _____

23. LIQUIDATED DAMAGES: (If initialled by all parties.)

Buyer's Initials _____ Seller's Initials _____ Buyer and Seller agree that if Buyer fails to complete this purchase by reason of any default of Buyer:

A. Seller shall be released from obligation to sell the Property to Buyer.

B. Seller shall retain, as liquidated damages for breach of contract, the deposit actually paid. However, the amount retained shall be no more than 3% of the purchase price if Property is a dwelling with no more than four units, one of which Buyer intends to occupy as Buyer's residence. Any excess shall be promptly returned to Buyer.

C. Seller retains the right to proceed against Buyer for specific performance or any other claim or remedy Seller may have in law or equity, other than breach of contract damages.

D. In the event of a dispute, Funds deposited in trust accounts or escrow are not released automatically and require mutual, signed release instructions from both Buyer and Seller, judicial decision, or arbitration award.

24. ATTORNEY'S FEES: In any action, proceeding, or arbitration between Buyer and Seller arising out of this agreement, the prevailing party shall be entitled to reasonable attorney's fees and costs.

REAL ESTATE PURCHASE CONTRACT AND RECEIPT FOR DEPOSIT – page 8

25. **MULTIPLE LISTING SERVICE:** If Broker is a Participant of a multiple listing service (MLS), Broker is authorized to report the sale, price, terms, and financing for publication, dissemination, information, and use of the MLS, its parent entity, authorized members, participants, and subscribers.

26. **OTHER TERMS AND CONDITIONS:** _____
_____

27. **TIME OF ESSENCE; ENTIRE CONTRACT; CHANGES:** Time is of the essence. All prior agreements between the parties are incorporated in this agreement, which constitutes the entire contract. Its terms are intended by the parties as a final, complete and exclusive expression of their agreement with respect to its subject matter and may not be contradicted by evidence of any prior agreement or contemporaneous oral agreement. The captions in this agreement are for convenience of reference only and are not intended as part of this agreement. This agreement may not be extended, amended, modified, altered, or changed in any respect whatsoever except by a further agreement in writing signed by Buyer and Seller.

28. **AGENCY CONFIRMATION:** The following agency relationship(s) are herby confirmed for this transaction:
Listing Agent: _____ is the agent of (check one): ❑ the Seller exclusively; or ❑ both the Buyer and Seller.
Selling Agent: _____ (if not same as Listing Agent) is the agent of (check one): ❑ the Buyer exclusively; ❑ the Seller exclusively; or ❑ both the Buyer and Seller.
(If the property contains 1-4 residential dwelling units, buyer and seller must also be given one or more disclosure regarding real estate agency relationships forms.)

29. **OFFER:** This is an offer to purchase the Property. All paragraphs with spaces for initials by Buyer and Seller are incorporated in this agreement only if initialled by both parties. If only one party initials, a Counter Offer is required until agreement is reached. Unless acceptance is signed by Seller and a signed copy delivered in person, by mail, or facsimile, and personally received by Buyer or by _____, who is authorized to receive it, by _____ , 19 _____ at _____ AM/PM, the offer shall be deemed revoked and the deposit shall be returned. Buyer and Seller acknowledge that Broker(s) is/are not a party(ies) to the purchase and sale agreement. Buyer has read and acknowledged receipt of a copy of the offer and agrees to the above confirmation of agency relationships. This agreement and any supplement, addendum, or modification, including any photocopy or facsimile, may be executed in two or more counterparts, all of which shall constitute one and the same writing.

Receipt for deposit is acknowledged: Broker: _____ Buyer: _____

ACCEPTANCE

The undersigned Seller accepts the above and agrees to sell the Property on the above terms and conditions and agrees to the above confirmation of agency relationships (❑ subject to attached counter offer). Seller agrees to pay compensation for services as follows:
_____ to _____ , Broker, and _____ to _____ , Broker, payable: (a) on recordation of the deed or other evidence of title, or (b) if completion of sale is prevented by default of Seller, upon Seller's default, or (c) if completion of sale is prevented by default of Buyer, only if and when Seller collects damages from Buyer, by suit or otherwise, and then in an amount equal to one-half of the damages recovered, but not to exceed the above compensation, after first deducting title and escrow expenses and the expenses of collection, if any. Seller hereby irrevocably assigns to Broker(s) such compensation from Seller's proceeds in escrow. In any recovered, but no to exceed the above compensation, after first deducting title and escrow expenses and the expenses of collection, if any. Seller hereby irrevocably assigns to Broker(s) such compensation from Seller's proceeds in escrow. In any action, proceeding, or arbitration relating to the payment of such compensation, the prevailing party shall be entitled to reasonable attorney's fees and costs, except as provided in paragraph 28. The undersigned Seller has read, acknowledges receipt of a copy of this agreement, and authorizes Broker(s) to deliver a signed copy to Buyer.

Date_____ Telephone_____ Fax _____ Seller_____

Real Estate Broker(s) confirm(s) agency relationship(s) as above. (Real Estate Brokers are not parties to the purchase and sale agreement between Buyer and Seller.):

Real Estate Broker (Selling) _____ By _____ Date _____

Address _____ Telephone _____ Fax_____

Real Estate Broker (Selling) _____ By _____ Date _____

Address _____ Telephone _____ Fax_____

FIGURE A.4 **REAL ESTATE PURCHASE CONTRACT** *(continued)*

FIGURE A.5

UNIFORM RESIDENTIAL LOAN APPLICATION

Uniform Residential Loan Application

This application is designed to be completed by the applicant(s) with the lender's assistance. Applicants should complete this form as "Borrower" or "Co-Borrower," as applicable. Co-Borrower information must also be provided (and the appropriate box checked) when ☐ the income or assets of a person other than the "Borrower" (including the Borrower's spouse) will be used as a basis for loan qualification or ☐ the income or assets of the Borrower's spouse will not be used as a basis for loan qualification, but his or her liabilities must be considered because the Borrower resides in a community property state, the security property is located in a community property state, or the Borrower is relying on other property located in a community property state as a basis for repayment of the loan.

I.   TYPE OF MORTGAGE AND TERMS OF LOAN

Mortgage Applied for:	☐ VA ☐ Conventional ☐ Other: ☐ FHA ☐ FmHA		Agency Case Number	Lender Case No.

Amount $	Interest Rate %	No. of Months	Amortization Type:	☐ Fixed Rate ☐ Other (explain) ☐ GPM ☐ ARM (type):

II.   PROPERTY INFORMATION AND PURPOSE OF LOAN

Subject Property Address (street, city, state, & zip code)	County	No. of Units

Legal Description of Subject Property (attach description if necessary)   Year Built

Purpose of Loan	☐ Purchase ☐ Construction ☐ Refinance ☐ Construction-Permanent	☐ Other (explain):	Property will be: ☐ Primary Residence ☐ Secondary Residence ☐ Investment

Complete this line if construction or construction-permanent loan.

Year Lot Acquired	Original Cost $	Amount Existing Liens $	(a) Present Value of Lot $	(b) Cost of Improvements $	Total (a + b) $

Complete this line if this is a refinance loan.

Year Acquired	Original Cost $	Amount Existing Liens $	Purpose of Refinance	Describe Improvements ☐ made ☐ to be made Cost: $

Title will be held in what Name(s)	Manner in which Title will be held	Estate will be held in: ☐ Fee Simple ☐ Leasehold (show expiration date)

Source of Downpayment, Closing Costs and/or Payoff Funds (explain)

III.   BORROWER INFORMATION

Borrower	Co-Borrower
Borrower's Name (include Jr. or Sr. if applicable)	Co-Borrower's Name (include Jr. or Sr. if applicable)

Social Security Number	Home Phone (incl. area code)	Age	Yrs. School	Social Security Number	Home Phone (incl. area code)	Age	Yrs. School

☐ Married ☐ Unmarried (include single, divorced, widowed) ☐ Separated	Dependents (not listed by Co-Borrower) no. ages	☐ Married ☐ Unmarried (include single, divorced, widowed) ☐ Separated	Dependents (not listed by Borrower) no. ages

Present Address (street, city, state, zip code) ☐ Own ☐ Rent _____ No. Yrs.	Present Address (street, city, state, zip code) ☐ Own ☐ Rent _____ No. Yrs.
If Mailing Address is different from above, please list on page 4.	If Mailing Address is different from above, please list on page 4.

If residing at present address for less than two years, complete the following:

Former Address (street, city, state, zip code) ☐ Own ☐ Rent _____ No. Yrs.	Former Address (street, city, state, zip code) ☐ Own ☐ Rent _____ No. Yrs.

Former Address (street, city, state, zip code) ☐ Own ☐ Rent _____ No. Yrs.	Former Address (street, city, state, zip code) ☐ Own ☐ Rent _____ No. Yrs.

IV.   EMPLOYMENT INFORMATION

Borrower	Co-Borrower

Name & Address of Employer ☐ Self-Employed	Yrs. on this job	Name & Address of Employer ☐ Self-Employed	Yrs. on this job
	Yrs. employed in this line of work/profession		Yrs. employed in this line of work/profession

Position/Title/Type of Business	Business Phone (incl. area code)	Position/Title/Type of Business	Business Phone (incl. area code)

If employed in current position for less than two years or if currently employed in more than one position, complete the following:

Name & Address of Employer ☐ Self-Employed	Dates (from-to)	Name & Address of Employer ☐ Self-Employed	Dates (from-to)
	Monthly income $		Monthly income $
Position/Title/Type of Business	Business Phone (incl. area code)	Position/Title/Type of Business	Business Phone (incl. area code)

Name & Address of Employer ☐ Self-Employed	Dates (from-to)	Name & Address of Employer ☐ Self-Employed	Dates (from-to)
	Monthly income $		Monthly income $
Position/Title/Type of Business	Business Phone (incl. area code)	Position/Title/Type of Business	Business Phone (incl. area code)

MARRIED APPLICANTS ARE HEREBY NOTIFIED THAT THEY ARE ENTITLED TO APPLY FOR A SEPARATE ACCOUNT.

Borrower's Initials X _____
Co-Borrower's Initials X _____

V. MONTHLY INCOME AND COMBINED HOUSING EXPENSE INFORMATION

Gross Monthly Income	Borrower	Co-Borrower	Total	Combined Monthly Housing Expense	Present	⑲ Proposed
⑪ Base Empl. Income*	$	$	$	Rent	$	
⑫ Overtime				First Mortgage (P & I)		$
Bonuses				⑮ Other Financing (P & I)		
Commissions				⑯ Hazard Insurance		
Dividends/Interest				Real Estate Taxes		
⑬ Net Rental Income				Mortgage Insurance		
⑭ Other (before completing, see the notice in "describe other income," below)				⑰ Homeowner Assn. Dues		
				⑱ Other:		
Total	$	$	$	Total	$	$

*Self Employed Borrower(s) may be required to provide additional documentation such as tax returns and financial statements.

Describe Other Income Notice: Alimony, child support, or separate maintenance income need not be revealed if the Borrower (B) or Co-Borrower (C) does not choose to have it considered for repaying this loan.

B/C		Monthly Amount
		$

VI. ASSETS AND LIABILITIES

This statement and any applicable supporting schedules may be completed jointly by both married and unmarried Co-Borrowers if their assets and liabilities are sufficiently joined so that the Statement can be meaningfully and fairly presented on a combined basis; otherwise separate Statements and Schedules are required. If the Co-Borrower section was completed about a spouse, this Statement and supporting schedules must be completed about that spouse also.

Completed ☐ Jointly ☐ Not Jointly

⑳ ASSETS Description	Cash or Market Value	Liabilities and Pledged Assets. List the creditor's name, address and account number for all outstanding debts, including automobile loans, revolving charge accounts, real estate loans, alimony, child support, stock pledges, etc. Use continuation sheet if necessary. Indicate by (*) those liabilities which will be satisfied upon sale of real estate owned or upon refinancing of the subject property.		
Cash deposit toward purchase held by:	$	㉓ LIABILITIES	Monthly Payt. & Mos. Left to Pay	Unpaid Balance
㉑		Name and address of Company	$ Payt./Mos.	$
List checking and savings accounts below				
Name and address of Bank, S&L, or Credit Union				
		Acct. no.		
		Name and address of Company	$ Payt./Mos.	$
Acct. no.	$			
Name and address of Bank, S&L, or Credit Union				
		Acct. no.		
		Name and address of Company	$ Payt./Mos.	$
Acct. no.	$			
Name and address of Bank, S&L, or Credit Union				
		Acct. no.		
		Name and address of Company	$ Payt./Mos.	$
Acct. no.	$			
Name and address of Bank, S&L, or Credit Union				
		Acct. no.		
		Name and address of Company	$ Payt./Mos.	$
Acct. no.	$			
Stocks & Bonds (Company name/number & description)	$			
		Acct. no.		
		Name and address of Company	$ Payt./Mos.	$
Life insurance net cash value				
Face amount: $				
Subtotal Liquid Assets	$			
㉒ Real estate owned (enter market value from schedule of real estate owned)	$	Acct. no.		
Vested interest in retirement fund	$	Name and address of Company	$ Payt./Mos.	$
Net worth of business(es) owned (attach financial statement)	$			
Automobiles owned (make and year)	$			
		Acct. no.		
Other Assets (itemize)	$	Alimony/Child Support/Separate Maintenance Payments Owed to:	$	
		Job Related Expense (child care, union dues, etc.) ㉔	$	
		Total Monthly Payments	$	
Total Assets a.	$	Net Worth (a minus b) ▶		Total Liabilities b.	$

Borrower's Initials X

Co-Borrower's Initials X

N34020

FIGURE A.5 **UNIFORM RESIDENTIAL LOAN APPLICATION** (continued)

VI. ASSETS AND LIABILITIES (cont.)

Schedule of Real Estate Owned (if additional properties are owned, use continuation sheet.)

Property Address (enter S if sold, PS if pending sale or R if rental being held for income) ▼	Type of Property	Present Market Value	Amount of Mortgages & Liens	Gross Rental Income	Mortgage Payments	Insurance, Maintenance, Taxes & Misc.	Net Rental Income
		$	$	$	$	$	$
	Totals	$	$	$	$	$	$

List any additional names under which credit has previously been received and indicate appropriate creditor name(s) and account number(s):

Alternate Name	Creditor Name	Account Number

VII. DETAILS OF TRANSACTION

a. Purchase price	$
b. Alterations, improvements, repairs	
c. Land (if acquired separately)	
d. Refinance (inc. debts to be paid off)	
e. Estimated prepaid items	
f. Estimated closing costs	
g. PMI, MIP, Funding Fee	
h. Discount (if Borrower will pay)	
i. Total costs (add items a through h)	
j. Subordinate financing	
k. Borrower's closing costs paid by Seller	
l. Other Credits (explain)	
m. Loan amount (exclude PMI, MIP, Funding Fees financed)	
n. PMI, MIP, Funding Fee financed	
o. Loan amount (add m & n)	
p. Cash from/to Borrower (subtract j, k, l, and o from i)	

VIII. DECLARATIONS

If you answer "yes" to any questions a through i, please use continuation sheet for explanation.

	Borrower Yes	Borrower No	Co-Borrower Yes	Co-Borrower No
a. Are there any outstanding judgments against you?	☐	☐	☐	☐
b. Have you been declared bankrupt within the past 10 years?	☐	☐	☐	☐
c. Have you had property foreclosed upon or given title or deed in lieu thereof in the last 7 years?	☐	☐	☐	☐
d. Are you a party to a law suit?	☐	☐	☐	☐
e. Have you directly or indirectly been obligated on any loan which resulted in foreclosure, transfer of title in lieu of foreclosure, or judgment? (This would include such loans as home mortgage loans, SBA loans, home improvement loans, educational loans, manufactured (mobile) home loans, any mortgage, financial obligation, bond, or loan guarantee. If "Yes," provide details, including date, name and address of Lender, FHA or VA case number, if any, and reasons for action.)	☐	☐	☐	☐
f. Are you presently delinquent or in default on any Federal debt or any other loan, mortgage, financial obligation, bond, or loan guarantee? If "Yes," give details as described in the preceding question.	☐	☐	☐	☐
g. Are you obligated to pay alimony, child support, or separate maintenance?	☐	☐	☐	☐
h. Is any part of the down payment borrowed?	☐	☐	☐	☐
i. Are you a co-maker or endorser on a note?	☐	☐	☐	☐
j. Are you a U.S. citizen?	☐	☐	☐	☐
k. Are you a permanent resident alien? #	☐	☐	☐	☐
l. Do you intend to occupy the property as your primary residence? If "Yes," complete question m below.	☐	☐	☐	☐
m. Have you had an ownership interest in a property in the last three years?	☐	☐	☐	☐
(1) What type of property did you own—principal residence (PR), second home (SH), or investment property (IP)?				
(2) How did you hold title to the home—solely by yourself (S), jointly with your spouse (SP), or jointly with another person (O)?				

IX. ACKNOWLEDGEMENT AND AGREEMENT

The undersigned specifically acknowledge(s) and agree(s) that: (1) the loan requested by this application will be secured by a first mortgage or deed of trust on the property described herein; (2) the property will not be used for any illegal or prohibited purpose or use; (3) all statements made in this application are made for the purpose of obtaining the loan indicated herein; (4) occupancy of the property will be as indicated above; (5) verification or reverification of any information contained in the application may be made at any time by the Lender, its agents, successors and assigns, either directly or through a credit reporting agency, from any source named in this application, and the original copy of this application will be retained by the Lender, even if the loan is not approved; (6) the Lender, its agents, successors and assigns will rely on the information contained in the application and I/we have a continuing obligation to amend and/or supplement the information provided in this application if any of the material facts which I/we have represented herein should change prior to closing; (7) in the event my/our payments on the loan indicated in this application become delinquent, the Lender, its agents, successors and assigns, may, in addition to all their other rights and remedies, report my/our name(s) and account information to a credit reporting agency; (8) ownership of the loan may be transferred to successor or assign of the Lender without notice to me and/or the administration of the loan account may be transferred to an agent, successor or assign of the Lender with prior notice to me; (9) the Lender, its agents, successors and assigns make no representations or warranties, express or implied, to the Borrower(s) regarding the property, the condition of the property, or the value of the property.

Certification: I/We certify that the information provided in this application is true and correct as of the date set forth opposite my/our signature(s) on this application and acknowledge my/our understanding that any intentional or negligent misrepresentation(s) of the information contained in this application may result in civil liability and/or criminal penalties including, but not limited to, fine or imprisonment or both under the provisions of Title 18, United States Code, Section 1001, et seq. and liability for monetary damages to the Lender, its agents, successors and assigns, insurers and any other person who may suffer any loss due to reliance upon any misrepresentation which I/we have made on this application.

Borrower's Signature	Date	Co-Borrower's Signature	Date
X		X	

X. INFORMATION FOR GOVERNMENT MONITORING PURPOSES

The following information is requested by the Federal Government for certain types of loans relating to a dwelling, in order to monitor the Lender's compliance with equal credit opportunity, fair housing and home mortgage disclosure laws. You are not required to furnish this information, but are encouraged to do so. The law provides that a Lender may neither discriminate on the basis of this information, nor on whether you choose to furnish it. However, if you choose not to furnish it, and you apply in person, under Federal regulations this Lender is required to note race and sex on the basis of visual observation or surname. If you do not wish to furnish the above information, please check the box below.

BORROWER ☐ I do not wish to furnish this information.

Race/National Origin: ☐ American Indian or Alaskan Native ☐ Asian or Pacific Islander ☐ Black, not of Hispanic origin ☐ White, not of Hispanic origin ☐ Hispanic ☐ Other (specify)

Sex: ☐ Female ☐ Male

CO-BORROWER ☐ I do not wish to furnish this information.

Race/National Origin: ☐ American Indian or Alaskan Native ☐ Asian or Pacific Islander ☐ Black, not of Hispanic origin ☐ White, not of Hispanic origin ☐ Hispanic ☐ Other (specify)

Sex: ☐ Female ☐ Male

This application was taken by:
☐ face-to-face interview
☐ mail
☐ telephone

Interviewer's Name (print or type)	Name and Address of Interviewer's Employer
	☐ Bank of America
Interviewer's Signature Date	☐ Loan Agent for Bank of America.
Interviewer's Phone Number (incl. area code)	☐ Other (specify)

Borrower's Initials X
Co-Borrower's Initials X

N34030

FIGURE A.5 **UNIFORM RESIDENTIAL LOAN APPLICATION** (continued)

261

Continuation Sheet/Uniform Residential Loan Application

Use this continuation sheet if you need more space to complete the Residential Loan Application. Mark B for Borrower or C for Co-Borrower.	Borrower:	Agency Case Number:
	Co-Borrower:	Lender Case Number:

If Mailing Address is different from property address, please list below (street, city, state & zip code)

I/We fully understand that it is a Federal crime punishable by fine or imprisonment, or both, to knowingly make any false statements concerning any of the above facts as applicable under the provisions of Title 18, United States Code, Section 1001, et seq.

Borrower's Signature	Date	Co-Borrower's Signature	Date
X		X	

Borrower's Initials X _____
Co-Borrower's Initials X _____

N34040

FIGURE A.5 **UNIFORM RESIDENTIAL LOAN APPLICATION** (continued)

FIGURE A.6

STATEMENT OF ASSETS AND LIABILITIES

Statement of Assets and Liabilities
(Supplement to Residential Loan Application)

Name

The following information is provided to complete and become a part of the application for a mortgage in the amount of $

with interest at _____ % for a term of _____ months and to be secured by property known as:

Subject Property Address (street, city, state, & zip code)

Legal Description of Subject Property (attach description if necessary)

ASSETS AND LIABILITIES

This statement and any applicable supporting schedules may be completed jointly by both married and unmarried Co-Borrowers if their assets and liabilities are sufficiently joined so that the Statement can be meaningfully and fairly presented on a combined basis; otherwise separate Statements and Schedules are required. If the Co-Borrower section was completed about a spouse, this Statement and supporting schedules must be completed about that spouse also.

Completed ☐ Jointly   ☐ Not Jointly

ASSETS	Cash or Market Value	Liabilities and Pledged Assets. List the creditor's name, address and account number for all outstanding debts, including automobile loans, revolving charge accounts, real estate loans, alimony, child support, stock pledges, etc. Use continuation sheet, if necessary. Indicate by (*) those liabilities which will be satisfied upon sale of real estate owned or upon refinancing of the subject property.	Monthly Payt. & Mos. Left to Pay	Unpaid Balance
Description		**LIABILITIES**		
Cash deposit toward purchase held by:	$	Name and address of Company	$ Payt./Mos.	$
List checking and savings accounts below				
Name and address of Bank, S&L, or Credit Union				
		Acct. no.		
		Name and address of Company	$ Payt./Mos.	$
Acct. no.	$			
Name and address of Bank, S&L, or Credit Union				
		Acct. no.		
		Name and address of Company	$ Payt./Mos.	$
Acct. no.	$			
Name and address of Bank, S&L, or Credit Union				
		Acct. no.		
		Name and address of Company	$ Payt./Mos.	$
Acct. no.	$			
Name and address of Bank, S&L, or Credit Union				
		Acct. no.		
		Name and address of Company	$ Payt./Mos.	$
Acct. no.	$			
Stocks & Bonds (Company name/number & description)	$			
		Acct. no.		
		Name and address of Company	$ Payt./Mos.	$
Life insurance net value	$			
Face amount: $				
Subtotal Liquid Assets	$			
Real estate owned (enter market value from schedule of real estate owned)	$			
		Acct. no.		
Vested interest in retirement fund	$	Name and address of Company	$ Payt./Mos.	$
Net worth of business(es) owned (attach financial statement)	$			
Automobiles owned (make and year)	$			
		Acct. no.		
Other Assets (itemize)	$	Alimony/Child Support/Separate Maintenance Payments Owed to:	$	
		Job Related Expense (child care, union dues, etc.)	$	
		Total Monthly Payments	$	
Total Assets a.	$	**Net Worth (a minus b)** ▶	**Total Liabilities b.**	$

Borrower's Initials _____

Co-Borrowers Initials _____

Schedule of Real Estate Owned (If additional properties are owned, use continuation sheet.)

Property Address (enter S if sold, PS if pending sale or R if rental being held for income) ▼	Type of Property	Present Market Value	Amount of Mortgages & Liens	Gross Rental Income	Mortgage Payments	Insurance, Maintenance, Taxes & Misc.	Net Rental Income
		$	$	$	$	$	$
	Totals	$	$	$	$	$	$

List any additional names under which credit has previously been received and indicate appropriate creditor name(s) and account number(s):

Alternate Name	Creditor Name	Account Number

ACKNOWLEDGEMENT AND AGREEMENT

The undersigned specifically acknowledge(s) and agree(s) that: (1) the loan requested by this application will be secured by a first mortgage or deed of trust on the property described herein; (2) the property will not be used for any illegal or prohibited purpose or use; (3) all statements made in this application are made for the purpose of obtaining the loan indicated herein; (4) occupancy of the property will be as indicated above; (5) verification or reverification of any information contained in the application may be made at any time by the Lender, its agents, successors and assigns, either directly or through a credit reporting agency, from any source named in this application, and the original copy of this application will be retained by the Lender, even if the loan is not approved; (6) the Lender, its agents, successors and assigns will rely on the information contained in the application and I/we have a continuing obligation to amend and/or supplement the information provided in this application if any of the material facts which I/we have represented herein should change prior to closing; (7) in the event my/our payments on the loan indicated in this application become delinquent, the Lender, its agents, successors and assigns, may, in addition to all their other rights and remedies, report my/our name(s) and account information to a credit reporting agency; (8) ownership of the loan may be transferred to successor or assign of the Lender without notice to me and/or the administration of the loan account may be transferred to an agent, successor or assign of the Lender with prior notice to me; (9) the Lender, its agents, successors and assigns make no representations or warranties, express or implied, to the Borrower(s) regarding the property, the condition of the property, or the value of the property.
Certification: I/We certify that the information provided in this application is true and correct as of the date set forth opposite my/our signature(s) on this application and acknowledge my/our understanding that any intentional or negligent misrepresentation(s) of the information contained in this application may result in civil liability and/or criminal penalties including, but not limited to, fine or imprisonment or both under the provisions of Title 18, United States Code, Section 1001, et seq. and liability for monetary damages to the Lender, its agents, successors and assigns, insurers and any other person who may suffer any loss due to reliance upon any misrepresentation which I/we have made on this application.

Borrower's Signature	Date	Co-Borrower's Signature	Date
X		X	

TO BE COMPLETED BY INTERVIEWER

Interviewer's Name (print or type)	Name and Address of Interviewer's Employer
This application was taken by:	☐ Bank of America NT&SA
☐ face-to-face interview	☐
Interviewer's Signature Date	Loan Agent for Bank of America NT&SA
☐ mail	☐ Bank of America Oregon
☐ telephone	
Interviewer's Phone Number (incl. area code)	☐ Other (specify)

Borrower's Initials_____
Co-Borrower's Initials_____

APPENDIX

FIGURE A.7

REQUEST FOR VERIFICATION OF DEPOSIT

INSTRUCTIONS TO LENDER:
1. Fill out Part I - Request
2. Have Applicant(s) sign each copy (no carbon signatures)
3. Forward both copies to Depository

VMP MORTGAGE FORMS • (800)521-7291

Ply 1 Printed on Recycled Paper

INSTRUCTIONS TO DEPOSITORY
1. Complete Part II - Verification
2. Return both completed copies to Lender

-47 (8908).02

OMB No. 2502-0059

DEPARTMENT OF VETERANS AFFAIRS AND U.S. DEPARTMENT OF HOUSING AND URBAN DEVELOPMENT
HUD COMMUNITY PLANNING AND DEVELOPMENT
HUD HOUSING - FEDERAL HOUSING COMMISSIONER
REQUEST FOR VERIFICATION OF DEPOSIT

PRIVACY ACT NOTICE STATEMENT - This information is to be used by the agency collecting it in determining whether you qualify as a prospective mortgagor for mortgage insurance or guaranty or as a borrower for a rehabilitation loan under the agency's program. It will not be disclosed outside the agency without your consent except to financial institutions for verification of your deposits and as required and permitted by law. You do not have to give us this information, but, if you do not, your application for approval as a prospective mortgagor for mortgage insurance or guaranty or as a borrower for a rehabilitation loan may be delayed or rejected. This information request is authorized by Title 38, U.S.C., Chapter 37 *(if VA)*; by 12 U.S.C., Section 1701 et seq., *(if HUD/FHA)*; and by 42 U.S.C., Section 1452b *(if HUD/CPD)*.

INSTRUCTIONS

LENDER OR LOCAL PROCESSING AGENCY: Complete Items 1 through 8. Have applicant(s) complete Item 9. Forward directly to the Depository named in Item 1. DEPOSITORY: Please complete Items 10 through 15 and return DIRECTLY to Lender or Local Processing agency named in Item 2.

PART I REQUEST

1. TO *(Name and Address of Depository)*	2. FROM *(Name and Address of Lender or Local Processing Agency)*

I certify that this verification has been sent directly to the bank or depository and has not passed through the hands of the applicant or any other party.

3. Signature of Lender or Official of Local Processing Agency	4. Title	5. Date	6. Lender's Number *(Optional)*

7. INFORMATION TO BE VERIFIED

Type of Account and/or loan	Account/Loan in Name of	Account/Loan Number	Balance
			$
			$
			$
			$

TO DEPOSITORY: I have applied for mortgage insurance or guaranty or for a rehabilitation loan and stated that the balance on deposit and /or outstanding loans with you are as shown above. You are authorized to verify this information and to supply the lender or the local processing agency identified above with the information requested in Items 10 through 12. Your response is solely a matter of courtesy for which no responsibility is attached to your institution or any of your officers.

8. NAME AND ADDRESS OF APPLICANT(S)	9. SIGNATURE OF APPLICANT(S)
	X
	X

TO BE COMPLETED BY DEPOSITORY
PART II - VERIFICATION OF DEPOSITORY
10. DEPOSIT ACCOUNTS OF APPLICANT(S)

Type of Account	Account Number	Current Balance	Average Balance for Previous Two Months	Date Opened
		$	$	
		$	$	
		$	$	
		$	$	

11. LOANS OUTSTANDING TO APPLICANT(S)

Loan Number	Date of Loan	Original Amount	Current Balance	Installments (Monthly/Quarterly)	Secured by	Number of Late Payments within Last 12 months
		$	$	$ per		
		$	$	$ per		
		$	$	$ per		

12. ADDITIONAL INFORMATION WHICH MAY BE OF ASSISTANCE IN DETERMINATION OF CREDIT WORTHINESS: *Please include information on loans paid-in-full as in Item 11 above)*

13. Signature of Depository Official	14. Title	15. Date
X		

The confidentiality of the information you have furnished will be preserved except where disclosure of this information is required by applicable law. The completed form is to be transmitted directly to the lender or local processing agency and is not to be transmitted through the applicant or any other party.

-47 (8908).02

VA-26-8497;a (7-80) HUD-92004-F (11-85) HB 4155.1

A P P E N D I X

FIGURE A.8

REQUEST FOR VERIFICATION OF EMPLOYMENT

EMPLOYER-RETURN BOTH COMPLETED COPIES TO LENDER
LENDER-DETACH THIS COPY AND FILE FOR FOLLOW-UP

RESOURCES

The following companies and government agencies can provide additional information.

APPRAISAL INFORMATION

Appraisal Institute
875 N. Michigan Avenue, Suite 2400
Chicago, IL 60611-1980
(312) 335-4100

Issues MAI and SRA designations. Will provide a list of members upon request.

American Society of Appraisers
555 Herndon Parkway, Suite 125
Herdon, VA 20170
(704) 478-2228

Private organization to which appraisers belong.

Appraisal Foundation
1029 Vermont Avenue NW, Suite 900
Washington, DC 20005-3517
(202) 347-7722

Private nonprofit foundation funded by 14 separate appraisal organizations. Sets uniform standards for appraisers. Offers training as well as subscription service for "what's happening" in the appraisal field.

CO-OP LENDING

National Cooperative Bank (NCB)
1630 Connecticut Avenue, NW
Washington, DC 20009
(202) 336-7700
Will provide information on co-op lending services.

CREDIT COUNSELING

Consumer Credit Counseling
(800) 388-2227
Will provide phone numbers for credit counselors in your area.

CREDIT REPORTING

Equifax
P.O. Box 740256
Atlanta, GA 30374
(800) 685-1111
Will provide free credit report to consumers whose credit is denied.

TRW
P.O. Box 2350
Chatsworth, CA 91313-2350
(800) 682-7654
Will provide free credit card report once a year.

HOME INSPECTIONS

American Society of Home Inspectors (ASHI)
85 W. Algonquin Road
Arlington Heights, IL 60005-4423
Will provide information on home inspections.

HOME WARRANTY

National Home Warranty Association (NHWA)
20 Ellerman Road
Lake St. Louis, MO 63367
(800) 325-8144
Private organization to which warranty companies belong.

For a free brochure on home warranties, send a self-addressed, stamped envelope to:

> NHWA/Fischman Public Relations
> 1141 Lake Cook Road, Suite C-1
> Deerfield, IL 60015
> (847) 945-1300

GOVERNMENT OR GOVERNMENT-ASSOCIATED AGENCIES

Federal National Mortgage Association (Fannie Mae)
Consumer Information and Education
3900 Wisconsin Avenue, NW
Washington, DC 20016
(202) 752-7000
   Will provide free information on loans and home buying.

Government National Mortgage Association (Ginnie Mae)
c/o HUD Consumer Information
451-7th Street SW
Washington, DC 20410
(202) 708-0926
   Will provide free information on loans and home buying.

Fair Housing Information Clearing House
P.O. Box 6091
Rockville, MD 20850
(800) 343-3442
   Will provide free brochures on numerous aspects of home buying, fair housing, and lending.

Federal Consumer Information Center
Pueblo, CO 81009
(719) 948-3334
   Will provide free catalog of information and brochures published by the government (thousands of free listings).

Federal Housing Administration (FHA)
Washington, DC 20410
(202) 401-0388

Will provide information on the many FHA loans available for home purchases and home improvements.

US Department of Housing and Urban Development (HUD)
451 7th Street SW, Room B100
Washington, DC 20410
(800) 767-7468 Fax (202) 708-2313

Will provide free information on housing and handles complaints of discrimination. Will also provide a list of HUD offices in your area.

US Department of Veteran's Affairs (VA)
810 Vermont Avenue, NW
Washington, DC 20420
(202) 273-5400

Will provide information on VA loans or other services available for qualified veterans.

GLOSSARY

Absentee Owner: A person who owns property and resides elsewhere, usually in another community.

Abstract of Title: A summary of all conveyances, transfers, and other facts (of record) relied on as evidence of title or that which would impair title of real property.

Acceleration: To hasten or speed up an event that normally would have occurred at a later date.

Acceleration Clause: A clause or provision in an agreement (note, deed of trust, mortgage) which would hasten or speed up the date of maturity (shall become all due and payable) upon the occurrence of a certain event.

Acceptance: The voluntary act of receiving something tangible or the voluntary agreement to specific terms and conditions.

Access Right: The right of a landowner to have "ingress to" and "egress from" privileges and right of way from his/her property to a public street.

Accretion: The gradual and imperceptible addition of land on a shore or riverbank by the natural action of water.

Accrue: The growing, adding to, accumulating, or causing to come into fact or existence.

Accrued Interest: All interest accumulated and unpaid to date.

Acknowledgment: A formal declaration made before an authorized official (usually notary public), by the person who has executed (signed) a document, that such execution is his or her own act and deed. In most instances, document must be acknowledged (notarized) before it can be accepted for recording.

Acquisition: The act of obtaining property; becoming an owner.

Acre: A measure of land equal to 160 rods, 4,840 square yards, 43,560 square feet, or 208.71 linear feet square.

Action: A judicial proceeding wherein one party prosecutes another for protection or enforcement of a right, the prevention or redress of a wrong, or the punishment of a public offense.

Action to Quiet Title (Quiet Title Action): A court action to remove a "cloud" from the title or to determine the actual status of the title.

Adjustable Rate Mortgage: Any real estate loan in which the interest rate varies over time according to a prescribed formula or set of conditions, usually changes in economic conditions (also known as a variable rate mortgage).

Adjusted Basis: The cost or value of property for taxation purposes after allowable expenses are deducted.

Administrator: A male who has been appointed (by the court) to handle the affairs of an estate for a person who died intestate (without a will).

Administratrix: A female who has been appointed (by the court) to handle the affairs of an estate for a person who died intestate (without a will).

Affiant: A person who makes and subscribes to a statement under oath; makes an affidavit.

Affidavit: A written statement taken under oath before an officer of the court or a notary public.

Affidavit of Mailing: Certifies that a copy of the Substitution of Trustee has been mailed (prior to its recordation) to all parties who also would receive a copy of any recorded Notice of Default.

Affidavit of Personal Service: In lieu of the record trustee's acknowledgment or an affidavit of publication of notice, this certifies that a copy of the Substitution of Trustee was personally served on the trustee who is being replaced.

Affirmation: A written declaration under penalty of perjury.

Agency: A relationship where one person acts (with authority) on behalf of another.

Agent: Someone who has the authority to represent another (the principal).

Agreement of Sale: An agreement entered into between two or more parties for the sale and purchase of property.

AKA: Abbreviation for "also known as."

Alienate: To voluntarily transfer one's interest in real property.

Alienation: The voluntary transfer of one's real property.

Alienation Clause: A provision in a note or a security document that automatically calls for maturity of the note (all due and payable) in the event of sale or title transfer by the borrower.

Allegation: An assertion or statement of fact in a pleading that the contributing party is prepared to prove.

All-Inclusive Deed of Trust: A security document for a new encumbrance that encompasses an existing debt ("wraparound" or secures payment of a senior or prior deed of trust). Upon recordation, the all-inclusive deed of trust is junior to said existing lien: also known as a "wrap-around deed of trust" or "wraparound mortgage."

A.L.T.A.: Abbreviation for the American Land Title Association.

Amenities: A property's desirable or attractive features; visible and/or hidden.

Amortization: The gradual payoff of a debt through regular and scheduled payments of principal and interest over a stated period of time until paid in full.

Amount of Judgment: The dollar amount awarded as settlement by the court.

Ancillary: Something that is "in addition to" or auxiliary to the main body or subject.

And When Recorded Mail To: After recording, the document will be mailed by the county to the addressee shown.

Annexation: The addition of property to an area already established by boundaries; the joining of one property to another.

Annuity: A payment of money made annually for a specified term.

Annum: A year, as in a period of time (per annum/per year).

Ante: A Latin prefix meaning "before."

Appearance: The presence of a party in court: either through summons or on a voluntary basis.

Appellant: One who files an appeal in a court of law.

Appraisal: An opinion or statement (written or oral) of the value of property.

Appraiser: A person who is qualified to determine the relative value of property.

Appreciation: An increase in the value of property.

Appurtenance: Anything incidental to, belonging to, or attached to land and therefore considered a part of the property (be it real property or a burden such as a covenant or an easement).

Appurtenant: "Incidental to," "belonging to," or "attached to."

Arbitrary Map: An unofficial parcel map made by a title company for its own convenience in identifying parcels of land; sometimes known as ARB MAP.

Arbitrator: An impartial person chosen by the parties in a dispute to resolve and make a final determination of the issues.

Assessed Value: Value of property for taxation purposes as determined by the tax assessor.

Assessments: Specific and special taxes (in addition to normal taxes) imposed on real property to pay for public improvements within a specific geographical area.

Assessor: The county official who determines the value of property for taxation purposes.

Assessor's Parcel Number (APN): Number assigned by the county assessor. In some counties, it must appear on the document as a prerequisite to recording.

Assets: Any property (real or personal) with value.

Assign: To transfer all of one's interest in property.

Assignee: The person to whom property interest has been assigned or transferred.

Assignor: The person who is transferring or assigning an interest in property.

Assumpsit: A promise or undertaking (expressed or implied, oral or written) to do an act or make a payment.

Assumption Agreement: An agreement to assume or take responsibility for a debt or obligation that was contracted originally by another person.

Assumption Fee: The fee charged by a lender when a buyer assumes or takes responsibility for an existing loan.

Assumption of Loan (Mortgage or Deed of Trust): An agreement wherein the buyer assumes or takes responsibility (becomes liable) for payment of an existing note secured by a mortgage or deed of trust.

ATA Title Policy: An American Title Association insurance policy that has greater coverage than a standard policy because it includes unrecorded liens and encumbrances.

Attachment: A judicial process wherein a creditor obtains a lien upon property prior to adjudication of the debt.

Attest: To bear witness to the execution of a document, to affirm as true.

Attestation Clause: A clause within a deed stating that the subscribing persons are witnesses in fact.

Attorn: The acceptance and acknowledgment of a new landlord.

Attorney-in-Fact: Identifies the party(s) (attorney-in-fact) designated to act on behalf of the principal as specified in a Power of Attorney. Identifies the party(s) whose specific authority is being revoked in the Revocation of Power of Attorney.

Authorization: The official statement of approval for the attorney-in-fact to act for the principal.

Avulsion: The sudden tearing away of land by the violent action of river or other watercourse; the abrupt change in the course of a waterbed that forms a boundary between two parcels of land, resulting in a change of land for each parcel (a gain for one and a loss for the other).

Balance Sheet: A statement of financial condition showing assets, liabilities, and net worth as of a specific time.

Balloon Payment: Any payment that is greater than twice the amount of the normal and periodic payment. Generally used to refer to the final payment of a note with an advanced due date.

Bankruptcy: A legal process in the U.S. District Court wherein assets of the debtor are liquidated to pay off the claims of his or her creditors.

Base Lines: Imaginary lines running east-west that intersect meridians (imaginary lines between the North and South poles) to form a starting point for the survey or measurement of land.

Basis: Usually the property owner's original cost, plus capital improvements, less depreciation, computed for income tax purposes according to one of many possible formulas. Also known as book value.

Benchmark: A durable and reliable location marker used by land surveyors.

Beneficiary: Generally, one who is in receipt of benefit, profit, or advantage. Used to identify the party to whom the trustor is obligated—usually the lender or the person intended to benefit from a trust.

Beneficiary Information — Notice of Default: The name, address, and phone number of the beneficiary who should be contacted to determine the amount necessary to reinstate or pay off the deed of trust in foreclosure.

Beneficiary Receives Damage Award: In the event the property or a portion of the property is condemned for public use, any award of damages connected with such action is assigned (by the trustor) to the beneficiary, who may apply said award to any indebtedness secured or, at beneficiary's option, may release the entire award, or a portion thereof, to the trustor.

Beneficiary's Demand: Usually the full payment (remaining balance including any accrued interest charges) required by a beneficiary (under a deed of trust) before authorizing a reconveyance.

Beneficiary's Statement: Statement by the beneficiary as to the principal balance due on a promissory note secured by a deed of trust. It also may contain other pertinent loan information. Also known as bene statement or offset statement.

Beneficiary Under the Deed or Trust: Identifies the present beneficiary on the Substitution of Trustee document.

Bequeath: The act of making a gift of personal property through a will.

Bilateral Contract: An agreement wherein promises are exchanged between the two parties.

Bill of Sale: A written instrument that transfers title of personal property from one person to another.

Binder: Memorandum of agreement to issue insurance that provides temporary coverage until the complete and formal policy can be issued; something that obligates or constrains the bound individual.

Blanket Deed of Trust or Mortgage: A security document that binds more than one parcel of land as the security for the loan obligation.

Blanket Policy: An insurance policy covering an entire subdivision for which individual policies are issued on separate parcels.

Blighted Area: A neighborhood in which the property values are declining due to economic or natural forces such as inharmonious property usages, rapidly depreciating buildings, and/or an influx of "undesirable inhabitants."

Body of Document: Generally, the main or operative text of provisions within a legal instrument.

Bona: Latin, meaning "good, virtuous."

Bona Fide: Made in good faith.

Bona Fide Purchaser: A person who purchases in good faith for a valuable consideration and has no notice of outstanding rights or claims of any third-party members.

Bond: A written agreement with sureties that guarantees faithful performance of acts or duties, including the payment of a certain sum of money.

Bonded Debt: A debt contracted under the obligation of a bond.

Breach: The breaking of a law, contract, or duty by omission or commission.

Brief: A written argument of legal points used by an attorney to convey to the court the essential facts of his or her client's case.

Broker: A person who brings parties together and assists in negotiating contracts between them for a commission or fee.

Building Code: A set of regulations setting forth minimum building construction standards in a city, county, or state.

Building Contract: An agreement for the construction or improvement of a structure.

Building Lines: Imaginary lines established by ordinance or by statute beyond which the building of structures is not permitted; also known as setback lines.

Building Restrictions: Zoning ordinances and regulatory laws that require that construction be protective of people's health and safety.

By-Law: A standing rule governing the regulation of a corporation's or society's internal affairs.

Call: To require payment of loaned money on demand.

Capacity: A person's capability or qualifications to enter into agreements —by being competent, of sound mind or legal age, etc.

Capita: Meaning "heads" or "persons," as in per capita or per person.

Capital Gain: Profit gained from the increase in value of a capital asset.

Capitalization: The process of amassing the funds necessary to purchase a property. Also, a means of appraising that determines the value of property by estimating net annual income and dividing by a capitalization rate; the "cap rate" usually is determined from current market prices.

Capital Loss: Loss resulting from the sale of an asset for a dollar amount below its purchase price or adjusted basis.

Caption: Heading or introduction to the main body of document that identifies the parties of interest.

Carryback: Usually known as seller carryback; seller acts as a lender of purchase money and holds or carries-back a loan for the purchaser.

Case Number: The case number as assigned by the court. Some documents also contain an explanation of the purpose of the document, which, for all practical purposes, becomes the title for the document.

Cause (of Action): A claim in law with sufficient facts to demand judicial attention; an action or suit.

Cautionary Notes — Rights in Foreclosure: Notations within a document regarding foreclosure due to default, rights to reinstate, rights to stop foreclosure, and the amount necessary to reinstate the obligations secured by the deed of trust under foreclosure.

Cautionary Note — Seek Legal Counsel: Note to all parties that legal rights and duties are established through the execution of this contract, and, therefore, all parties are advised to seek independent and legal counsel.

Cautionary Note — Subordination Agreement: Note to the subordinating party as to the effect of the Subordination Agreement on his or her security interest (becomes subject to and of lower priority than the new Deed of Trust).

Caveat: Latin, meaning "let him beware."

Caveat Emptor: Latin, meaning "let the buyer beware." This is the basic rule of commerce and law: The purchaser buys at his or her own risk.

Certificate of Sale: Document issued as evidence of purchaser's acquisition of legal title at a judicial sale, subject to redemption rights, if any exist.

Certificate of Title: Document issued as evidence of land ownership according to examination of record title.

Certification: Certification by a deputy of the clerk of the Superior Court that the decree is a full, true, and correct copy of the original on file in the clerk's office. The date of filing and entering of the document in the judgment books is also shown (a requirement for recordation).

Chain of Title: The chronological list of recorded documents affecting title to a specific parcel of real property.

Change of Venue: The movement of a trial from one judicial jurisdiction to another.

Character of the Property: A description of the nature or character of the property being homesteaded. Examples of character would include: nature of residence (single family or multiresidential), type of construction (stucco, brick, frame), etc.

Chattel: Any tangible, movable, personal property article.

Chattel Mortgage: An obsolete name for a mortgage or security interest in personal property.

Chattel Real: An interest in real property that is less than a freehold or fee interest (estate at sufferance, etc.)

Chose: A thing either presently possessed or claimed as a possession.

Chose in Action: A claim or debt of which recovery may be made in a lawsuit.

Civil Law: Roman law currently used in most Western states; also distinguishes noncriminal (civil) and criminal law.

Claim: The assertion of a right to money or property.

Class Action: A lawsuit wherein the plaintiff is bringing suit on behalf of all persons in similar situations.

Clear Title: A title that is free from any encumbrance, obstruction, or limitation that would "cloud the title."

Closing: Closing of escrow; the final act of a transaction wherein papers are signed, monies are exchanged, and the title is transferred.

Closing Costs: The expenses incurred in a real estate transaction including costs or title examination, title insurance, attorney's fees, lender's service charges, documentary transfer tax, etc.

Cloud of Title: An outstanding claim of title that has yet to be proven invalid.

Coadministrator: One of two or more administrators.

Code: A systematic compilation or collection of laws on a specified subject, organized for clarity and understanding.

Codicil: An instrument that amends a will without revoking it. A codicil may add to, enlarge, alter, restrict, qualify, etc.

Coexecutor: One of two or more executors.

Collateral: The property secured as a security interest for a debt.

Collateral Assignment: The transfer of interest in personal property for security reasons.

Collusion: An attempt by two or more people to defraud another of his or her rights.

Color of Title: Lending the appearance of title; an instrument that appears to pass title when, in effect, there is no legal basis for said title transfer.

Commercial Acre: In land development terms, that net portion of an acre remaining after deducting areas devoted to streets, sidewalks, etc.

Commissioner's Deed: A deed executed by a court-appointed official in consummation of a court-ordered sale.

Commitment: Something given in trust; a pledge, promise, a firm agreement. A title insurer's contractual obligation to insure title to real property.

Common Law: The English system of jurisprudence that is based on judicial precedent rather than legislative enactments; therefore, it is generally derived from principles rather than rules.

Community Property: Property acquired after marriage by either party (husband or wife), other than by gift or by inheritance.

Competent: The capacity to reason, understand, and do a certain thing; therefore, the capacity to enter into a contract with legal basis.

Completion Bond: A bond posted by a contractor as a guarantee that he or she will satisfactorily complete a project and it will be free of any liens.

Composition: Negotiated agreement between a debtor and creditors wherein the creditors each agree to mutually accept a certain percentage less than is due or an altered payment schedule and/or structure.

Comprehensive Coverage: An insurance policy that covers a range of contingencies.

Conclusive Presumption: A conclusion drawn by a court of law from a set of facts that cannot be overcome by contrary proof.

Concurrent: To run together, in conjunction with; as in concurrent closing of a new Deed of Trust and a Subordination Agreement; must record together.

Condemnation: Under the laws of eminent domain, a municipality takes over private property for public use. Also: Result of official determination that the building is unfit for human habitation.

Condemnation Guarantee: A document executed as evidence of title issued to a governmental agency naming defendants in an eminent domain proceeding.

Condition: A qualification or restriction attached to the conveyance of property wherein it is predetermined that upon the occurrence of a specified event, an estate shall commence, enlarge, or be defeated.

Conditional Sales Contract: Also known as a Contract of Sale or a Land Sales Contract; title remains in the name of the vendor (seller) until the vendee (buyer) fulfills all the conditions of the contract.

Condition Precedent: A condition wherein an act or event must exist or occur before a right accrues or an estate vests.

Condition Subsequent: A condition that defeats a previously vested estate or accrued right.

Condominium: Fee ownership of an individual unit (within the confines of the perimeter walls) and tenants-in-common ownership in all the underlying fees and in the common building and grounds designated for use for all the unit owners.

Confirmation of Sale: Court approval of a sale through a personal representative, guardian, or conservator.

Congressional Grant: A grant of public land or the United States via an act of Congress.

Conservatee: A person without capacity to care for self and/or property and for whom the probate court has appointed a conservator.

Conservator: A person appointed by the probate court to handle the affairs (take care of person and/or property) of a conservatee.

Consideration: Something of value that is given in return for a specific performance or a promise of performance by another in the formation of a contract.

Constructive: That which is not actual but is accepted in law as if it actually were real; inferred or implied.

Constructive Notice: Public notice given by public records.

Constructive Trust: A trust imposed by law to prevent unjust enrichment or to redress a wrong.

Contiguous: That which is bordering, touching, adjacent to.

Contingency: An item in a contract dependent on a specific condition for its fulfillment.

Contingent: That which is dependent on a future event that may never occur.

Contingent Beneficiary: A person who may or may not share in an estate or trust based on the occurrence of a specific yet uncertain event.

Contingent Estate: An interest in land that may or may not begin at some time in the future based on the occurrence of specific, yet uncertain event.

Contingent Interest: An interest in an estate that may or may not occur at some time in the future based on the occurrence of a specific yet uncertain event.

Contract: A promise, or a set of promises; an agreement to do or not to do certain things, as between two or more parties.

Contract of Sale: Also known as a Conditional Sales Contract and a Land Contract of Sales; title remains in the name of the vendor (seller) until the vendee (buyer) fulfills certain conditions of the contract.

Convey: To transfer title to property from one person to another.

Conveyance: A written document that transfers title to property from one person to another.

Co-Owner — Pertinent Information: Sets forth the full name and address of anyone holding title to the property as co-owner with the person giving notice. This applies only if title is held as joint tenants or tenants-in-common. If there are no co-owners, the word "none" should be inserted.

Corporate Seal: The purpose of a seal is to attest in a formal manner the execution of a document; thus a corporate seal attests said execution by the corporation.

Corporation: An artificial being created by law and endowed with certain rights, privileges, and duties of natural person, yet is entirely separate and distinct from the individuals who compose it. A corporation has the unique quality of continuous existence or succession.

Corporeal Hereditaments: Anything that can be inherited, including real or personal property or a combination of both.

Cost: The actual purchase price paid for a property.

Cotenancy: Ownership interests by two or more persons.

Cotrustee: One of two or more trustees.

Counteroffer: A new offer as to price, terms, and/or conditions, made in reply to and supersedes a prior offer.

County Recorder's Stamps: The large stamp reflects the recording reference of the document and makes reference to the names of the county and the county recorder. The smaller stamps are placed on the document by the clerk in the county recorder's office.

Courses and Distances: Description of land measurement, angles, and parameters by metes and bounds.

Court Identification: Identifies the court and the judicial district number where the court case was conducted.

Court Seal: The official seal of the court handling the case is placed over the date of issuance of the abstract.

Covenant: To enter into a formal agreement to do or not to do a certain thing; a promise.

Coverage: Items insured under a policy. "Additional coverage" refers to extra premiums charged where extraordinary risk or labor is involved in issuance of a policy.

Creditor: One to whom a debt is owed; a person who grants credit.

Credit Report: A report on the credit history of a person or business.

Custody: The personal control, care, guarding, inspection, preservation, and security of a property or person under the delegated authority and responsibility of the custodian.

Cut Out: A parcel or a portion of a property taken or "cut out" from a larger parcel on an arbitrary map.

Damages: The amount of money ordered by a court to be paid to a person who sustained an injury, either to property, person, or relative rights, through the actions or failures to act of another.

Date Down: The date through which an examination of title is to be conducted.

Date of Approval: Date the decree is prepared and also usually the date of approval by the judge of the Superior Court.

Date of Completion: The actual date of completion to the improvement work done on the property. In order to be valid, the Notice of Completion must be recorded within 10 days of the date of actual completion.

Date of Delivery: Date on which a document was officially received.

Date of Entry: The date on which the judgment was entered in the judgment books of the court.

Date of Execution: Usually the date on which the document is executed (signed); however, quite often it is the date on which it is prepared (drawn).

Date of Issuance of Abstract: Specifies the date on which the abstract of the judgment was executed by the court.

Debit: A charge or debt.

Debtor: Someone who owes a debt or is liable for a claim.

Debt Service: The amount of money periodically required as payments to amortize.

Decedent: A deceased person.

Declarants: Identifies the individuals who are recording the Declaration of Homestead as well as the name of the head of the family and a mention of other family members. A statement is included that identifies the city and county where the property is located and that the person or persons are now residing on the premises on which the homestead is being declared.

Declarants Abandoning: Identifies the original declarants who recorded the Declaration of Homestead, certifies their relationship (husband and wife, etc.), and states that they do hereby abandon the homestead of the subject property.

Declaration: At common law, the formalized document that sets forth the plaintiff's cause of action.

Declaration of Homestead: A legal, written and recorded document that provides the "homesteader" certain protections against a forced sale of a primary residence.

Declaration of Trust: A written document wherein a person acknowledges that he or she holds title to the subject property (as trustee) for the benefit of someone else (beneficiary).

Decree: A judicial decision.

Decree of Distribution: A judicial decision of probate court that distributes the assets of the deceased to the proper persons (distributees).

Dedication: Donation of private property (by the landowner) to a municipality for public usage.

Deed: A written document that transfers the interest in property from one person to another.

Deed in Lieu of Foreclosure: The conveying of title to a mortgage or beneficiary in order to prevent foreclosure.

Deed of Trust: A security document used to transfer "bare legal" title from the trustor (borrower) to the trustee (a neutral party, usually a corporation) to be held in trust for the benefit of the beneficiary (lender) until the trustor completes performance of an obligation (monetary or otherwise).

Deed of Trust — Pertinent Information: Cross-reference information regarding the deed of trust in question. It includes: recording reference, date of execution, names of original trustor and beneficiary, and the county in which said deed of trust was recorded. This same basic identification information is listed whenever any of the following notices are filed: request for notice; notice of default; noted of recession; assignment of deed of trust.

Deed Restrictions: Limitations on the use of real estate written into the deed.

De Facto: Latin, meaning "in fact," "in reality," "actually."

Default: Anything wrongful; failure to discharge a duty; failure in the performance of an obligation.

Default/Breach Statement: Statement containing information regarding the specifics of the obligation that has been placed into default.

Default Judgment: A judgment entered against a defendant who failed to respond to the plaintiff's action or failed to appear in court.

Defeasance: An instrument that negates or reverses the effectiveness of another document.

Defeasance Clause: A provision in a deed of trust of mortgage that allows the trustor/mortgagor to redeem the title to the subject property upon satisfaction of the obligation that it secures.

Defeasible: Subject to being defeated, annulled, or revoked if certain conditions are not met.

Defeat: To make null and void.

Defective Title: A title that is unmarketable; title is not able to be transferred in its present condition.

Deferred Payments: Payments that are extended over a period of time or put off until some date in the future.

Defendant: The party against whom the court action was initiated; the party being sued.

Deficiency Judgment: A personal judgment against a debtor for the difference between the amount owed and the amount received in a foreclosure.

Definition of Obligation: Defines the trustor's obligation. Since the obligation to be performed is usually the payment of a promissory note, the amount is set forth here.

Defunct: No longer in effect or use; dead.

De Jure: Latin, meaning "by right," "lawful" and "legitimate."

Demand: A term used in escrow to identify the consideration payoff required to execute a reconveyance, relinquishment of an interest, or a right to property.

Demand of Claimant: The total amount owing to the claimant is specified along with any interest rate that might be assigned to the debt if it is being paid through an installment arrangement.

Demurrer: A formal allegation that the pleadings of the opponent are not legally sufficient to allow the case to proceed any further.

Deponent: A witness, one who gives information under oath.

Deposition: Out-of-court question-and-answer testimony (usually held before court proceedings) taken under oath.

Depository Statement: Escrow instructions directing the usage and flow of documents, instruments, or property.

Deposit Receipt: A written document used to secure a firm offer to purchase property and provide a receipt for the buyer's earnest money; also known as a purchase agreement or purchase offer.

Depreciation: A decline in the value of a property.

Deraign: To dispute or contest a claim; to trace; to prove.

Dereliction: The recession of waters of the sea, a navigable river, or stream wherein the land that was previously covered by water is now dry.

Descent: The orderly manner of title succession of an intestate decedent.

Determinable Fee: An interest in property that may last forever, however, if certain contingencies are not satisfied, title automatically terminates. Also known as fee simple determinable.

Devise: A gift of real property by a will.

Devisee: A person who receives a gift of real property by a will.

Dictum: A judicial opinion that is not necessary for the decision of the case.

Diluvian: The gradual washing away and loss of soil along the banks of a river.

Discharge Statement: A statement indicating that the obligation secured by mortgage has been fully paid, therefore the mortgage is satisfied and discharged (released).

Divestiture: A remedy wherein the court orders the offending party to rid itself of rights or title to property or assets prior to the time when it would normally do so.

Divisa: A recognized boundary.

Documentary Transfer Tax: Tax levied by the county (also sometimes by the city) on the transfer of title of real property.

Domicile: The fixed and permanent home of a person.

Domiciliary Administrator: A probate court–appointed administrator of a decedent's domicile.

Dominant Tenement: The land benefited by an appurtenant easement; an estate whose owners are entitled to the beneficial use or another property.

Dona: A gift.

Donee: A person who receives a gift.

Donor: A person who gives a gift.

Down Payment: The portion of the purchase price of a home that the buyer pays in cash and does not finance.

Draft: A written order directing a person other than the maker (of the draft) to pay a specified amount of money to a named person.

Dragnet Clause: A provision in a security document making it applicable to all past and present obligations between a debtor and creditor.

Due Date: Fixed time for a payment.

Due-on-Sale Clause: A provision in a security document calling for the automatic maturity (note is all due and payable) in the event of sale or transfer of title.

Durable Power of Attorney: A power of attorney that will exist for an indefinite period of time; one where the duration is not limited.

Earnest Money: Something of value given as part of the purchase price to show "good faith" and to secure an agreement.

Easement: A limited right or interest in the land of another entitling the holder to some use, privilege, or benefit.

Easement Appurtenant: A "pure easement" created for the benefit of and attaching to a parcel of land known as the dominant tenement.

Easement in Gross: An easement created for the benefit of a person rather than for a parcel of land; therefore, often it is not assignable or inheritable.

Economic Life: The time remaining during which a property is expected to yield a return on an investment or to be used profitably.

Economic Obsolescence: A loss in value of property due to such causes as high unemployment, unfavorable zoning, deteriorating neighborhood, etc.

Economic Rent: The estimated income that a property should generate in the current rental market, based on the rent for comparable properties.

Effective Age: The age assigned to a building by an appraiser, based on the physical condition of the property rather than its chronological age.

Egress: The means of exiting from a property.

Ejectment: Legal action brought about by one claiming a right to possess real property against the one who currently possesses it.

Eminent Domain: The legal right and procedures for a municipality to take title and possession of private property for public use.

Emptor: Latin, meaning "buyer."

Encroachment: The unlawful extension of an improvement onto the land owned by another.

Encumber: The placing of a legal claim on a property.

Encumbrance: A right, interest in, or legal liability upon land limiting the fee simple title without hindering or affecting its sale or transfer.

Endorsement: The placing of a signature on the back of a check, bill, or promissory note in order to transfer to another party, the value represented on the face of the instrument.

Enfeoff: The conveyance of fee title to land; sometimes used on deeds as the "granting" verbiage.

Entirety: The ownership of property (real or personal) by a husband and wife (unity of one) wherein neither party is allowed to alienate any part of the property without the consent of the other.

Equal Credit Opportunity Act (ECOA): A federal law that prohibits lenders form denying mortgages on the basis of the borrower's race, color, religion, national origin, age, sex, marital status, or receipt of income from public assistance programs.

Equitable Lien: A lien recognized in a court of equity.

Equitable Owner: One who has pledged his or her property as security for a debt while retaining the right to use and enjoy the property.

Equitable Title: Ownership of property that is recognized by a court of equity; the right to acquire legal title.

Equity: Natural right or justice based on ethics and morals: also commonly used to denote the difference between the value of property and the amount owed on the property.

Equity of Redemption: The right of the judgment debtor to redeem property (within specific guidelines) after a judicial sale.

Equity Sharing: A type of purchase wherein two or more parties (absentee investor-owner and owner-occupant) share in the equity and appreciation of the property.

Erosion: The gradual eating away of soil by natural causes.

Escalator Clause: A provision in a contract or lease that provides for an upward or downward adjustment of price, costs, rents, expenses, prorations, etc., based on factors beyond the control of the parties.

Escheat: The reversion of title to the state, usually upon death of a person without heirs; however, can also be by virtue of a breach of condition.

Escrow: A transaction wherein an impartial third party (escrow agent) acts as agent to both parties (seller/buyer—lender/borrower, etc.) acting only under instructions in delivering papers, drawing and/or recording documents, and disbursing funds.

Estate: The degree, quantity, nature, and extent of a person's interest and/or ownership in real property.

Estate at Will: The right of possession by a tenant for an indefinite time that is terminable upon notice by either landlord or tenant.

Estate for Life: An estate that is measured in time by the uncertain duration of a specific person's lifetime.

Estate for Years: An estate that is created and is measured for a certain, definite, and fixed period of time.

Estate of Inheritance: A freehold estate of indefinite duration, of absolute inheritance to particular heirs (free of any condition, limitations or restrictions); fee simple.

Estate Tax: A tax upon the transfer of title to a decedent's property rather than a tax on the property itself.

Estoppel: A bar (preclusion) that prevents a person from denying the truth of a fact (or an action of a right) that already has become settled in judicial proceedings.

Et Al.: Latin; abbreviation for "and others."

Et Con.: Latin; abbreviation for "and husband."

Et Seq.: Latin; abbreviation for "and the following."

Et Ux.: Latin; abbreviation for "and wife."

Examination of Title: The process of determining the vesting, encumbrances, and liens upon a title.

Examiner: A person who analyzes a chain of title to land and offers an opinion on said chain of title.

Exception: Allowance for a deduction, subtraction, or exclusion from the main body or group.

Exchange Agreement: A contract for the exchanging of title and equity positions in properties, as compared to selling and buying.

Exclusive Agency Agreement: A written agreement between an owner and an agent that gives the agent the right to sell a property within a specified period of time, while allowing the owner the right to sell the property him- or herself without paying the agent a commission.

Exclusive Right to Sell: A written agreement between an owner and an agent that gives the agent the exclusive right to sell the property within a specified time period.

Exculpatory Clause: A contract provision that absolves a party from liability.

Execute: To perform that which is required in order to have and demonstrate completion or validity.

Executed: Complete, fully performed, nothing unfulfilled.

Execution Proceedings: Judicial enforcement of a money judgment wherein the debtor's property is seized and sold.

Executor: A male who is appointed by a testator (one who dies leaving a will) to handle the affairs of the testator's estate.

Executory: An agreement or contract that is contingent upon the occurrence of a specific event(s) or performance of some act(s) before it is fully accomplished or completed.

Executrix: A female who is appointed by a testator (one who dies leaving a will) to handle the affairs of the testator's estate.

Exemption: Something that is set aside or immune from a burden or obligation.

Ex Officio: Latin, meaning "from the office of" or "by virtue of the office."

Expediente: A Spanish or Mexican land grant file.

Ex Post Facto: Latin, meaning "after the fact" (event); when an event or decision is affected by something that occurs after the first event is finished.

Expropriate: To take land or other property from a property owner for public use.

Extension Agreement: A mutual agreement that grants additional time for the completion of performance.

Facsimile: An exact copy of the original.

Facto: Latin, meaning "in fact," "by an accomplishment/deed."

Fair Credit Reporting Act: A consumer protection law that sets a procedure for correcting mistakes on one's credit record.

False Personation: The unauthorized assumption of another's identity for fraudulent purposes.

Federal Housing Administration: FHA. A federal agency that sets guidelines and insures loans on residential housing.

Fee: An estate of inheritance; one in which ownership can be sold or devised to heirs.

Fee Simple: Absolute ownership without limitations, conditions, or restrictions burdening particular heirs.

Fee Simple Absolute: The clearest, most recognized estate in land without any limitations.

Fee Simple Defeasible: A fee simple estate subject to being defeated, annulled, or revoked if certain conditions are met or not met.

Feme Sole: An unmarried woman.

Feme Covert: A married woman.

Fictitious: Artificial or contrived; that which is false, feigned, or pretended.

Fictitious Deed of Trust: A deed or trust that is recorded to have "on record" all the general terms and conditions that never change during the life of this specific document. It generally represents the second page of a deed of trust and eliminates the unnecessary repetitious recording of this page as it can be referred to by recording reference identification.

Fictitious Name: A name created for business or other usage and not the true name of the owner or individual.

Fiduciary: One who holds a position of trust and confidence to act primarily for the benefit of another in matters of responsibility.

Final Decree: The final and complete judicial decision.

Financing Statement: A personal property security instrument that replaced the chattel mortgage (as a security instrument) upon the adoption of the Uniform Commercial Code.

Fixed Expense: The ongoing and normally stable charges or costs required to own or have possession of a property: rent, insurance, taxes, maintenance, etc.

Fixed-Rate Mortgage: A mortgage in which the interest rate does not change during the term of the loan.

Fixture: Property that was originally personal in nature but converted to a real property category due to the intention and manner in which it was affixed to real property.

For a Valuable Consideration: A statement that reflects that money or some legal consideration is being given in exchange for the property. (This is a holdover from earlier times and is no longer necessary in a voluntary conveyance.)

Foreclosure: The nonvoluntary procedure to sell real property according to the terms and conditions of the deed of trust that identified the subject property as security for a lien.

Foreclosure Sale: The nonvoluntary selling of property (in default) that was used as security for a lien.

Forfeiture: The loss of a right, title, or interest in property as a result of neglect of a duty or nonperformance of an obligation.

Franchise: A privilege of a public nature conferred on an individual or group by a governmental grant; also, the right granted by a company to a dealer (franchisee) to conduct business under the company name within certain territory.

Fraud: Intentional deception with the intent to gain advantage that results in injury to another.

Free and Clear: Title to real property that is unencumbered by liens.

Freehold Estate: An estate of indefinite duration; a fee or life estate.

Functional Obsolescence: A loss of value in property due to conditions regarding the property itself: style, age, size, poor floor plan, outdated heating/air conditioning, etc.

Future Interest: An estate in real property that provides for the benefits of possession and enjoyment at some future date.

Garnishment: The process of attaching money or goods that are due a defendant and yet in the hands of a third party.

General Index: Matters affecting title to land that are maintained by a title company according to names of individuals and entities instead of by property description.

General Partner: The managing partner of a limited partnership of all partners in a general partnership; the one(s) who is ultimately liable for all obligations of the partnership.

General Plan Restrictions: Restrictions (attached to the grant deed) on the development and usage of all lots within a subdivision.

Gift: A voluntary transfer of property without compensation received in return.

Good Faith: Clear intention to fulfill one's obligations; a total absence of any intention to seek unfair advantage or to defraud another.

Gore: A small triangular piece of land.

Graduated Lease: A lease with provisions for changing and varying rental rates according to a time structure and/or other conditions.

Graduated Payment Plan: GPM. A fixed rate, fixed-term mortgage that provides for reduced payments in the beginning year, with payments increasing to a set level in later years.

Grant: The operative word or conveyance in a grant deed; in general, the transfer of interest in real property by deed.

Grant Deed: A voluntary written instrument transferring title to real property.

Grantee: The party buying or receiving the property. The grantee's status (husband and wife, etc.) and legal method of acquiring title (joint tenants, tenants in common, etc.) comprises the vesting. In a public auction such as a trustee's sale or a tax sale, the successful bidder at said sale is the grantee.

Grantor: The party selling or transferring the interest in property.

Grants Are Condition Subsequent: Specific Use: In the land contract of sale, one provision specifies certain granting to occur automatically upon the completion of specified events (i.e., upon the recordation of a deed of full reconveyance, the vendor will grant title to the vendee).

Gross Income: Total income before any expenses are deducted.

Guarantee or Title: Evidence of title based solely on matters of public record.

Guaranteed Loan: A loan backed by a guarantee from a party other than the borrower.

Guardian: A person appointed by probate court to care for and be responsible for the person and/or property of a minor or incompetent person.

Habendum Clause: A clarifying clause in a deed that names the grantee and defines the limits of the estate to be granted; the clause begins with the wording "to have and to hold . . . "

Head of Household: One who is responsible for dependents; not necessarily a married person.

Heir: A person entitled by law to inherit property of a decedent who dies either testate or intestate.

Heir Apparent: The person who has the right to inheritance providing that he or she lives longer than the ancestor.

Hereditaments: Includes anything that can be inherited: real, personal, or mixed property.

Hereditary Succession: The passing of title according to the laws of descent.

Highest and Best Use: An appraisal term indicating the most productive and logical usage of land.

Holder in Due Course: One who has taken a check, note, or bill of exchange in good faith and for value, without notice that it is overdue or has been dishonored, and free of any claims to it or defenses against it by any person.

Holding: Possession of property to which one has legal title.

Holding Agreement: A form of trust where the trustee holds legal title to real property without active control or management responsibilities.

Holographic Will: A will entirely written, dated, and signed in the handwriting of the testator.

Homestead: The primary residence of a declarant who has filed a Declaration of Homestead, which offers protection (within specific guidelines) against a forced sale.

Homestead — Pertinent Information: Sets forth the recording reference and the county where the Declaration of Homestead (which is being abandoned) was recorded.

Hostile Possession: Possession of real property without permission (of the owner in title) coupled with a claim, express or implied, of ownership.

HUD: The U.S. Department of Housing and Urban Development.

Hypothecate: To pledge property as security for a debt without giving up possession of the property.

Idem Sonans: Latin, meaning "items the same." The doctrine that if two names sound alike, any slight variance in spelling is immaterial, i.e. Lawrence and Laurance.

Implied: Not explicitly written or stated. To say or address indirectly.

Impound Account: An account into which a borrower deposits periodic payments toward annual taxes and/or hazard insurance, usually at the insistence of the lender.

Improved Real Estate: Land upon which buildings and/or other improvements have been made.

Improvement: Any development of land or buildings.

Incapacity: The quality or status of being unable to care or act for oneself; incompetence.

Inchoate: Something that is incomplete, unfinished, not perfect.

Income and Expense Statements: An itemized statement of income received from a property and the expenses incurred in its operation.

Incompetent: A person deemed by law incapable of caring of managing him- or herself and/or property.

Income Property: Property owned or purchased for the generation of income.

Incorporate: To combine together to form a whole; to incorporate writings together; or to form a corporation.

Incorporeal: That which is intangible, without a physical existence.

Indefeasible: An estate that cannot be defeated or altered by any condition.

Indemnify: To secure against a loss of damage that may occur in the future, or to provide compensation for a loss already suffered.

Indemnity: Compensation that is given for a loss sustained.

Indemnity Agreement: An obligation to compensate. Also known as a hold harmless agreement. An agreement whereby one party agrees to compensate the other party for specific potential losses the second party sustains.

Indenture: A deed between two parties conveying an interest in real property wherein both parties assume obligations.

Independent Contractor: One who contracts to do a specific act and who is responsible to his or her employer only as to the results.

Indorsement: Signature written on back of an instrument with the intent and effect to transfer the right to the instrument to another; also, a rider attached to an insurance policy expanding or limiting the coverage. See *endorsement*.

In fee: Fee simple estate; absolute ownership in an estate in land.

Inference: A proposition or deduction based on the given facts; usually is less than certainty; however, may be sufficient to support a finding of fact.

Ingress and Egress: The entering upon and departure from; such as a landowner's physical right to enter and exit onto a public street; also contractual, such as the right of a lessee to enter and leave a leasehold.

Inherit: To take as an heir; originally by law of descent (intestate); however, modern usage includes devise (testate).

Inheritance Tax: A tax imposed on the right to receive property from a decedent; not a tax on the property itself.

Injunction: A court order restraining one or more parties from doing an act deemed unjust to the rights of some other party.

In Personam: Latin, meaning "against the person"; an action against the person.

In Propia Persona: Latin, meaning "in his own person; himself." Abbreviated as "pro per."

In Re: Latin, meaning "in the matter of"; usually used in legal proceedings where there is no opponent.

In Rem: Latin, meaning "against a thing/property"; signifies actions that are against property rather than actions against a person.

Insolvent: A situation where liabilities exceed assets; inability to pay one's debts: impoverished.

Installment Loan: A loan that requires periodic payments until both principal and interest are completely paid.

Installment Sales Contract: An agreement of purchase wherein the purchase price is paid in specific and timely installments and the title is not transferred until the final payment.

Institutional Lenders: Banks, savings and loans, and insurance companies that provide real estate loans.

Instrument: A formal, legal and written document that records an act or agreement.

Insurable Interest: A sufficient interest in property so that loss or damage to said property would create a financial loss to the owner.

Intangible Property: Property that does not have value in and of itself; rather, it simply represents value.

Intangible Value: Goodwill, franchises, licenses, patents, trademarks, and similar benefits of an established business.

Intent Recital: A statement that clarifies the intent and purpose of the document and/or parties.

Interest: A share of, a right to, or a concern with something of value; also the premium paid for the use of money (based on an annual rate).

Interest-only Note: A promissory note that requires that only the interest by paid during the term of the note, with the principal amount due in a lump sum at the end of the term.

Interim Loan: A short-term loan while borrower is waiting for subsequent long-term loan to be granted.

Interlocutory: Something that is temporary, not final; waiting for issues to be determined and resolved at some future time.

Interlocutory Decree: A degree that is temporary, pending the outcome of issues before it is finalized.

Intestate: To die without leaving a will; also, a decedent who did not leave a will.

Intra: Latin, meaning "within"; used in the formation of compound words.

Intrinsic Value: The actual, true, or inherent value of something that is not based on temporary economic swings.

Inure: To serve to the use or benefit of someone; to vest.

Investment: The amount of money put into property with the expectation of making a profit.

Involuntary Lien: A lien imposed upon property without the consent or choice of the owner; federal/state/property tax liens, etc.

Irrevocable: Unchangeable, or incapable of being recalled or revoked.

Joinder: The uniting of several causes or persons into a single unit or suit.

Joint: A united combination in interest or action.

Joint Protection Policy: A policy insuring more than one party's interest; such as the interest of both the owner and the lender.

Joint Tenancy: A form of co-ownership by two or more persons, each with equal shares and the unique quality of the right of survivorship upon death of a cotenant.

Joint Venture: A form of business organization composed of two or more persons in which profits, losses, and control are shared.

Judgment: A final determination in a court (of competent jurisdiction) to an action or proceeding.

Judgment Creditor: Identifies the party (creditor) to whom the debt (court settlement) is owned by the judgment debtor. The identification of the creditor often includes his or her address.

Judgment Debtor: Identifies the party (debtor) who owes the debt (court settlement) to the judgment creditor. Certain identification information (of the judgment debtor) is usually declared: social security number, driver's license number, and address.

Judgment Lien: A statutory lien ordering the payment a of a sum of money, created by recording an abstract or a complete judgment.

Judgment — Pertinent Information: Sets out recording reference information including: date of entry, book and page numbers of the court judgment books, and the names of the judgment debtor and creditor.

Junior Lien: A recorded lien of inferior priority.

Jurat: The clause appearing at the end of an affidavit reciting the date, location, and person before whom the statement was sworn. A jurat is not the same as an acknowledgment, although the terms are often (mistakenly) used interchangeably.

Jurisdiction: The power of a court to hear and determine a case.

Just Compensation: The fair and equitable compensation paid to a landowner when the power of eminent domain is exercised.

Laches: Inexcusable delay in asserting a right; the doctrine suggests that long-neglected rights cannot be enforced.

Land: Real estate without any improvements attached to it.

Land Contract of Sale: Also known as a Conditional Sales Contract and a Contract of Sale; title remains in the name of the vendor (seller) until the vendee (buyer) fulfills certain conditions of the contract. The vendee has possession and equitable interest.

Landlord: A lessor who leases or rents property to a tenant (lessee).

Land Usage: The uses being made, or those allowable under zoning ordinances.

Lease: An agreement whereby the lessor (landlord) relinquishes the right of possession of the property (in exchange for rent) to the tenant, while retaining title and full ownership.

Leaseback: A sale arrangement wherein the buyer leases the property back to the seller.

Leasehold: The lessee's estate in real property that was created by virtue of the lease agreement.

Lease Option: A lease allowing the tenant the right to buy the property if and when certain conditions are met.

Legacy: A gift of personal property by a will.

Legal Advice Notice: A cautionary note suggesting that the trustor should seek legal advice from an attorney or government agency.

Legal Description: Legally describes the real property or interest being conveyed. Usually accomplished by lot/tract, metes and bounds, or U.S. Government Survey type or legal description.

Legal Rate of Interest: The maximum rate of interest that can legally be charged for the use of money.

Legatee: A person to whom personal property is given by a will.

Lessee: The person acquiring possession of real property by virtue of the lease agreement that creates a leasehold estate for the lessee.

Lessor: One who grants a lease and the exclusive right of possession of real property to another, subject only to rights expressly retained by the lessor in the agreement.

Less Than Interest Note: A promissory note that allows or requires the borrower to make periodic payments that actually are less than the accrued interest.

Let: To grant a lease to another.

Letters of Administration: The written approval from the probate court that appoints an administrator (administratrix) as the personal representative of the affairs of one who dies intestate.

Letters of Conservatorship: The written approval from the court that appoints a conservator to handle the affairs or care for the person who is a conservatee.

Letters of Guardianship: The written approval from the court that appoints a guardian for the person and/or estate of a minor or of an incompetent.

Letters Testamentary: The written approval from the court that appoints a personal representative of the estate of a testate decedent.

Levy: To assess, collect, gather: i.e., the seizure of property by judicial procedure.

Liable: Held responsible or accountable under the law.

Liability: An obligation or duty that must be performed, that which must be paid. The opposite of asset.

License: Permission by a recognized authority to act or engage in a business, profession, or other activity. A certificate or document that gives the right to receive or perform a specific activity. Also, a right to a use of real property.

Lien: A charge, hold, or claim of another for the purpose of securing a debt or obligation.

Lien Subordination ("Good Faith") Clause: Provides for the protection of the lien holder's value and position from any future reversion or forfeiture resulting in a breach of the restrictions attached to the agreement.

Life Beneficiary: A person entitled to receive specified benefits for the duration of that individual's life.

Life Estate: An estate measured in duration by the lifetime of a natural person.

Limitations, Statutes of: Statutes that limit the time within which parties having a cause of action must institute judicial proceedings or lose such rights.

Limited Partnership: A partnership arrangement in which some of the partners (the limited partners) have a limited investment, limited liability, and no management controls.

Lineal: Descent by a direct line of succession in ancestry.

Liquid Assets: Assets that are readily convertible to cash.

Liquidate: To convert property or other assets into cash.

Liquidated Damages: The amount of money agreed upon in a contract as payment or compensation for a breach of contract; thus eliminating further legal action.

Lis Pendens: Latin, meaning "action pending;" suspended or pending lawsuit.

Listing: A written contract between an owner (principal) and an agent (broker) authorizing the agent to sell, lease, or rent the owner's property in exchange for compensation.

Lite Pendente: Latin, meaning "while the action is ending."

Litigant: Party involved in a lawsuit.

Litigation: Civil action; a controversy in court to determine the rights of each party.

Living Trust: A trust that is operative during the lifetime of the person creating it.

Loan: Delivery of something of value with the expectation of repayment or return. Money given to another in expectation of return of the principal amount plus interest for given period of time.

Loan Policy: A policy of title insurance, which insures the interest of the lender on a particular debt obligation.

Loan to Value (LTV): The ratio of the amount borrowed to the property's appraised value or selling price.

Lock-in Clause: A loan provision specifying a time period during which no repayment or complete payoff is permitted.

Loss Payable Clause: An endorsement to a fire insurance policy identifying additional parties (lenders) entitled to participate in claims proceeds in the event of loss.

Lot Books: A title company's set of books reflecting every real estate document that has been recorded within the county.

Lot Split: The legal division or splitting of a parcel of land into more than one legal parcel of land.

Maintenance: The ongoing painting, cleaning, and repair work done to property and equipment to keep it productive, useful, and in good repair.

Maker: One who executes or endorses a note.

Management: The supervision of people or property for another.

Map Act: The Subdivision Map Act that sets forth the guidelines and regulations for the subdivision of land.

Margin: The amount that the lender adds to the index to determine the rate on an adjustable rate mortgage (ARM) when it adjusts.

Marketability: The status and condition of title to property in relationship to its acceptability (for conveyance) to an informed and able purchaser.

Market Data: Information regarding the listed price, sales price rental fees, market time, etc., of real property.

Market Data Approach: A method used in appraisal that determines the price of a home or lot by comparing it with other property similar to it that have sold recently.

Market Title: Title to a piece of property that a reasonable informed purchaser would be willing to accept.

Market Value: The price for a property that a willing buyer and a willing seller would agree upon when neither is under abnormal pressure.

Master Plan: A long-range general plan for physical development and usage of property within a community based on projected population changes and growth trends.

Material Fact: A fact that in all likelihood would affect the decision of an owner in giving his or her consent to an agent to enter into a particular transaction.

Maturity: The date at which time a note becomes due and payable; the same concept is valid with regard to when legal rights become enforceable.

Meander: To follow a variable and winding course.

Mechanic's Lien: A statutory lien to secure payment for persons contributing labor and/or material toward improvements upon real property when the compensation was not paid in a timely manner.

Mechanic's Lien — Pertinent Information: Sets forth the name of the mechanic's lien claimant, name of the party who requested the improvement work, and a recording reference for the mechanic's lien including the county where said lien was recorded.

Memorial: A short written statement; a memorandum.

Merger of title: The absorption of a lesser estate into a larger estate.

Meridians: The imaginary lines (north-south) used (along with base lines east-west) to measure and identify land.

Metes and Bounds: Measurement, angles, boundaries, and distances used in describing land perimeters.

Mineral Lease: A lease that permits a lessee to explore and extract minerals from an owner's land. Mineral leases usually are payable on a royalty basis.

Monument: A fixed mark or object used by a surveyor to fix or establish boundaries or land location.

Moratorium: The legal authorization to delay the performance of some obligation, especially payment of debts.

Mortgage: A two-party security instrument pledging land as security for the performance of an obligation.

Mortgagee: The creditor (lender) who takes a lien on the subject property in return for expected performance on the obligation by the mortgagor.

Mortgage — Pertinent Information: Sets forth recording reference, names of mortgagor and mortgagee, and the county where the mortgage was recorded.

Mortgagor: The debtor (borrower) who executes a mortgage, has possession of the property used as security, and promises the performance of the obligation.

Muniments of Title: Deeds and other original documents comprising a chain of title to a parcel or real property.

Mutual Consent: Agreement by two or more people.

Mutual Water Company: A company organized for the purpose of providing water to its members and customers.

Name of Assignee ("New Beneficiary"): Identifies the party receiving the beneficial interest under the deed of trust (assignee). The status and method of acquiring title to the beneficial interest also should be specified.

Name of Attorney: Specific use: The name and address of the attorney who is representing the party identified.

Name of Claimant: Specific use: Identifies the contractor (claimant) who is claiming the mechanic's lien.

Name of Contractors: Specific use: Identifies the original contractor for the work of the improvement. If there was no contractor for the work of improvement as a whole, insert "none."

Name of Court: Name and location of the court adjudicating a specific case.

Name of Deceased: Specific use: The nature of the court action is specified. For probate proceedings, the decedent's name generally is preceded by the wording "in the matter of the Estate of . . ." The name of the decedent will appear exactly as it appears on county records in order to provide a complete chain of title.

Name of Distributee: Specific use: Identifies the party (distributee) who is receiving the property described in the Decree of Distribution.

Name of Party Executing and Interest Held in Property: Specific use: Identifies the party giving the Notice of Non-Responsibility and indicates his or her interest in the property.

Name of Party Requesting Work Under Contract: Specific use: Identifies the party who requests, by agreement (contract), that work be performed and/or materials be supplied by the claimant. This is usually the owner of the property.

Name of Property Owner: Specific use: Identifies the owner, or supposed owner, of property on which the work or improvement has been completed.

Name of Subdivider: Identifies the subdivider (often the developer and/or owner of the tract) who is creating the restrictions for the tract development.

Naturalization: The conferring of rights and privileges of citizenship on one who was an alien.

Naturalized Citizen: One who has been legally proclaimed a citizen of the United States by an act of Congress.

Negative Amortization: Payment terms under which the borrower's payments do not cover the interest due. The "deferred interest" is added to the principal balance.

Negotiable: Capable of transfer between parties by indorsement of the holder in the ordinary course of business.

Negotiable Instrument: An instrument that contains an unconditional promise or order to pay a certain sum of money, payable at a definite time, or on demand, and is payable to order or to bearer.

Negotiation: The process of creating a meeting of the minds between two or more parties in order to reach an agreement.

Net Income: The amount of money from income property that remains after expenses and charges have been deducted.

Net Lease: A lease that requires the tenant to pay all the costs of maintaining the building, including the payment of taxes, insurance, repairs, and other expenses normally paid by the owner.

Net Listing: A listing that states the minimum amount the seller is to receive and stipulates that any amount above this goes to the broker as commission.

Net Worth: That which remains after subtracting liabilities from assets.

New Deed of Trust — Pertinent Information: Sets forth the amount of the note, date, and beneficiary of the new deed of trust, which is to record concurrently with the Subordination Agreement.

Nominee: A person designated to act in the place and stead of another.

Nonconforming Use: Actual use of land that lawfully existed prior to the enactment of a zoning ordinance (which now prohibits or restricts said usage) and, therefore, said usage may be continued.

Nondisclosure: Misrepresentation by silence.

Nonjudicial Foreclosure: Sale of property pursuant to the power-of-sale provisions contained in a security instrument.

Nonrecourse Loan: A loan that limits the lender, in the event of default by the borrower, to foreclosure on the property that was used as security. The lender cannot sue for deficiency of funds and cannot attach the borrower's personal assets.

Notarize: To provide proof of execution of a document by means of notary public's certificate of acknowledgment.

Notary Public: A public officer authorized to administer oaths to attest or certify certain types of documents, to take depositions, and to perform certain other civil functions.

Notary Seal or Stamp: The official seal of the notary public or other authorized official.

Note: A common reference to a promissory note.

Notice of Cessation: A recorded notice shortening the time for the filing of mechanic's liens when work has ceased prior to completion of the improvement.

Notice of Completion: A notice recorded within 10 days of completion of a work of improvement signals commencement of the time period within which claims of mechanic's liens must be recorded.

Notice of Default: A recorded notice of a trustor's failure to perform his or her obligation under a deed of trust. It is the initial step in nonjudicial foreclosure.

Notice of Default Recording Information: Includes the book and page notation for the recordation of the Notice of Default in the Official Records. This statement also acknowledges that the legal procedures connected with the Notice of Default have been completed in a timely manner.

Notice of Intent to Sell: States intent to sell defaulted property at public auction to the highest bidder. Must be posted and published according to specific regulations.

Notice of Nonresponsibility: A recorded notice by an owner of real property that he or she will not be responsible for payment of costs of improvements contracted for by anyone other than the owner him- or herself.

Notice Regarding Construction and Responsibility: Sets forth a statement of the nature of the improvement work being done on the property and demonstrates that the owner executing the notice has obtained knowledge of this work within the past 10 days. Furthermore, a declaration is made that the owner will not be responsible for any material or labor furnished in regard to this specific improvement work project.

Notice to Current Beneficiary: Cautionary note concerning the possible use of new loan proceeds for reason other than improvement of the land.

Notice to Quit: Notice given by a landlord to a tenant to pay rent within three days or vacate the premises. This term also is used after a foreclosure to give notice to tenants (may be previous owner who was foreclosed) to vacate the premises and give possession to the new owners.

Notorious Possession: Possession or real property that is open and conspicuous.

Novation: The substitution of a new obligation for an old one, or the substitution of another party for one of the original parties.

Now Therefore … : Sets forth various terms relating to the subordination agreement: priority levels, extensions, contingent agreements, etc.

Nuncupative Will: A verbal will before sufficient number of witnesses; generally reduced to writing later, if ever.

Oath: A declaration appealing to God to be witness of the truth of a fact, statement, or act. A solemn affirmation or serious pledge.

Obsolescence: A loss of value or property due to its being outmoded.

Official Records: The books in which all documents filed in a county recorder's office are recorded that impart constructive notice of matters pertaining to real property.

Offset Statement: An owner statement, deposited into escrow, showing the status of rents, security deposits, and other balances and obligations connected with the investment property.

Omnibus Clause: As applies to the Decree of Distribution, this clause is intended to protect the distributee's interest by including property that may have been improperly or not specifically described. It is included so that it will not be necessary to reopen probate proceeding or to amend the decree. An example of the protective language: "The following described property and all other property of the estate, whether described herein or not, is distributed to … "

Open-End Mortgage (Deed of Trust): Provision that allows for additional loan advances to be funded to the borrower, while keeping the same security and security documents.

Open Listing: A listing given by a property owner that states that the first agent to secure a buyer on the terms and conditions agreeable to the seller will be paid a commission.

Operative Property: Property that is reasonably necessary to operate and conduct a specific type of business.

Operative Words of Conveyance: An essential part of any deed, indicating an intent to transfer the title to real property. In a grant deed: The wording "hereby grant(s)" is qualified by" … without any covenant or warranty . . ." In a deed of trust (trust deed), the trustor conveys or transfers "bare legal" title to the trustee. The wording "hereby grants, transfers and assigns to trustee, in trust, with power of sale" is generally used.

Operative Words of Endorsement: The formal words that transfer the beneficiary's interest under a deed or trust to the assignee; " … has endorsed said note and does hereby assign and transfer to …"

Option: A choice, right, or consideration to do or not to do a certain thing, either now or sometime in the future; the option to lease or to buy property.

Optionee: The person who acquires or holds a legal option; the person who has the choice.

Optionor: The person who grants an option and is bound by the decision of the optionee during the lifetime of the option.

Order Confirming Sale: A court order confirming the sale of estate property by a personal representative or other fiduciary.

Ordinance: A legislative enactment of a city or county.

Original Trustee Under the Deed of Trust: Identifies the original trustee who is being replaced under the deed of trust by use of the Substitution of Trustee document.

Origination Fee: A charge made for obtaining and processing a new loan.

Ostensible: That which is, or seems to be apparent.

Outlawed: A claim, right, or cause of action unenforceable due to lapse of time.

Owner's Equity: The value held by the owner that represents the difference between the market value and the existing liens on a property.

Ownership: The exclusive right to use and enjoy property.

Owner's Policy: A policy insuring the title of the owner of the property.

Paper: Slang for a note or mortgage used in lieu of cash.

Parcel: Any area of land contained within a single description.

Parol: That which is verbal rather than written.

Partial Reconveyance: A document that identifies a particular parcel of land and releases said parcel as security from a blanket deed of trust.

Partial Release Clause: A clause in a blanket mortgage allowing for the release of a portion of the property (as security for the lien) when certain conditions are met.

Partition Action: A judicial separation of the respective interests in land of co-owners; it may be a physical division into separate parcels or a sale of the entire parcel and a division of proceeds.

Partnership: As association of two or more competent persons to carry on as co-owners of a business for profit.

Party Giving Notice — Pertinent Information: Sets forth: The full name of the party (owner of property) giving notice on line 2; his or her full address on line 3; the nature of the interest held in the subject property on line 4.

Party Wall: A dividing wall located on a boundary line and used by both owners.

Patent: A federal or state government conveyance of public lands to a private party.

Payee: One who receives a payment.

Payor: One who makes a payment.

Pendente Lite: Latin, meaning "matters that are contingent upon the determination of pending litigation."

Per Annum: Latin, meaning "through the course of a year," "annual."

Per Capita: Latin, meaning "by the head," "by the number of individuals"; a method or reporting figures or statistics.

Percentage Lease: A lease that provides for the rental rate to be determined, in whole or in part, from the dollar volume of business conducted.

Percolation Test: A test that determines the ability of the ground to absorb and drain water.

Performance: The fulfillment of an obligation or promise.

Performance Bond: A bond posted by a contractor as a guarantee that he or she will satisfactorily complete a project and it will be free of any liens.

Periodic Tenancy: Tenancy for successive periods of equal duration (week to week, month to month, year to year).

Personal Property: Anything that is movable and not attached to real property; therefore, anything that is not real property.

P.I.T.I.: Abbreviation for principal, interest, taxes, and insurance in regard to a loan payment.

Plaintiff: The party who brought the court action, or the party who is suing another.

Plat: A plot, map, or chart.

Pleadings: The formal writings filed in court containing the various claims and defenses of the opposing parties.

Pledge: The delivery of personal property as security for the performance of an obligation.

Plottage: The assemblage of adjoining land to increase the area of holding and often the inherent value.

Policy of Title Insurance: A contract indemnifying against loss resulting from a defect in title or outstanding liens on the real property insured.

Point: A charge (to borrowers by lenders) pursuant to obtaining a loan. One point is equal to 1 percent of the loan value.

Police Power: The power of the state and local governments to impose such regulations and restrictions upon private rights that are reasonably related to the promotion and maintenance of the health, safety, morals, and general welfare of the public.

Possession: Having, holding, or detaining property in one's command.

Possession (Actual): As concerns real property, actual possession is the physical occupation of the property or the direct appropriation of the property's benefits.

Possession (Constructive): The ability to have the power and the intention to exercise control over said property. Constructive possession does not include physical occupation.

Possessory Action: Lawsuits to obtain or maintain possession or real property.

Power of Attorney: A document authorizing a person (the attorney-in-fact) to act on behalf of another (the principal). To be directive in real estate, the power of attorney must be recorded.

Power of Attorney — Pertinent Information: Sets forth the recording reference and county where the power of attorney (which is being revoked) was recorded.

Power of Sale: A right granted in a deed of trust or mortgage that permits the trustee or mortgagee to sell the property at a public auction in the event the buyer defaults.

Powers: Specifies exactly the authority given to the attorney-in-fact.

Preceding Estate: A prior estate upon which a future estate is determined. An estate in remainder is based on a preceding life estate.

Preemptive Right: A right to purchase on the same terms as offered by another party.

Preliminary Report: A formal report that sets out in detail the condition of title to a particular parcel of land.

Premises: Basically, land and all its appurtenances; however, different entities have specific definitions.

Prepayment Clause: A clause within an agreement permitting payment of a debt prior to a due date; may be with or without a penalty.

Prepayment Penalty: A provision inserted in a note whereby a penalty is to be paid by the borrower in the event the note is paid off before the due date (or, usually, more than 20 percent in any one year). Most prepayment penalties expire at the end of five years into the term.

Prescription: The securing of a property right by using the property openly, continuously, hostilely, and notoriously for a period of time prescribed by the civil code.

Presumption: That which is assumed without actual proof.

Prima Facie: That which is assumed to be correct until proven otherwise.

Primary Financing: The first note, mortgage, or trust deed.

Principal: One who has permitted or directed another to act for his or her benefit and subject to his or her direction or control. Power of Attorney: Identifies the person (principal) who is giving authority to the attorney-in-fact to act in his or her behalf. Generally, the name of the county and state of the principal's residence is also specified. Revocation of Power of Attorney: Identifies the party (principal) who is revoking the powers set forth in a previously recorded power of attorney. Also, the amount of loan to be repaid exclusive of the interest.

Priority: The relative positions of liens and encumbrances, usually according to recording date and time.

Private Mortgage Insurance (PMI): Insurance written by a private company that protects the lender against losses if a borrower defaults.

Probate: A period of time during which the court has jurisdiction over the administration of an estate of a deceased person.

Probate Court: The court that has jurisdiction over wills and estate settlements.

Probate Sale: A sale to liquidate the estate of a decedent for the settlement of the estate.

Processing: The preparation of a mortgage loan application and supporting documentation for consideration by a lender or insurer.

Procuring Cause: An action by an agent that originates a series of events that eventually finalizes in a sale.

Promissory Note: A document promising to pay a sum of money at a specified time in the future; an IOU.

Pro-Rata: Directly proportional to a certain rate or amount of ownership or use.

Proration: Dividing something (income/expense, etc.) according to relative time or amount of use.

Public Domain: All federal government–owned land that is subject to the general land laws.

Public Report Subdivision: A report (prepared by the real estate commissioner on the details of a new subdivision) that must be given to each buyer in a new subdivision.

Purchase Money Loan: A loan originated at time of purchase for all or a portion of the purchase price.

Purchase Note Terms: Specific use: A promissory note included within the displayed version of a land contract of sale specifying the terms and conditions of payment.

Purchase Offer: A written document used to secure a firm offer to purchase property and provide a receipt for the buyer's earnest money; also known as a purchase agreement or deposit.

Purpose: Sets forth the purpose and intent of the Contract of Sale and specifies the vendor's security interest protection through the power of sale.

Purpose and Identification of Restrictions: Sets out the nature and purpose of the development restrictions, along with the "General Plan" restrictions and the method by which the restrictions shall be imposed on the tract.

Qualified: Approval by meeting certain requirements. Legally competent or capable.

Quasi: That which is or has a similar nature.

Quasi-Community Property: Property acquired by either spouse that would be considered community property if the person had been living in this state, however, it was purchased while domiciled outside of the state.

Quasi-Contract: A contractual-type relationship based on conduct, which receives its power by implication of the law.

Quiet Title Action: A court action to establish clear title or to remove a defect or "cloud" on a title to real property.

Quitclaim Deed: A deed that transfers the grantor's rights and interest in property without any warranty or covenants of title.

Range: A column of townships running north and south in a row parallel to, and east or west of, a principal meridian.

Ratification: To certify or validate.

Real Estate Settlement Procedures Act (RESPA): A federal law that requires lenders to give borrowers advance notice of closing costs.

Real Property: Land and whatever is erected, growing, or affixed to the land.

Realtor®: A real estate licensee who is a member of the National Association of Realtors® and who has agreed to abide by the ethics and standards of that organization.

Recession of Contract: To rescind or annul a contract by mutual consent of all parties or for cause by any one party.

Recognized Gain: The amount of monetary gain (subject to tax) that is realized from the sale or exchange of real property.

Reconveyance: A document that returns the "bare legal" title to the owner (trustor) upon fulfillment of all obligations under a deed of trust.

Record: To give public notice of a document by placing the document on file with the county recorder.

Recorder's Office: The government office that publicly records deeds, mortgages, trust deeds, and all other legal documents as part of the public record process.

Recording Information: The book and page numbers of the Official Records where the document is entered, the file number (sometimes called the document or instrument number) assigned by the county recorder, and the date and time of recordation are noted on the document.

Recording of Judgment — Pertinent Information: If the Satisfaction of Judgment is to be recorded, the recording reference information and the county where the judgment (or abstract) was recorded should be documented.

Recording Requested By: Identifies the party requesting that the document be recorded and often shows the names of title companies when they submit groups of documents to the county for recording.

Record Trustee's Acknowledgment: The signature of the trustee (being replaced) certifies receipt of a copy of the Substitution of Trustee document.

Recourse Loan: A loan that allows the lender to seek a deficiency judgment in the event that money is still owed on a debt after a foreclosure sale.

Redemption: The time period during a nonjudicial foreclosure process in which the owner must pay the entire sum due and payable to the lender to prevent the final sale; also, the buying back of one's property after it has been lost through foreclosure (usually judicial foreclosure).

Redemption Right: The legal right of a debtor to reacquire title to property lost in a judicial foreclosure.

Refinancing: The process of taking out a new loan on property already owned; paying off the existing financing and retaining the cash balance, if one exists.

Reformation: An action to correct a mistake or modify a document.

Regression: An appraisal concept: When a property of a given value is placed in a neighborhood with properties of a lower value, the higher-value property will tend to be devalued to the level of the lower-valued properties.

Register Number: A trustee's cross-reference number used for quick file location of a blanket deed of trust whenever a partial reconveyance is issued for that specific trust deed.

Reinstatement: Restoration of a previous position or status after losing said position to default; also, the first three-month period of a nonjudicial foreclosure process of a deed of trust with a power of sale.

Release Clause: A clause in a blanket mortgage allowing for the release of a portion of the property (as security for the lien) when certain conditions are met; also known as a partial release clause.

Reliction: The gradual recession of a body of water leaving a body of land.

Remainder Estate: A future interest in property created in someone other than the grantor, which is or may become possessory upon the natural expiration of the prior particular estate.

Remainderman: The person who owns an estate in remainder; therefore, the person who will receive title upon termination of the prior, particular estate.

Renegotiable Rate Mortgage: A mortgage whose interest rate may be renegotiated periodically, typically every three to five years.

Renovate: Restore to a former condition or to upgrade the condition.

Rent: Income received for the use of property.

Replacement Cost: A method used in appraising whereby a property is given a value based on the estimated cost to replace a similar or equivalent property in the current market.

Request for Notice of Default: A request to receive a copy of any Notice of Default that may be filed against any lien encumbering said property. Contract of Sale: Both vender and vendee request a copy of the Notice of Default that was in existence and either assumed or taken "subject to" as part of the contract agreement.

Request for Reconveyance: Written instructions from the beneficiary to the trustee to issue a reconveyance deed to the trustor because the loan obligation has been satisfied.

Reservation: A right or an interest retained by a grantor as part of a conveyance.

Reservation of Vendor's/Vendee's Right: Sets forth certain important and reserved rights of the vendor and vendee (from conveyance to the trustee) since title does not pass until the conditions of the contract are complete.

Restriction: A limitation on the use of real estate; may be part of the conditions, covenants, and restrictions ("CC & R's") adopted by the developer, or may be a governmental ordinance.

Revenue Stamps: Tax levied by the county (sometime by the city) on the sale of real property, the same as documentary tax stamps.

Reversion: A future estate, generally reserved in the grantor, that becomes possessory at the end of a grantee estate.

Rider: A supplement or an addition to, an indorsement to a document.

Right of Survivorship: The right of a surviving joint tenant(s) to automatically acquire the interest of a deceased joint tenant.

Right of Way: A right granted by an owner (to another person) to pass over or through the owner's land.

Riparian Rights: The right of a landowner to a reasonable use of the water comprising a waterway either through or adjacent to said property.

Rule Against Perpetuities: The rule of law that places time limits on the vesting of future interest in real and personal property.

Sale Contract: An agreement entered into for the purchase and sale of real property. Also known as a purchase agreement and deposit receipt.

Sandwich Lease: A sublease that is subject to the original lease and that has been further sublet. An "in-between" lease.

Satisfaction: A paid-off debt. Also, a document recorded with the county recorder when a mortgage (satisfaction of mortgage), or trust deed (deed off reconveyance), or lien has been paid in full.

Scheduled Rate: A list of prices for title insurance policies.

Seal: An embossed or stamped impression made to authenticate a document or attest to a signature.

Searcher: A person who collects all the facts and documents regarding the title to real property for submission to a title examiner.

Secondary Financing: Mortgages or trust deeds that are secondary in priority, or subordinate, to first mortgages and trust deeds; also known as junior liens.

Secondary Money Market: The market where existing secured notes are bought and sold. This is accomplished on the institutional and private level.

Section: A measure of land containing 640 acres, one mile square.

Security Deposit: A deposit made to assure future performance of an obligation.

Seller Carryback: Any situation in which a seller acts as a lender, holding or "carrying back" a part of the purchase price on a note.

Separate Property: All property owned prior to marriage or acquired after marriage by gift, will, inheritance, or acquired as rents, issues, or profits from separate property.

Servient Tenement: The estate burdened with an easement.

Setback Line: A line established by a zoning regulation prohibiting any building beyond a prescribed distance from the edge of the property.

Severalty Ownership: Sole or single ownership.

Shared Appreciation Mortgage: A loan, usually at lower-than-market interest rates, wherein the lender and the seller share in the future appreciation of the property.

Sheriff's Deed: The deed issued at a court-ordered sale of real property.

Short-rate Insurance: The rate of an insurance premium that is charged when one cancels a policy.

Signature of Assignor ("Old Beneficiary"): Signature of assignor with his or her name printed beneath the signature. This is the party releasing interest in the deed of trust.

Signature of Attorney: Signature of the attorney for the judgment creditor with his or her (attorney's) name printed beneath the signature.

Signature of Beneficiary: Signature of beneficiary with his or her name printed beneath the signature. Notice of Default: Either the beneficiary or the trustee may sign as the official on this notice. Notice of Recession: Beneficiary's signature indicates cancellation of Notice of Default. Substitution of Trustee: Beneficiary's signature causes change or substitution of trustee.

Signature of Claimant: Signature of claimant with his or her name printed beneath the signature. Claimant's legal capacity (individual, firm, corporation, etc.) is also designated. Mechanic's Lien: Signature of person setting forth claim. Release of Mechanic's Lien: Signature demonstrating the claim is being released.

Signature of Deputy Clerk of the Court: Signature of the deputy clerk with his or her official title printed beneath. Occasionally the deputy clerk of the court will acknowledge the document; his or her signature would be sufficient to take the place of the signature and stamp of the notary public.

Signature of Grantor: Signature of grantor with his or her name printed beneath the signature.

Signature of Judge: Signature of the judge of the Superior Court (who approves the document) with his or her name printed beneath the signature. Occasionally the name of the judge is simply stamped on the document.

Signature of Mortgagee: Signature of the mortgagee (lender) with his or her name printed beneath the signature.

Signature of Owner: Signature of the owner with his or her name printed beneath the signature. Notice of Nonresponsibility: Signature of owner giving notice. Abandonment of Homestead: Signature of declarants of the recorded Declaration of Homestead that is being abandoned. Subordination Agreement: Signature of owner receiving new financing.

Signature of Party Executing Document: Signature of the surviving joint tenant with his or her name printed beneath the signature.

Signature of Principal: Signature of the principal with his or her name printed beneath the signature.

Signature of Subordinating Party: Signature of the beneficiary of the deed or trust that is subordinating to a new loan. Name is printed beneath the signature.

Signature of Trustee: Signature of trustee with his or her name printed beneath the signature. Notice of Recession: Indicates receipt of the notice on a specific date. Full Reconveyance: Under directions from the beneficiary, the trustee reconveys or releases the subject property. Partial Reconveyance: Under directions from the beneficiary, the trustee reconveys or releases a specific property as security under a "blanket deed of trust."

Signature of Trustor: Signature of trustor with his or her name printed beneath the signature. Deed of Trust: Acknowledges security of note. Substitution of trustee: Occasionally the trustor may be involved in the decision (along with the beneficiary) to change or substitute the trustee; and therefore, the trustor would sign the document.

Signature of Vendee: Signature of vendee with his or her name printed beneath the signature.

Signature of Vendor: Signature of vendor with his or her name printed beneath the signature.

Soldiers' and Sailors' Civil Relief Act: Federal law initiated to protect members of the armed forces from loss of property to satisfy obligations incurred prior to service entry.

Solvent: Able to pay all of one's debts and financial obligations.

Special Assessments: Fees collected by the tax collector (along with taxes) that are to pay for improvements and other benefits (school district assessments, etc.).

Specific or Special Lien: A lien that affects only one specific asset, as opposed to a general lien, which affects a number of assets.

Specific Performance: A sale of real property that fulfills the terms agreed upon.

Spouse: A husband to a wife; a wife to a husband.

Starter: The base or policy of the last title order, used as a starting point from which examination of the current order is begun.

Statement of Identity: A questionnaire used by title companies to help establish the identity of a person in order to protect the title from liens on persons with similar names; also known as a statement of information.

Statement of Improvement Work Completed: An explanation of the work completed or material supplied by the claimant. Also, when appropriate, an itemized breakdown of expenses that are incorporated in the claims.

Statement Regarding Signatures: By affixing their signatures to this Contract of Sale, both the vendor and vendee agree to Request for Notice of Default.

Status: The legal position of a person (minor, adult, incompetent, etc.).

Statute of Limitations: A law that requires that certain court actions be initiated before expiration of certain time period.

Straight-line Depreciation: A depreciation method that assigns an equal loss in value for each year of a property's useful life; paper loss for tax purposes.

Straight Note: A promissory note that requires that only one payment of principal and all accrued interest be paid at the end of the term.

Street Improvement Bonds: Interest-bearing bonds issued by a city or count to secure the payment of assessments levied against land for street improvements.

Subcontractor: An individual or contracting firm agreeing to perform all or part of a principal or general contract; someone hired by the general contractor on an independent contractor basis.

Subdivision: The division of a single parcel of land into four or more separate parcels.

Subject to: When one purchases property with existing loans and takes the responsibility to make the payments without accepting personal liability for said indebtedness.

Sublease: A lease, junior to and shorter than the original lease, made by the original lessee to a new lessee.

Subordinate: To make inferior in priority, position, and recognition.

Subordinating Beneficiary Declares, Agrees, Etc.: Sets forth agreements of the beneficiary of the subordinating deed of trust; consents to subordinate to the new deed of trust; to new loan disbursements, etc.

Subordinating Deed of Trust — Pertinent Information: Sets forth recording reference, trustor, trustee, beneficiary amount of note, and the county where the subordinating deed of trust was recorded. Note: On this form, a legal description is inserted in between the above information.

Subordinating Party: Identifies the beneficiary (lender) of the existing deed of trust that is subordinating to a new deed of trust. The Subordinating Agreement and the new Deed of Trust are to record concurrently.

Subordination Agreement: A provision allowing a new agreement to move into a superior position of priority over an existing or concurrent agreement.

Subrogate: To substitute one person into a position for another; to substitute a claim against one person for a claim against another person.

Substitution: The appointment of a person to act in place of, or for, another.

Succession: The legal act of taking, or right to take, property by will or inheritance.

Summons: An instrument from the court (usually via the sheriff) notifying the defendant that an action has been filed against him or her.

Surety: A person or entity guarantees the performance on a obligation by another; often accomplished with the purchase of a bond.

Survey: The measurement of land and the establishing, or the ascertaining, of its area and boundaries.

Sweat Equity: Labor or services put into improving real property and used in place of money to gain title.

Take-off: The abstract of all instruments or other matters affecting title to real property that are filed each day in the clerk's and recorder's office. If full photocopies are used instead of abstracts, it is known as complete take-off.

Takeout Loan: A long-term loan that pays off and takes the place of the short term construction loan.

Tax Deed: The deed conveying title to property purchased at a tax sale.

Taxes: As applied to real property, a charge assessed against the value of real property to pay the cost of governmental services.

Tax Lien: A statutory lien, in favor of the state or municipality, upon the land of a person charged with unpaid personal or real property taxes.

Tax Statement Address: The party (and address) to whom statements regarding real property taxes will be mailed by the county tax office. It is usually the same party mentioned in the "And when recorded mail to" section.

Tenancy: The occupying of real estate under a lease or rental. Ownership of an estate less than freehold.

Tenancy in Common: A form of co-ownership of real property by two or more persons in undivided interests; the percentage of interests can be unequal and each tenant has the right to alienate or devise his or her interest.

Tenancy in Partnership: The interest held by two or more partners in property purchased by the partnership.

Tender: An unconditional offer to perform coupled with the ability to perform.

Tenements: All the land, rights, and benefits that are conveyed with said land.

Tentative Map: A proposed subdivision map that is placed before local planning commissions/building departments for approval, which leads to a final map.

Term: Provisions and conditions within a contract; also, the length of time of a contract.

Terminable Interests: An interest in property that is extinguished by death or the occurrence of a specified event.

Termite Report: A report of structural inspection concerned with wood-destroying pests. Also the common verbiage for a "structural pest control report" that identifies all wood damaging situations.

Terms and Conditions of Sale — Contract of Sale: A distinction must be made between a Contract of Sale in the legal concept of the purchase agreement and "Contract of Sale" (as used in the real estate profession) as an alternative method of financing. The latter is the usage in this text according to the following explanation. During the life of the contract, the Contract of Sale is unique in that possession and equitable interest is delivered to the vendee while the vendor retains title to the subject property. Therefore, it is necessary to set forth specific areas to rights and responsibilities as well as to identify the consequences for the violation of said agreements during the term of the contract.

Testament: As commonly used, the statements and wishes of a person in his or her will; however, in the literal sense, testament deals with the person's wishes as to the dispensation of personal property.

Testamentary Trust: A trust created by a decedent's will and testament.

Testator: One who died leaving a will.

Tier: A row of townships running east and west that are parallel to, and positioned either north or south of, a designated base line.

Time, Date, and Place of Sale: The actual time, date, and location of the trustee's sale is documented to demonstrate compliance with the original Notice of Sale.

Time Is of the Essence: A standard clause in teal property contracts that indicates that punctual compliance is required.

Title: The basic rights of enjoyment and possession or interest in property; also used to describe a document that furnishes proof of ownership.

Title Insurance: Indemnification for loss occasioned by defects in the title to real property or to an interest in real property.

Title Plant: The lot books or property accounts, maps, general index, individual/corporation files, and other records necessary for the issuance of title insurance policies by a title company.

Title Policy: An insurance policy or contract indemnifying against loss resulting from a defect in the title to the interest, or lien, in the real property thus insured.

Title Search: The examination and research in the history of title to a specific property in order to develop the chain of title.

Topography: The physical appearance and elevations of land.

Torrens: A system under which the title to land is registered with a registrar of land title. After the first registration, theoretically it is unnecessary to go beyond the registry to investigate the validity of a title. This system is used in only a few states.

Township: In the U.S. Government Survey, a plot of land six miles square, containing 36 sections; also, a unit of local government.

Tract: A parcel of land that is subdivided into smaller parcel of land called lots.

Trade Fixtures: Articles of personal property that are affixed to real property, which, however, remain personal property due to their necessity to carry on a trade or business.

Trade Name: The name under which business is conducted.

Transferor — Pertinent Information: If the Notice of Completion is signed by a successor in interest of the party (previous owner) who initiated the work of improvement, the full name and address of the previous owner is documented.

Transfer Tax: Tax levied by the county (also by the city sometimes) on the transfers of title to real property.

Trust: A right of property, real or personal, held by one party for the benefit of another.

Trust Account: A special account wherein monies held in trust are maintained separately from other monies.

Trust Deed: A three-part security document conveying "bare legal" title to be held in trust as security for the performance of an obligation; also known as a deed of trust.

Trustee: Identifies the party (usually a corporation) who is receiving the "bare legal" title (to be held in trust for the trustor and the beneficiary). The trustee usually is given a "power of sale" pursuant to which a Trustee's Sale (nonjudicial foreclosure) may be conducted in the event of default by the trustor. Under a Full Reconveyance, the trustee is identified as the party "reconveying," or releasing, the subject deed or trust. Partial Reconveyance: Identities trustee who is reconveying or releasing a specific property from the effect of the subject deed of trust.

Trustee's Deed: The deed issued to a purchaser of real property at a trustee's sale.

Trustee's Sale: Nonjudicial foreclosure sale, conducted by the trustee under a deed of trust with a power-of-sale clause.

Trustor: Identifies the obligor (trustor, usually the borrower) who is conveying the "bare legal" title of the property to the trustee who holds this title in trust for the benefit of the trustor and the beneficiary. Under a Full Reconveyance, the original trustor (on the deed of trust being reconveyed) is identified. Partial Reconveyance: Identifies original trustor (as shown on the subject deed of trust) for the specific property that is being reconveyed or released.

Trustor Under the Deed of Trust: Identifies the original trustor (borrower) as shown on the deed of trust that was foreclosed upon.

Undivided Interests: The unsegregated interest in the ownership of property by the various co-owners in joint tenancy and tenants in common.

Undue Influence: Taking undue advantage of another's need, distress, or weakness to further personal gain; using excessive persuasion to overcome the will of a vulnerable person.

Unilateral Contract: A contract in which only one party promises to do something or undertakes a performance and, therefore, only one party has an obligation.

Unities: Time, title, interest, and possession; the four basic elements of joint tenancy.

Unlawful Detainer: An action brought for recovery of possession of property from a person who is in unlawful possession.

Usury: Charging an interest rate higher than that allowed by law.

VA: The U.S. Veterans Administration.

Valid: Legally sufficient; authorized by law; effective.

Valuation: An opinion of an asset's worth; an appraisal.

Variable-rate Mortgage: Any real estate loan in which the interest rate varies over time according to a prescribed formula or set of conditions; usually changes in economic conditions. Also known as an adjustable rate mortgage.

Variance: A change of the zoning of a specific parcel from the zoning of the rest of the immediate area.

Various Restrictions Imposed and Enforcement: Specifies the development restrictions imposed (usually by the owner of the property or the subdivider/developer) and the means for enforcing said restrictions.

Vendee: Identifies the contractual purchaser (vendee) of property under a Contract of Sale. The status of the vendee (husband and wife, etc.) and the legal method of acquiring title (joint tenants, tenants in common, etc.) is also set forth.

Vendee Protection on Underlying Loan Payments: Specific use: The displayed Land Contract of Sale has a provision for an all-inclusive deed of trust; therefore, the protection allows the vendee to make up any underlying loan payments not made by the vendor and the vendee. See *All-Inclusive Deed of Trust* for more information.

Vendor: The contractual seller (vendor) of property under a Contract of Sale.

Venue: The state and county where the acknowledgment is taken.

Verification: A confirmation of correctness, truth or authenticity of the contents of the attached document.

Vest: To give title to, or to transfer ownership of property.

Vested Interest: Unconditional, fixed interest in a property, for both now and in the future.

Vestee: Present record owner.

Vesting: A statement of the name(s) of the owner(s) of property and the nature of said ownership: joint tenancy, tenancy in common, etc.

Void: Null, having no force of effect.

Voidable: That which may be declared void but is not void itself.

Voluntary Lien: A lien created by choice.

Waive: To relinquish or set aside a right.

Warranty: An assurance or promise that certain defects do not exist, or will be corrected.

Warranty Deed: A deed in which express covenants of good title and the right of possession are detailed and guaranteed.

Water Right: The right of an owner to use water adjacent to and below the surface of his or her property.

Water Table: The changeable level at which natural water is present, whether above or below the ground level.

Whereas ... : Specific use: Sets forth the purpose and intent of the Subordination Agreement and generally establishes benefits and agreements.

Will: Written instructions on the disposition of the effects of one's estate upon death.

Without Recourse: A provision often found in endorsements of negotiable instruments that means that the endorser does not assume responsibility or liability for collection.

Wraparound Mortgage of Deed of Trust: A deed of trust (or mortgage) that "wraps around" or secures payment of a senior or prior deed of trust; also known as an all-inclusive mortgage.

Writ: A court order.

Writ of Execution: A court order instructing an official to carry out a judicial decision.

Yield: The profit or income that an investment will return; the rate of return.

Zone: An area, region, or district officially designated for specific types of use.

Zoning: Governmental regulations controlling the use of property according to specified areas within the community.

INDEX

ABOUT THE AUTHOR

TERRY EILERS is a best-selling author and internationally recognized seminar speaker who has educated over 600,000 sales and sales management professionals in all 50 states and in six countries. His real estate training classes, personal development workshops, marketing guidebooks, and cassette tape programs have become the "standard" for sales success. He has published several real estate handbooks for the professional market and is also the author of *How to Buy the Home You Want, for the Best Price, in Any Market* and the forthcoming books, *Mastering Peak Performance* and *Stones Across the Creek*. He lives in Lake Tahoe, California.